Paulo Freire's Intellectual Roots

Paulo Freire's Intellectual Roots

Toward Historicity in Praxis

Edited by
Robert Lake
and
Tricia Kress

BLOOMSBURY
LONDON • NEW DELHI • NEW YORK • SYDNEY

Bloomsbury Academic

An imprint of Bloomsbury Publishing Plc

175 Fifth Avenue 50 Bedford Square
New York London
NY 10010 WC1B 3DP
USA UK

www.bloomsbury.com

First published 2013

Library of Congress Cataloging-in-Publication Data
A catalogue record for this book is available from the Library of Congress.

ISBN: HB: 978-1-4411-1184-5
PB: 978-1-4411-9523-4
ePDF: 978-1-4411-1380-1
epub: 978-1-4411-5442-2

Typeset by Newgen Imaging Systems Pvt, Ltd, Chennai, India
Printed and bound in the United States of America

CONTENTS

ACKNOWLEDGMENTS

First of all we want to thank the 14 people who contributed to this book. We are keenly aware that you had to take time away from other projects, deadlines, family responsibilities, and so many other commitments to write for this project. Many of you have known Freire's work for many years, and some have recently become more intimately acquainted with the body of his work, yet all of you have helped construct this volume that provides a portrait of Freire's intellectual genealogy and, in so doing, shows your place in the critical pedagogy family tree.

We also want to thank David Barker and everyone at Bloomsbury Publishers for their vision of advancing the heritage and future of Paulo Freire's work in ways that make a project like this possible and for allowing us to reprint a rare autobiographical piece by Freire. Thank you to Robert Lake's graduate assistant Amber Bryan for transcribing this piece.

We are grateful to Pablo Fontdevila for allowing us to use his artistic rendering of Paulo for the cover of this book. We are deeply appreciative of two of Freire's personal colleagues, Henry Giroux and Stanley Aronowitz for providing the prologue and the introduction to this book. We also thank Ana Cruz for her work of translating the documents that provided the basis for her chapter.

Prologue
The Fruit of Freire's Roots

Henry Giroux

Paulo Freire is one of the most important critical educators of the twentieth century.[1] Not only is he considered one of the founders of critical pedagogy, but he also played a crucial role in developing a highly successful literacy campaign in Brazil before the onslaught of the junta in 1964. Once the military took over the government, Freire was imprisoned for a short time for his efforts. He was eventually released and went into exile, primarily in Chile and later in Geneva, Switzerland, for a number of years. Once a semblance of democracy returned to Brazil, he went back to his country in 1980 and played a significant role in shaping its educational policies until his untimely death in 1997. His book, *Pedagogy of the Oppressed*, is considered one of the classic texts of critical pedagogy, and has sold over a million copies, influencing generations of teachers and intellectuals both in the United States and abroad. Since the 1980s, there has been no intellectual on the North American educational scene who has matched either his theoretical rigor or his moral courage. Most schools and colleges of education are now dominated by conservative ideologies, hooked on methods, slavishly wedded to instrumentalized accountability measures, and run by administrators who lack either a broader vision or a critical understanding of education as a force for strengthening the imagination and expanding democratic public life.

As the market-driven logic of neoliberal capitalism continues to devalue all aspects of the public good, one consequence has been that the educational concern with excellence has been removed from matters of equity, while the notion of schooling as a public good has largely been reduced to a private good. Both public and higher education are largely defined through the corporate demand that they provide the skills, knowledge, and credentials that will provide the workforce necessary for the United States to compete and maintain its role as the major global economic and military power. Consequently, there is little interest in both public and higher education, and most importantly in many schools of education, for understanding pedagogy as a deeply civic, political, and moral practice—that is, pedagogy as a practice for freedom. As schooling is increasingly subordinated to a corporate order, any vestige of critical education is replaced by training and the promise of economic security. Similarly, pedagogy is now subordinated to the narrow regime of teaching to the test coupled with an often harsh system of disciplinary control, both of which mutually reinforce each other. In addition, teachers are increasingly reduced to the status of technicians and deskilled as they are removed from having any control over their classrooms or school governance structures. Teaching to the test and the corporatization of education becomes a way of "taming" students and invoking modes of corporate governance in which public school teachers become deskilled and an increasing number of higher education faculty are reduced to part-time positions, constituting the new subaltern class of academic labor.

But there is more at stake here than a crisis of authority and the repression of critical thought. Too many classrooms at all levels of schooling now resemble a "dead zone," where any vestige of critical thinking, self-reflection, and imagination quickly migrate to sites outside of the school only to be mediated and corrupted by a corporate-driven media culture. The major issue now driving public schooling is how to teach for the test, while disciplining those students who because of their class and race undermine a school's district ranking in the ethically sterile and bloodless world of high stakes testing and empirical score cards.[2] Higher education mimics this logic by reducing its public vision to the interests of capital and redefining itself largely as a credentializing factory for students and a petri dish for downsizing academic labor. Under such circumstances, rarely do educators ask questions about how schools can prepare students to be informed citizens, nurture a civic imagination or teach them to be self-reflective about public issues and the world in which they live. As Stanley Aronowitz puts it:

> Few of even the so-called educators ask the question: What matters beyond the reading, writing, and numeracy that are presumably taught in the elementary and secondary grades? The old question of what a kid needs to become an informed "citizen" capable of participating in making the large and small public decisions that affect the larger world as well as everyday life receives honorable mention but not serious consideration. These unasked questions are symptoms of a new regime of educational expectations that privileges job readiness above any other educational values. (2008, p. xii)

Against this regime of "scientific" idiocy and "bare pedagogy" stripped of all critical elements of teaching and learning, Freire believed that all education in the broadest sense was part of a project of freedom and eminently political because it offered students the conditions for self-reflection, a self-managed life, and particular notions of critical agency. As Aronowitz puts it in his analysis of Freire's work on literacy and critical pedagogy:

> Thus, for Freire, literacy was not a means to prepare students for the world of subordinated labor or "careers," but a preparation for a self-managed life. And self-management could only occur when people have fulfilled three goals of education: self-reflection, that is, realizing the famous poetic phrase, "know thyself," which is an understanding of the world in which they live, in its economic, political and, equally important, its psychological dimensions. Specifically "critical" pedagogy helps the learner become aware of the forces that have hitherto ruled their lives and especially shaped their consciousness. The third goal is to help set the conditions for producing a new life, a new set of arrangements where power has been, at least in tendency, transferred to those who literally make the social world by transforming nature and themselves. (see Aronowitz, 2009, p. ix)

What Paulo made clear in *Pedagogy of the Oppressed*, his most influential work, is that pedagogy at its best is not about training, teaching methods, or political indoctrination. For Freire, pedagogy is not a method or an a priori technique to be imposed on all students, but a political and moral practice that provides the knowledge, skills, and social relations that enable students to expand the possibilities of what it means to be critical citizens, while expanding and deepening their participation in the promise of a substantive democracy. Critical thinking for Freire was not an object lesson in test taking, but a tool for self-determination and civic engagement. For Freire, critical thinking was not about the task of simply reproducing the past and understanding the present. On the contrary, it offered a way of thinking beyond the present, soaring beyond the immediate confines of one's experiences, entering into a critical dialogue with history and imagining a future that did not merely reproduce the present. Theodor Adorno captures the spirit of Freire's notion of critical thinking by insisting that

> Thinking is not the intellectual reproduction of what already exists anyway. As long as it doesn't break off, thinking has a secure hold on possibility. Its insatiable aspect, its aversion to being quickly and easily satisfied, refuses the foolish wisdom of resignation. Open thinking points beyond itself. (Adorno, 1998, pp. 291–2)

Freire rejected those regimes of educational degradation organized around the demands of the market, instrumentalized knowledge, and the priority of training over the pursuit of the imagination, critical thinking, and the teaching of freedom and social responsibility. Rather than assume the mantle of a false impartiality, Freire believed that critical pedagogy involves both the recognition that human life is conditioned not determined, and the crucial necessity of not only reading the world critically but also intervening in the larger social order as part of the responsibility of an informed citizenry. According to Freire, the political and moral demands of pedagogy amount to more than the school and classroom being merely the instrument of official power or assuming the role of an apologist for the existing order, as the Obama administration seems to believe—given its willingness to give Bush's reactionary educational policies a new name and a new lease on life. Freire rejected those modes of pedagogy that supported economic models and modes of agency in which freedom is reduced to consumerism and economic activity is freed from any criterion except profitability and the reproduction of a rapidly expanding mass of wasted humans. Critical pedagogy attempts to understand how power works through the production, distribution, and consumption of knowledge within particular institutional contexts and seeks to constitute students as informed subjects and social agents. In this instance, the issue of how identities, values, and desires are shaped in the classroom is the grounds of politics. Critical pedagogy is thus invested in both the practice of self-criticism about the values that inform teaching and a critical self-consciousness regarding what it means to equip students with analytical skills to be self-reflective about the knowledge and values they confront in classrooms. Moreover, such a pedagogy attempts not only to provide the conditions for students to understand texts and different modes of intelligibility but also opens up new avenues for them to make better moral judgments that will enable them to assume some sense of responsibility to the other in light of those judgments.

Freire was acutely aware that what makes critical pedagogy so dangerous to ideological fundamentalists, the ruling elites, religious extremists, and right-wing nationalists all over the world is, central to its very definition, the task of educating students to become critical agents who actively question and negotiate the relationships between theory and practice, critical analysis and common sense, and learning and social change. Critical pedagogy opens up a space where students should be able to come to terms with their own power as critically engaged citizens; it provides a sphere where the unconditional freedom to question and assert is central to the purpose of public schooling and higher education, if not democracy itself. And as a political and moral practice, way of knowing, and literate engagement, pedagogy attempts to "make evident the multiplicity and complexity of history" (Said, 2001, p. 141). History in this sense is engaged as a narrative open to critical dialogue rather than predefined text to be memorized and accepted unquestioningly. Pedagogy in this instance provides the conditions to cultivate in students a healthy skepticism about power, a "willingness to temper any reverence for authority with a sense of critical awareness"(ibid., p. 501). As a performative practice, pedagogy takes as one of its goals the opportunity for students to be able to reflectively frame their own relationship to the ongoing project of an unfinished democracy. It is precisely this relationship between democracy and pedagogy that is so threatening to so many of our

educational leaders and spokespersons today and it is also the reason why Freire's work on critical pedagogy and literacy are more
relevant today than when they were first published.

According to Freire, all forms of pedagogy represent a particular way of understanding society and a specific commitment to the
future. Critical pedagogy, unlike dominant modes of teaching, insists
that one of the fundamental tasks of educators is to make sure that
the future points the way to a more socially just world, a world in
which the discourses of critique and possibility in conjunction with
the values of reason, freedom, and equality function to alter, as part
of a broader democratic project, the grounds upon which life is lived.
This is hardly a prescription for political indoctrination, but it is
a project that gives critical education its most valued purpose and
meaning, which, in part, is "to encourage human agency, not mold it
in the manner of Pygmalion"(Aronowitz, 2009, pp. 10–11). It is also
a position that threatens right-wing private advocacy groups, neocon-
servative politicians, and conservative extremists. Such individuals
and groups are keenly aware that critical pedagogy, with its emphasis
on the hard work of critical analysis, moral judgments, and social
responsibility, goes to the very heart of what it means to address real
inequalities of power at the social level and to conceive of education
as a project for freedom, while at the same time foregrounding a
series of important and often ignored questions such as:

> What is the role of teachers and academics as public intellectuals?
> Whose interests does public and higher education serve? How
> might it be possible to understand and engage the diverse contexts
> in which education takes place? What is the role of education as
> a public good? How do we make knowledge meaningful in order
> to make it critical and transformative? (Giroux, 2010, p. 184)

In spite of the right-wing view that equates indoctrination with
any suggestion of politics, critical pedagogy is not concerned with
simply offering students new ways to think critically and act with
authority as agents in the classroom; it is also concerned with providing students with the skills and knowledge necessary for them
to expand their capacities both to question deep-seated assumptions and myths that legitimate the most archaic and disempower-
ing social practices that structure every aspect of society and to
then take responsibility for intervening in the world they inhabit.

Education is not neutral. It is always directive in its attempt to teach students to inhabit a particular mode of agency; enable them to understand the larger world and one's role in it in a specific way; define their relationship, if not responsibility, to diverse others and to presuppose through what is taught and experienced in the classroom some sort of understanding of a more just, imaginative, and democratic life. Pedagogy is by definition directive, but that does not mean it is merely a form of indoctrination. On the contrary, as Freire argued, education as a practice for freedom must attempt to expand the capacities necessary for human agency and, hence, the possibilities for democracy itself. Surely, this suggests that at all levels of education from the primary school to the privileged precincts of higher education, educators should nourish those pedagogical practices that promote

> a concern with keeping the forever unexhausted and unfulfilled human potential open, fighting back all attempts to foreclose and pre-empt the further unraveling of human possibilities, prodding human society to go on questioning itself and preventing that questioning from ever stalling or being declared finished. (Bauman & Tester, 2001, p. 4)

In other words, critical pedagogy forges both an expanded notion of literacy and agency through a language of skepticism, possibility, and a culture of openness, debate, and engagement—all those elements now at risk because of the current and most dangerous attacks on public and higher education. This was Paulo's legacy, one that invokes dangerous memories and, hence, is increasingly absent from any discourse about current educational problems.

I first met Paulo in the early 1980s, just after I had been denied tenure by John Silber, the then notorious right-wing president of Boston University. Paulo was giving a talk at the University of Massachusetts, and he came to my house in Boston for dinner. His humility was completely at odds with his reputation and I remember being greeted with such warmth and sincerity that I felt completely at ease with him. We talked for a long time that night about his exile, my firing, what it meant to be a working-class intellectual, the risk one had to take to make a difference, and when the night was over a friendship was forged that lasted until his death 15 years later. I was in a very bad position after being denied tenure and had no idea what my future would hold for me. I am convinced that if it had not been for Freire and Donaldo Macedo, also a friend and co-author with Paulo[3] I am not sure I would have stayed in the field of education. But Freire's passion for education and Macedo's friendship convinced me that education was not merely important, but a crucial site of struggle.

Unlike so many intellectuals I have met in academia, Paulo was always so generous, eager to publish the work of younger intellectuals, write letters of support and give as much as possible of himself in the service of others. The early 1980s were exciting years in education in the United States and Paulo was at the center of it. Together, we started a critical education and culture series at Bergin and Garvey and published over a hundred young authors, many of whom went on to have a significant influence in the university. Jim Bergin became Paulo's patron as his American publisher, Donaldo became his translator and a coauthor and we all took our best shots at translating, publishing, and distributing Paulo's work, always with the hope of inviting him back to the United States so we could meet, talk, drink good wine, and recharge all the struggles that marked us in different ways. Of course, it is difficult to write simply about Paulo as a person because of who he was and how he entered one's space and the world could never be separated from his politics. Hence, I want to try to provide a broader context for my own understanding of him as well as those ideas that consistently shaped our relationship and his relationship with others.

Occupying the often difficult space between existing politics and the as yet possible, Paulo Freire spent most of his life working in the belief that the radical elements of democracy are worth struggling for, that critical education is a basic element of social change and that how we think about politics is inseparable from how we come to understand the world, power, and the moral life we aspire to lead. In many ways, Paulo embodied the important but often problematic relationship between the personal and the political. His own life was a testimonial not only to his belief in democracy but also to the notion that one's life had to come as close as possible to modeling the social relations and experiences that spoke to a more humane and democratic future. At the same time, Paulo never moralized about politics, never employed the discourse of shame, or collapsed the political into the personal when talking about social issues. For him, private problems had to be understood in relation to larger public issues. Everything about him suggested that the first order of politics was humility, compassion, and a willingness to fight against human injustices.

Freire's belief in democracy as well as his deep and abiding faith in the ability of people to resist the weight of oppressive institutions and ideologies was forged in a spirit of struggle tempered by both the grim realities of his own imprisonment and exile, mediated by both a fierce sense of outrage and the belief that education and hope are the conditions of both agency and politics. Acutely aware that many contemporary versions of hope occupied their own corner in Disneyland, Freire fought against such appropriations and was passionate about recovering and rearticulating hope through, in his words, an "understanding of history as opportunity and not determinism" (Freire, 1994, p. 91). Hope for Freire was a practice of witnessing, an act of moral imagination that enabled progressive educators and others to think otherwise in order to act otherwise. Hope demanded an anchoring in transformative practices, and one of the tasks of the progressive educator was to "unveil opportunities for hope, no matter what the obstacles may be" (Freire, 1994, p. 9). Underlying Freire's politics of hope was a view of radical pedagogy that located itself on the dividing lines where the relations between domination and oppression or power and powerlessness continued to be produced and reproduced. For Freire, hope as a defining element of politics and pedagogy always meant listening to and working with the poor and other subordinate groups so that they might speak and act in order to alter dominant relations of power. Whenever we talked, he never allowed himself to become cynical. He was always full of life, taking great delight in dialogue with a passion that both embodied his own politics and confirmed the lived presence of others.

Committed to the specific, the play of context, and the possibility inherent in what he called the unfinished nature of human beings, Freire offered no recipes for those in need of instant theoretical and political fixes. For him, pedagogy was strategic and performative: considered as part of a broader political practice for democratic change, critical pedagogy was never viewed as an a priori discourse to be reasserted or a methodology to be implemented, or for that matter a slavish attachment to knowledge that can only be quantified. On the contrary, for Freire, pedagogy was a political and performative act organized around the "instructive

ambivalence of disrupted borders," (Bhabha, 1994, p. 28) a practice of bafflement, interruption, understanding, and intervention
that is the result of ongoing historical, social, and economic struggles. I was often amazed at how patient he always was in dealing with people who wanted him to provide menu-like answers to
the problems they raised about education, not realizing that they
were undermining his own insistence that pedagogy could never be
reduced to a method. His patience was always instructive for me
and I am convinced that it was only later in my life that I was able
to begin to emulate it in my own interactions with audiences.

Paulo was a cosmopolitan intellectual, who never overlooked the
details in everyday life and the connections the latter had to a much
broader, global world. He consistently reminded us that political
struggles are won and lost in those specific yet hybridized spaces
that linked narratives of everyday experience with the social gravity
and material force of institutional power. Any pedagogy that called
itself Freirean had to acknowledge the centrality of the particular
and contingent in shaping historical contexts and political projects.
Although Freire was a theoretician of radical contextualism, he
also acknowledged the importance of understanding the particular
and the local in relation to larger, global and cross-national forces.
For Freire, literacy as a way of reading and changing the world had
to be reconceived within a broader understanding of citizenship,
democracy, and justice that was global and transnational. Making
the pedagogical more political in this case meant moving beyond
the celebration of tribal mentalities and developing a praxis that
foregrounded "power, history, memory, relational analysis, justice (not just representation), and ethics as the issues central to
transnational democratic struggles" (Alexander & Mohanty,
1997, p. xix).

But Freire's insistence that education was about the making and
changing of contexts did more than seize upon the political and
pedagogic potentialities to be found across a spectrum of social
sites and practices in society, which, of course, included but were
not limited to the school. He also challenged the separation of
culture from politics by calling attention to how diverse technolo-
gies of power work pedagogically within institutions to produce,
regulate, and legitimate particular forms of knowing, belonging,
feeling, and desiring. But Freire did not make the mistake of many
of his contemporaries by conflating culture with the politics of

recognition. Politics was more than a gesture of translation, representation, and dialogue; it was also about creating the conditions for people to govern rather than be merely governed, capable of mobilizing social movements against the oppressive economic, racial, and sexist practices put into place by colonization, global capitalism, and other oppressive structures of power.

Paulo Freire left behind a corpus of work that emerged out of a lifetime of struggle and commitment. Refusing the comfort of master narratives, Freire's work was always unsettled and unsettling, restless yet engaging. Unlike so much of the politically arid and morally vacuous academic and public prose that characterizes contemporary intellectual discourse, Freire's work was consistently fueled by a healthy moral rage over the needless oppression and suffering he witnessed throughout his life as he traveled all over the globe. Similarly, his work exhibited a vibrant and dynamic quality that allowed it to grow, refuse easy formulas, and open itself to new political realities and projects. Freire's genius was to elaborate a theory of social change and engagement that was neither vanguardist nor populist. While he had a profound faith in the ability of ordinary people to shape history and to become critical agents in shaping their own destinies, he refused to romanticize the culture and experiences that produced oppressive social conditions. Combining theoretical rigor, social relevance, and moral compassion, Freire gave new meaning to the politics of daily life while affirming the importance of theory in opening up the space of critique, possibility, politics, and practice. Theory and language were a site of struggle and possibility that gave experience meaning and action a political direction, and any attempt to reproduce the binarism of theory versus politics was repeatedly condemned by Freire.[4] Freire loved theory, but he never reified it. When he talked about Freud, Marx, or Erich Fromm, one could feel his intense passion for ideas. And, yet, he never treated theory as an end in itself; it was always a resource, the value of which lay in understanding, critically engaging, and transforming the world as part of a larger project of freedom and justice. To say that his joy around such matters was infectious is to understate his own presence and impact on so many people that he met in his life.

I had a close personal relationship with Paulo for over 15 years, and I was always moved by the way in which his political courage and intellectual reach were matched by a love of life and generosity of spirit. The political and the personal mutually informed Freire's life and work. He was always the curious student even as he assumed the role of a critical teacher. As he moved between the private and the public, he revealed an astonishing gift for making everyone he met feel valued. His very presence embodied what it meant to combine political struggle and moral courage, to make hope meaningful and despair unpersuasive. Paulo was vigilant in bearing witness to the individual and collective suffering of others, but shunned the role of the isolated intellectual as an existential hero who struggles alone. For Freire, intellectuals must match their call for making the pedagogical more political with an ongoing effort to build those coalitions, affiliations, and social movements capable of mobilizing real power and promoting substantive social change. Freire understood quite keenly that democracy was threatened by a powerful military-industrial complex and the increased power of the warfare state, but he also recognized the pedagogical force of a corporate and militarized culture that eroded the moral and civic capacities of citizens to think beyond the common sense of official power and its legitimating ideologies. Freire never lost sight of Robert Hass' claim that the job of education, its political job, "is to refresh the idea of justice going dead in us all the time" (Hass cited in Pollock, 1992, p. 22). At a time when education has become one of the official sites of conformity, disempowerment, and uncompromising modes of punishment, the legacy of Paulo Freire's work is more important than ever before.

Notes

1 One of the best sources on the life and work of Paulo Freire is Peter Mayo, "Liberating Praxis: Freire's Legacy for Radical Education and Politics" (Rotterdam: Sense Publishers, 2008). Two of the best translators of Freire's work to the American context are Donaldo Macedo, *Literacies of Power* (Boulder, CO: Westview, 1994) and Ira Shor, *Freire for the Classroom* (Portsmouth, NH: Boynton/Cook, 1987).
2 On the issue of containment and the pedagogy of punishment, see: Jenny Fisher, "The Walking Wounded: The Crisis of Youth, School Violence, and Precarious Pedagogy," *Review of Education, Cultural Studies, and Pedagogy* (33 (5), 2011: 379–432).

3 See Paulo Freire and Donald Macedo, *Literacy: Reading the Word and the World* (Amherst, MA: Bergin and Garvey, 1987).
4 Surely, Freire would have agreed wholeheartedly with Stuart Hall's insight that: "It is only through the way in which we represent and imagine ourselves that we come to know how we are constituted and who we are. There is no escape from the politics of representation." Stuart Hall, "What is this 'Black' in Popular Culture?" in Gina Dent, ed. *Black Popular Culture* (Seattle: Bay Press, 1992), pp. 30.

References

Adorno, T. (1998). *Education after Auschwitz: Critical models interventions and catchwords*. New York: Columbia University Press.
Alexander, M. J. and Mohanty, C. T. (1997). "Introduction: genealogies, legacies, movements." In M. J. Alexander and C. T. Mohanty (eds), *Feminist genealogies, colonial legacies, democratic futures* (pp. xiii–xlii). New York: Routledge.
Aronowitz, S. (2008). *Against schooling: For an education that matters*. Boulder, CO: Paradigm Publishers.
— (2009). "Foreword." In S. L. Macrine (ed.), *Critical pedagogy in uncertain times: Hope and possibilities* (pp. ix–xii). New York, NY: Palgrave Macmillan.
Bauman, Z. and Tester, K. (2001). *Conversations with Zygmunt Bauman*. Malden, MA: Polity Press, p. 4.
Bhabha, H. (1994). *The enchantment of art: The artist in society*, in C. Becker and A. Wiens (eds). Chicago: *New Art Examiner*, pp. 24–34.
Freire, P. (1994). *Pedagogy of hope: Reliving pedagogy of the oppressed*. New York: Continuum Press.
Giroux, H. (2010). "Bare Pedagogy and the Scourge of Neoliberalism: Rethinking Higher Education as a Democratic Public Sphere." *The Educational Forum*, 74 (3), 184–196.
Pollock, S. (1992). "Robert Hass." *Mother Jones*, March/April, 22.
Said, E. (2001). *Reflections on exile and other essays*. Cambridge, MA: Harvard University Press.

Introduction

Paulo Freire's Pedagogy: Not Mainly a Teaching Method

Stanley Aronowitz

Paulo Freire

By the time Paulo Freire died in 1997 he was recognized as perhaps the world's leading educator. Some even called him the Latin
American John Dewey, although as we shall see shortly, this analogy is as deeply flawed as was the dominant liberal conception
of education. Unlike Dewey, whose conception of democracy in
education was oriented to the integration of the vast immigrant
United States population into liberal democratic values and into a
workforce that was largely subordinate to capital, until the end,
Freire was a transformative intellectual. His work was always in
the service of a way of life that was thoroughly egalitarian. He
sought to abolish the capitalist system of exploitation and was
convinced that to truly establish an egalitarian education system
was a vital aspect of the society he wished to bring about. This
society could be brought about only by revolution, but, especially
in his later work, Freire's version of the revolution and its aftermath was not congruent with either the prevailing Communist
dogma that maintained the distance between the leader and the
led, and sought to capture the state and to install the sovereignty
of the vanguard party. Nor did he adhere to the social-democratic
idea that representative democracy plus social welfare was adequate to realize a just society. Although he worked closely with
social movements that were allied with the existing oppositional

parties of the radical left, and cooperated with the World Council of Churches and other social progressive organizations, Freire was never comfortable. Gradually, while retaining his revolutionary vision, he became a vocal radical democratic humanist for whom the journey toward liberation was more important than the goal. Or put another way, the means of the revolution had to be democratic in the participatory meaning of the term; otherwise achieving power would certainly be authoritarian. In contrast to mechanical revolutionary Marxism, Freire's philosophy was continuous with what has been euphemistically termed "western" Marxism, which embraces the quest for a sufficient theory of subjectivity identified in the post-war periods with the Critical Theory of the Frankfurt school, psychoanalysis, and phenomenology.

In his early years he divided his time between university teaching and working in Brazil's rural Northeast region. One of the most famous of his discoveries was that rural people, although unlettered, were not without knowledge. The teacher was not to be an autocrat but a participant along with her students, in the search for truth. And that "truth" consisted in several moments: the learner's knowledge of the social conditions that constitute the determinants of class position; her awareness of the necessary and contingent steps to liberation from those conditions toward the achievement of freedom; and the objective and subjective obstacles to achieving these ends. In our era of top-down, high stakes testing, and increasingly vocationalized education for the masses, the radicalism of this concept is plain to see. Of course, the teacher brings to the process a wealth of learning, but so does the student. Their contributions to education are different; the student's experience in the world of labor, of economic hardship, and of impoverished but proud communities, is valued as a corrective to the arrogance of the teacher who has been trained to the privileges of unquestioned authority. The teacher is, above all, a listener and then brings his command of the philosophical and literary achievements of (bourgeois) humankind to the table. Both types of knowledge are necessary, but there is no question of the superiority of one over the other. The student must learn how to read and write, but also must eventually master the basic concepts of science and the traditions of philosophy, social theory, and literature, not in reverence, but always critically. The teacher must, literally, study the lives of ordinary people in order to ferret out the sources and the rich content of their indigenous knowledge.

Freire honed his political and educational capacities and practices in close alliance with the revolutionary movements of his time, with the progressive and radical educators who went into the peasant countryside and worked with the poor and, equally importantly, with his extensive reading in Marxism, existentialism, and psychoanalytic theory. As is well known, in the course of these experiences and intellectual influences Freire developed a theory of education that, among other features, renounced what he termed the "banking model" of pedagogy. Freire urged us to abjure the concept that the Great Tradition and its bearers were, in advance, authorized to hand down the received wisdom of the past. The student, accordingly, was conceived as a receptacle, an instantiation of Locke's bland sheet of paper who brought almost nothing of value to the learning process except the desire to imbibe knowledge, delivered from above. In essence what has been called "critical pedagogy" is a dialogue between selective philosophical and scientific literatures and the practical experiences of the people. The dialogic aspect of Freire's perspective has been largely ignored by most of his North American interlocutors; Freire was often annoyed by their pervasive anti-intellectualism and had to insist on the salience of theoretical knowledge.

Exiled from his own country after the fall of the democratically elected Goulart government to a military dictatorship in 1964, the 43-year-old Freire spent nearly 30 years as an itinerant scholar and teacher: agitating, writing 20 books on a broad scope of educational matters, and numerous articles, lecturing in Europe and North America, and advising reform and revolutionary movements, principally in Africa. In 1985, under both internal and international political and economic forces, Brazil's military gave way to civilian government. Since the repression that all but destroyed the legal Left inhibited its claim to power, a Center/Right coalition led by Fernando Henrique Cardozo, a former Marxist, and other neoliberals mounted the first successful nonmilitary regime. Less than a decade later the now legal and emergent Workers Party won control of the country's largest city, San Paulo. The newly installed municipal government invited Freire to become secretary of education and he readily accepted. He spent his first year visiting almost all of the schools, talking to teachers and administrators, and pressuring the new city government for more money. But a year later, Freire stepped down because, as he reported, the new government lacked the political will to revamp the schools root and branch. Freire believed that the education system was not only seriously flawed, it was almost completely broken and only a radical turn would establish even a semblance of learning. Most teachers were ill-prepared and underpaid, the school week was limited to three days, many of which were half-days, and the available materials were woefully inadequate.

Which raises an important question: can the education systems of countries in both advanced and developing capitalist societies be reformed, without linking a program to political as well as educational transformation? In this regard, the broken public education system of the United States has spawned a critical mass of critics, some of whom proffer proposals for reform. Meanwhile, national and local governments persist in their own program of transformation: to reduce mass education to training and reserve education for critical thinking to the private schools that, in the main, serve the sons and daughters of the corporate and political elite (of course the term "critical" means that these schools offer organized skepticism as a value). The din of protest, most prominently by Diane Ravitch, seems to have had little or no effect on the rulers. Numerous studies have shown the tendency of public schooling to dumbing down the curriculum and imposing punitive testing algorithms on teachers and students alike. Whether intended or not, we live in an era where the traditional concepts of liberal education and popular critical thinking are under assault. Neoliberals of the Center, not less than those of the Right, are equally committed to the reduction of education to a mean-spirited regime of keeping its subjects' noses to the grindstone. As the postwar "prosperity" that offered limited opportunities to some from the lower orders to gain a measure of mobility fades into memory, the chief function of schools is repression. Except for a highly selective number of professional schools where there are still jobs at the end of the course of study, they have only credentials to offer, most of which are next to worthless in an increasingly jobless economy. As we have learned, the shutting down of jobs has affected many graduates of colleges and universities and has even touched the elite schools.

Freire has been received in the United States in a manner more consistent with Dewey's educational philosophy and the pernicious anti-intellectualism that pervades American thought than Freire's own world view or his politics. For example, one prominent education writer of the Left describes Freire's contribution as a provocative teaching method. The left and liberal tendencies in American thought share an overriding suspicion of philosophy and social theory that do not conform to an instrumental perspective on all aspects of social life, especially education. Consequently, Freire is labeled the inventor of a superb teaching method, a learning regime that concentrates almost exclusively on the dialogic technique in the classroom. So Freire is a master of techniques. Learning is identified, as in mainstream schooling with the acquisition of skills; the difference is that Left and liberal educators have imbibed Freire's respect for the student.

In 1995 Freire appeared at a conference dedicated to him and his work at New York's New School. The 400 people in attendance were mostly education activists, teachers, and graduate students. In the course of the conversation many expressed their disdain for "theory" and praised Freire as a superb populist teacher. Freire responded, vehemently, by denouncing the anti-intellectualism of those who expressed these views and reminded his audience of the importance of philosophy and social theory for the project of social transformation that, he said, was the object of his educational philosophy.

Marx, Fromm, and Sartre

Previously, I have indicated that Freire did not praise all theories and ideas; his intellectual sources were highly selective. From Marx he took the understanding that history mattered and was marked by class and class struggle. Against the neoliberal notion that the interests of capital and labor were similar, if not identical, Freire recognized the veracity of Frederick Douglass's apt phrase: "without struggle there is no progress" (1857/1999, p. 367). And progress consisted in the achievement of a world in which private property in the major means of material and intellectual production was no more, that social relations would be construed according to the principles of social and economic equality and of human freedom. (The Left almost never invokes the idea of freedom, having ceded it to the Right.) In his later radical democratic humanist texts, Freire extolled individual dissent and, thus, preserves one of the more eternal of the doctrines of liberalism. In a time of galloping authoritarianism, even in liberal democratic societies, the declaration of human freedom as, in the first place, the right not to conform to prevailing mores and ideas becomes a radical concept. The Left would acknowledge its validity in the context of capitalist and military-totalitarian regimes, but largely has forsaken the intrinsic value of dissent. Freire's *Pedagogy of Freedom* (1998), one of his last books, is plainly at odds with this view. The book may be read as a partial repudiation of some of the views expressed in his *Pedagogy of the Oppressed* (1970), which is still influenced by some aspects of Communist ideology.

But historical materialism, at least in its conventional form, is only the necessary condition for freedom. As noted, even if the conditions for its achievement are present, the sufficient conditions for social transformation are an oppressed population that has shed its fear of freedom and is willing to fight for it, and as Sartre argued, even at the price of surrendering life itself. Although, some writers have argued that Marx's concept of the commodity fetish, brilliantly resumed by Georg Lukacs after years of neglect, provides a crucial opening toward a theory of subjectivity. After all, Marx (1978) himself called for such a theory in one of the theses on Feuerbach, in which he noted that idealism has addressed subjectivity as opposed to a materialism that ignores it or, perhaps more accurately, remains stuck in mechanisms. Objectivist Marxism, still the most forceful and leading tendency among Left revolutionists, the logic of capital that plunges the system into periodic crises—depression and war—that becomes deeper and deeper is enough to obviate the need for a theory of subjectivity. The workers and other oppressed social formations are, according to this formulation, driven to action with the help of the revolutionary party. So organization substitutes rather than complements consciousness; Freire was not convinced. From Eric Fromm he drew the insight that what prevented the masses from achieving their liberation was not, primarily, the astounding success of capitalism; indeed, alienated labor still obtains under all forms of capitalism even under the most favorable economic circumstances. What prevents rebellion is a deeply lodged fear in the mass unconscious (Fromm, 1942), to which Sartre adds the refusal to risk life, as Hegel reminds us. The Lord dominates because the bondsman is incapable of risking life and does not conceive of freedom as anything beyond material security. Although I doubt Freire invokes Hegel very much, the search for subjectivity and its vicissitudes has direct lineage to Hegel's *Phenomenology of the Spirit* (1807/1977), surely the inspiration for Sartre's evocative introduction of death as a threshold for life in his first major treatise *Being and Nothingness* (1956). Since the proletariat, broadly conceived, remains in thrall of a system that has distorted truth, fragmented its ranks, and imposed ideological as well as physical coercion on a wide front, Freire understood education as a companion to organized resistance. Freire's educational "method is, first of all, revolutionary empowerment."

A movement that conducts the struggle for power or for structural reform without a complementary educational effort that valorizes the experiences of the people and offers literacy and access to the range of knowledge that marks civilization, is likely to fail in the short or medium term. But movements for social change must also dedicate themselves to changing life. A social-democratic program that confines itself to more nationalization of the means of production and provision of social benefits but refuses to address subjectivity, and fully embraces representative government as the best of all possible worlds, may win a measure of equality, but if it fails to address the underlying problems of alienation it can, unintentionally, strengthen the system of domination. The social democratic objection to the communist demand to change life has, since 1917, cited the totalitarianism of the point of view of the totality. But the thrust of Freire's discourse is deeply embedded in this point of view, while just as fiercely maintaining a radical democratic stance. If, for instance, a regime calling itself socialist abolishes private property in the decisive means of production like the Soviet Union and the Eastern European bloc but perpetuates the system of wage slavery and commodity production, and refuses to challenge the sanctity of the bourgeois family, it has left a huge opening for the reemergence of capitalist social relations. Some radicals even argued that the Soviet empire was in no way a workers' society, but was a version of state capitalism or bureaucratic collectivism.

But to introduce ideas such as "moral incentives" to replace material incentives as was attempted in the early years of the Cuban revolution entails a protracted educational process that addresses the long bourgeois past of individualism, the authority of the father in child-rearing, royal sovereignty, and other forms of bondage. The Cuban experiment was ended because the fragile revolution could not withstand the popular demands for higher living standards. The Bolsheviks were similarly constrained, even though many of its intellectuals like Alexandra Kollontai tried to challenge bourgeois familial mores, especially in sexuality. In this respect Lenin was instrumental in halting the sexual revolution in Bolshevik Russia because, as he declared, it was producing too many orphan babies at a time when the revolution was severely tested by civil war and foreign invasion. But bureaucratic domination and outright physical repression played a major role in the so-called return to normalcy. Kollantai was shipped off to Sweden to serve as Soviet ambassador.

Although Freire devoted a significant portion of his itinerant years to supporting revolutionary movements in Africa and Europe, there is no country anywhere today whose educational system works with Freire's concepts. Individual teachers apply his classroom practice and academics show his connection to Marx and Fromm but the problem is there that there is no political oppositional formation; either party or social movement has consistently introduced his ideas even to their own activists. In an epoch of triumphal capitalism where reform is no longer even on the agenda of the progressive Left/liberals who contest elections for national and local office, what are the avenues for educational praxis?

Praxis must, first of all, be attentive to the concrete conditions that prevail at any given time and place. We live in a time of increasing dissent and opposition to the prevailing powers, but the institutions, at least in the advanced industrial countries, are still in their hands. As the economic and political system comes under criticism and opposition, we have observed a growing rigidity in liberal democratic regimes. Thus, the possibility for systemic reform is extremely limited unless the various movements go beyond single issues and modest proposals. This statement is not to deny the chance for local structural change. But, if possible, it will become realistic not only by mass movements but also by the initiation of a number of prefigurative institutions that operate outside the public sector.

The United States has a long history of educational experiments outside of the public schools in the nineteenth and twentieth century. Anarchists and communists created a series of schools that were conceived as alternatives, if not oppositional to the public schools. Paul Avrich in his path-breaking work *The Modern Schools Movement* (1980) provides rich detail about some of these anarchist-inspired institutions. New York still has a number of "private" k-12 schools that once were intentional alternatives: Walden, Little Red Schoolhouse, Horace Mann, Fieldston, Lincoln, and Dalton were not for the rich and upper middle class, but for middle class and working people. The Socialist and Communist parties ran networks of adult, nondegree schools. Among them, the Rand School, The Workers School, and, its successor, the Jefferson School of Social Science in New York were among the more durable. A. J. Muste, a pacifist and labor activist organized the Brookwood Labor College, and Myles Horton started the Highlander Folk School in Tennessee in an effort to educate and to train a new generation of socially conscious labor activists and organizers. Highlander, under Cold War attack, became a central center for training and dialogue among civil rights organizers in the 1950s and 1960s and seriously adopted some of Freire's ideas. In the 1960s, some New Left schools were started. The free university was founded in 1965 to provide a nondogmatic array of courses and programs to the burgeoning student, anti-war, and intellectual movements of the period. Today, its main legatee, The Brecht Forum, founded in 1975 by Arthur Felberbaum, offers courses in Hegel, Marxism, and philosophy and stages forums and conferences, but remains almost singular in an otherwise dismal environment.

To conceive of a strategy of creating and sustaining alternative educational institutions would likely require a political formation dedicated to providing material and intellectual support. In the United States and many other economically developed countries where, with a few exceptions, the libertarian left, Marxist, and anarchist alike, are relatively weak, such an undertaking remains difficult, if not temporarily improbable. To be sure, especially in universities, Freirean educational efforts might be realistic, but even in higher schooling the heavy hand of corporatization has made important strides. Yet, if praxis is the touchstone of movements toward freedom, intellectuals might consider the iconic phrase of the last freedom movement in the West; May 1968 "be realistic demand the impossible" (Cited in O'Brien, 2002, p. 67).

References

Avrich, P. (1980). *The modern school movement: Anarchism and education in the United States.* Princeton, NJ: Princeton University Press.

Douglass, F. (1857/1999). *Frederick Douglass: Selected speeches and writings.* Chicago, IL: Lawrence Hill Books.

Freire, P. (1970). *Pedagogy of the oppressed.* New York, NY: Seabury Press.

— (1998). *Pedagogy of freedom: Ethics, democracy, and civic courage.* Lanham, MD: Rowman & Littlefield.

Fromm, E. (1942). *The fear of freedom*, London, UK: Routledge & Kegan Paul.

Hegel, G. (1807/1977). *Phenomenology of spirit.* Oxford, UK: Oxford University Press.

Marx, K. (1978). "Theses on Feuerbach." In R. Tucker (ed.). *The Marx-Engels Reader* (pp. 143–5). New York, NY: W. W. Norton.

O'Brien, J. (2002). "Be realistic, demand the impossible: Staughton Lynd, Jesse Lemisch, and a committed history." *Radical History Review*, 82, 65–90.

Sartre, J. P. (1956). *Being and nothingness: A phenomenological essay on ontology.* New York, NY: Pocket Books.

1

Contradiction, Consciousness, and Generativity: Hegel's Roots in Freire's Work

Andy Blunden

Paulo Freire owes a great deal to the nineteenth-century German philosopher Hegel, whose work has directly or indirectly inspired every current of genuinely critical thought since his death in 1831.

Hegel's legacy

The most radical movement in Marx and Engels' student days was a group of Hegel's students known as the Young Hegelians. But by the mid-nineteenth century Hegel's philosophy had been eclipsed by positivism and the rising influence of natural science. Marx sought to retain the revolutionary dialectical character of Hegelianism, while responding to the need for a scientific theory for the workers' movement, by interpreting Hegel in terms of activity (or practice). It is via Marx's interpretation that Hegel's philosophy was most influential during the twentieth century.

Still, very few of the leaders of the socialist movement 100 years ago had any real knowledge of Hegel's philosophy. Probably the most influential leader of Social Democracy who had studied Hegel independently was Georgi Plekhanov, the leader of the Russian Social Democrats. Plekhanov was Lenin's teacher, and Lenin went on to lead the 1917 Russian Revolution. During his exile in Switzerland in 1914–15, Lenin read Hegel's *The Science of Logic* (1969/1816) (both the long and short versions) and his *History of Philosophy* (1955), and made annotations on his reading. There is no doubt that Lenin learnt a lot from Hegel, and Lenin meant it when he wrote: "It is impossible completely to understand Marx's (1996/1867) *Capital*, and especially its first chapter, without having thoroughly studied and understood the whole of Hegel's Logic. Consequently, half a century later none of the Marxists understood Marx!"

Lenin's annotations were published in Volume 38 of his *Collected Works* (1972/1916), and were the basis on which Marxists of the Third and Fourth Internationals understood Hegel. These annotations tended to function, however, as a substitute for an actual study of Hegel, which may be forgivable, as Hegel is very difficult to read and understand. Nonetheless, Lenin's attention to Hegel legitimized and inspired the serious study of Hegel, and some outstanding Hegelians emerged out of the Soviet Union and other parts of the Communist International and the Trotskyist movement.

It was however the independent study of Hegel by Georg Lukács, a leader of the Hungarian communists, and a genuine intellectual in his own right, that recovered the full depth of Hegel's legacy for the Communist movement. Lukács inspired the formation of the Frankfurt School, and although Lukács himself never joined it, the Frankfurt School continued a tradition of Critical Theory and the study of Hegel in the tradition initiated by Lukács.

Hegelian thought appeared in the late nineteenth century in the United States of America where the Pragmatists, especially John Dewey and George Herbert Mead, developed a form of Hegelianism in which Hegel's name is rarely mentioned. Rather, similar to Marx's original appropriation of Hegel, they substituted for Hegel's Spirit the sum total of interactions between individuals.

Hegel also developed his own theology and while he remained a minority figure in theology generally, his ideas are influential among proponents of Liberation Theology, where Christianity and Marxism found an area of common ground. Quite separately from these currents, in the 1930s, Hegel's influence in France took a surprising turn. The only translations of Hegel available in French had been the very poor translations of Augusto Vera, and as a result the French had taken no interest in Hegel. Despite the efforts of the French Hegelian Alexandre Koyré, like England, France remained firmly in the grip of analytical philosophy. But in 1933, the Russian emigré Alexander Kojève presented an astounding series of lectures on the master-servant narrative in Hegel's *Phenomenology of Spirit* (2011/1807), which electrified the French Left. Jean Hyppolite published a fine translation of *Phenomenology* and very soon new interpretations and translations of this book exploded in France. This movement fostered a new understanding of the anti-colonial movement, including support for the Algerian resistance to French rule, and Simone de Beauvoir's *The Second Sex*. This exclusive focus on the master-servant narrative, or more generally, focus on Recognition as elaborated in Hegel's early works, has tended to overshadow all other interpretations of Hegel and flowed over into the Frankfurt School and the American Pragmatists, leading to a current of social theory based on interactionism and the struggle for recognition.

Freire's Hegelianism is sensitive to this current, evidenced in his interest in Sartre and Fanon, but tends to draw on the same broad sources of Hegelianism that inspired Marx and twentieth-century Marxists.

An easy way to get a grasp of Hegel's idea is the concept of Zeitgeist, or "spirit of the times." Geist, or spirit, is the central concept for Hegel and its meaning is retained in the concept of Zeitgeist with which we will all be familiar. The Zeitgeist is the overall dominant consensus on what are the main questions in life and the kind of answers that can be given. This includes oppositional ideas as well as the dominant view, as those who oppose the answers given by those in power, still find themselves having to answer the same questions and in much the same terms. The Zeitgeist reflects the whole way of life of a community, the way they make a living, the kinds of behavior that are rewarded, and the sense of justice and what kind of thing is seen as despicable or threatening. Zeitgeist carries the implication that one and the same spirit affects everyone, and of course this is not true of modern societies. The point is: if you want to understand how a society ticks it is better to start from the whole, and then move down to finer and finer grains of detail—the various classes, subcultures, and so on—than to try to understand society by adding up the nature of isolated individuals, because individuals, on their own, have no nature whatsoever.

Further, Hegel believed that while individuals all shared a common culture, a people was only really alive to the extent that their most basic beliefs and principles were under continual criticism and skeptical challenge. As soon as a society stopped questioning its fundamental beliefs then "the spirit left them" and moved on elsewhere. Cultural criticism was thus the heart and soul of the community for Hegel.

How Hegel transcended the problems of philosophy

Since the beginning of modern philosophy with Descartes in the 1630s, philosophy had posed for itself the problem of an individual human being confronting a natural world, and how it was possible for an individual to have knowledge of that world. If the world is given to us only in sensations, then how do we know what exists "behind" sensation? And how do people acquire Reason, and is Reason a reliable source of knowledge? Is Reason innate, and if not how can a capacity for Reason spring from sensations alone? These questions proved insoluble because they were wrongly posed in terms of an individual person passively observing Nature from outside—just like the typical philosopher.

Hegel saw that a person's relation with Nature was mediated by the use of tools and all the artifacts that had been created by previous generations, while a person's relation to their community was mediated by language, education, and their participation in common projects. People did not confront Nature as naked individuals. Rather an individual's relationship was with the culture into which he had been raised. And how this culture—the various tools, domestic animals, crops, buildings, and so on—worked was no mystery, because these were objects created by human activity. The problem of Nature was one of the adequacy of the entire way of life and way of thinking of which they were part, living in some

community, at some definite juncture in the history and development of culture.

Hegel then began his study with the whole community, and
asked how a certain form of life, a certain way of thinking was
possible and then asked how individual consciousness developed
out of the whole collective way of life in which the individual participated. The individual "subject" then was not an isolated person confronting Nature, but a subject situated in some historically
developed form of society, dealing with Nature from within a definite form of life.

Hegel called this collective form of life a "formation of consciousness" ("formation" is a translation of the German word,
Gestalt). Hegel conceived of this "formation of consciousness" as
simultaneously a way of thinking and acting, a way of life or a
form of social practice, and a constellation of artifacts (this means
everything from land and crops to artworks and language). It was
this moving Gestalt that was the substance and subject of his philosophy. Individuality and the whole variety of ways of life within
any given community arises through differentiation within this
whole. The development of this whole is driven by contradictions
within its core principles, which, sooner or later, comes under challenge and the whole system fails and opens the door for a new
system. And so it goes on. As Goethe said, "All that exists deserves
to perish" (cited in Engels, 1997, p. 185).

Hegel saw the state not as a limitation on freedom, as libertar-
ians do, but rather as an expression and guarantor of freedom: a
person only has freedom to live and flourish to the extent that they
are part of a state (meaning not just a government but a whole system of life governed by the rule of law) that expresses their aspirations and protects them from outside threats, crime, and injustice.
Hegel did not see the class struggle in the way it later came to be
seen. Hegel lived before the Chartist movement in England, before
the first proletarian uprisings in France in the 1830s, and he had no
conception of the poor masses becoming a progressive force.

This may seem odd to people living in a modern bureaucratic
state today, but Hegel's situation was more like that of people in
Vietnam or Cuba in the 1950s, fighting for a state of their own. In
Hegel's lifetime, Germany did not have a state. Until 1815, Germany
was part of what was still called the Holy Roman Empire, made
up of over 300 small principalities, some Catholic some Protestant,

each with their own class structure and traditions. They had a total population of about 25 million, that is, an average of about 86,000 per state, about one-third that of the London Borough of Hackney today. So the "state" that Hegel talks about is more comparable to the ancient Greek polis, the ideal size of which was, according to Aristotle, such that the entire city could be surveyed from a hilltop. After 1815, the German Federation was composed of 38 states, comparable in size to the Paris of the Paris Commune, and, given a decent constitution, capable of controlling its own destiny, despite predatory neighbors like England, France, Russia, and Austria-Hungary.

In fact, what Hegel calls a "formation of consciousness" is best imagined as a social movement, or something like a branch of science or a religious community: a group of people bound together by the common pursuit of an idea, adhering to a system of social practices in line with that ideal. A modern multicultural state is made up of a whole bunch of such communities, social movements, and institutions, with individuals defining themselves in relation to a number of such projects.

Spirit and activity

In his earliest works, Hegel theorized "spirit" in much the same way we would today, as a something that expressed a way of life and its ideas, but then he turned this around: Spirit became something that pre-existed human life and manifested itself in human activity. The difference between these two ways of understanding "spirit" is subtle, but it does have methodological implications. Marxists interpret "spirit" as activity, or practice. In fact, this idea of understanding life as activity, or praxis, pre-dates Hegel.

As is well-known, Descartes' philosophy was plagued by a dualism between thought and matter. Spinoza had endeavored to overcome this dualism by declaring that thought was just a property of matter, not a separate substance. However, Spinoza had retained Descartes' mechanical conception of Nature, and this left human beings trapped in a fatalistic determinism. It was Johann Gottfried Herder—a friend of Goethe and a contemporary critic of Immanuel Kant—who made a crucial revision of Spinoza: Nature was active. Whereas Descartes had seen intentions as something that could only be attributed to human beings, Herder said that intentions, struggle, and contradiction were part of Nature. Spinoza and Herder were Pantheists, so God did not make Nature, God is Nature.

Another critic of Kant, Fichte, took up this idea and made activity the foundation of his system. Activity, or practice is both subjective and objective; it is subjective in the sense that it expresses a person's intentions, but objective in the sense that it is in the world, subject to the constraints of Nature. But Fichte was an extreme individualist. The Ego was pure activity and Fichte aimed to build a social theory and an entire philosophy on the basis of this Ego, an extreme version of liberalism, and in fact, Fichte was a supporter of the Jacobins. So Hegel appropriated this idea of activity that was both subjective and objective, but instead of beginning with the activity of individuals and adding them up to the state, Hegel took activity as Spirit, expressed in the subjective/objective activity of individuals.

In 1843, Moses Hess, a student of Fichte's, published a founding work of communism, *The Philosophy of the Act,* and he was one of the people Marx met in Paris in the early 1840s, who won Marx to communism. In the spring of 1845 Marx responded with his own version of the philosophy of the act, *Theses on Feuerbach* (1975/1845). The change from Spirit to Activity, or praxis, was not just a semantic point. When Marx and Engels wrote the *Communist Manifesto* (1976/1848) they did not declare that the workers movement had to do what was logical, and Marx did not try to foresee the future of the workers' movement. On the contrary, he studied the workers movement as it actually was, its ideas and its aspirations, and gave voice to these in the Manifesto. This was the main methodological difference: the point was to understand activity, make it intelligible, and give voice to it. But Marx remained dedicated to the study of Hegel to the end of his days, and his theories are much closer to Hegel's ideas than is generally realized.

The cell form

"[P]roblem-posing education seeks out and investigates the 'generative word.'"

Freire, 2011, p. 110

So far so good, but this still left Hegel with the problem of how to grasp a complex entity like a nation-state as a whole, as a Gestalt. Here the answer came from Goethe. Although renowned as a poet and novelist, Goethe was an avid student of Nature as well, but he was hostile to the "Newtonian" style of science that had become dominant (and is still dominant to this day). Goethe objected to the attempt to explain complex phenomena by means of invisible forces acting "behind the scenes." He was also less than impressed by the practice of classifying things according to attributes, as in Linnaeus' taxonomy, rather than trying to determine what made an organism just as it was. Goethe developed the idea of Urphänomen, or cell, which was the smallest unit of the complex whole that could exhibit all the essential properties of the whole, and in fact constituted the whole. Microscopes were still not powerful enough in his day for Goethe to have any idea of the complex microstructure of living organisms, but it was shortly after his death that the cell was discovered and biology put on a scientific basis for the first time.

Hegel appropriated this idea and developed it further: one could say that the Urphänomen was the Urphänomen of Hegel's philosophy, the cell from which the fully developed organism was developed. The cell from which Hegel was to understand the formation of consciousness (Gestalt) was the concept. That is, a formation of consciousness was to be understood as a combination of concepts, with one concept—it's self-concept—lying at the heart of it. Self-evidently, Hegel did not mean by "concept" something that simply existed inside the head. On the contrary, a concept was manifest in actions, social practices, and cultural products such as language. A community could be understood by cultural critique— the systematic, critical study of its concepts.

Marx rendered Hegel's "formation of consciousness" as a social formation, and like Hegel, Marx understood the way of thinking and the social practices to be intimately tied up with one another, which is one of the reasons that Marx devoted his life to the study of bourgeois political economy, taking it quite seriously, but seeking out the internal contradictions in the bourgeois concept of "value."

And like Hegel, Marx needed to identify the cell of bourgeois society, and this he found to be the commodity relation. Note that Marx did not claim that the commodity relation was the cell of everything that happened in modern society, it was the "economic cell-form," the unit of economic life. And of course, he understood the central role that the economy played in social and political life in general. Hegel, on the other hand, took as his unit private property, and aimed to unfold the entirety of social and political life—from morality, family life, and economics up to world history—from the relation of private property. One might say that Hegel went too far here.

But the methodological insight that Marx adopted from Hegel is the heart of the matter. Just one relation, one concept, if exhaustively interrogated, reveals a whole network of relations and ramifications that link it to the social formation of which it is a part. Within the myriad of the phenomena of daily life, just one of relations may prove to be crucial. But any relation, if exhaustively examined reveals the entirety of the society to which it belongs. Surely it was this idea that Freire had in mind when he encouraged learners to take up a problem and investigate it to the end. The idea of the "generative word" is pure Hegel. Do not set out from general surveys and impressions, statistical summaries, and so on—just take one relation, or one artifact, and investigate it to the end!

The situation and contradiction

"Human beings are because they are in a situation."

Freire, 2011, p. 109

The driving, creative force of Hegel's thought is contradiction. Each new concept arises through the resolution of a contradiction or problem. The concept of "situation" captures this idea very well. People and their circumstances have to be understood as a "situation," and Hegel understood situations in a very specific way. In normal, bourgeois social science, if you asked "what is the situation?" you would be given a series of factors—the level of unemployment, productivity, the rate of inflation, workforce participation, and so on. This kind of description is abstract and superficial.

In the understanding of the economy, Hegel understood the contradiction that was driving development, not only in the economy but in political life as well, to be the contradiction between human

needs and the means of their satisfaction. In a given situation, people's needs are determined by their activity, directed toward meeting social needs, just as much as their activity is directed toward
meeting their needs. The two aspects of activity form a unity, and
neither one nor the other is primary. Needs and labor form an integral system of activity. But at a certain point, needs arise that cannot be met within the current arrangement and this forces change.
The political system arises on the basis of problems that arise in the
system of needs and labor, which cannot be resolved within that
system. To understand any specific crisis or situation, it is necessary to identify the contradiction that is at work, and form a concept of that situation. This allows understanding of the new forms
of activity that arise from the contradiction.

It is the same for an individual person, or a community. You
cannot understand a person—and nor can persons understand
themselves—by listing their characteristics: you are your situation.
How do you meet your needs? Where do your needs come from?
Do they match up? Or is there a contradiction here, which is driving you to change. But a human being could not even exist were
they not in some situation. In contrast to isolated individualism,
our freedom arises only in and through the definite form of life of
which you are a part, but that does not mean that freedom is just
given. On the contrary, freedom means a continual overcoming of
contradictions, such as that between needs and labor.

Hegel laid the foundation for his philosophy with his Logic. In
this work he began with an empty concept—Being. Not being this
or being that, but just Being. Put like this, without any content,
Being is seen to be Nothing. And thus already we see the system
of concepts Becoming. The simplest thing that can be without
being something, is a Quality, and if a Quality changes while
remaining the same then this is Quantity. And so on. And thus
he proceeded, beginning from no presuppositions other than a
living community of people capable of questioning their own way
of life, and generated the whole series of concepts that makes up
Logic. Each concept generated from the contradiction inherent
in posing the previous concept as universal. In the Logic, Hegel
developed the method that he then went on to utilize in analysis
of the whole range of problems and sciences. The central concept
of the Logic is the Concept itself, which marks a nodal point in
the development of the Logic. The first part of the Logic has a

series of opposites that follow one another, each pair of opposites pushing the previous set into the background so to speak,
until all this is transcended with the emergence of a new concept. Then this concept develops by becoming more and more
concrete, in interaction with others. The structure of the Logic
can be seen at first as the stream of meaningless data (the stuff of
bourgeois social science) followed by the search for the new concept, marked by contradictions, and culminated in the discovery
of the Urphänomen or cell: then a reconstruction of the whole
(Gestalt) in the light of this cell, which sheds light of a particular
hue on the whole situation.

It is in the Logic above all that Hegel demonstrates the dialectic.
There are hundreds of definitions of dialectics, but the best I think
is that dialectics is the art of handling concepts. Studying a situation and working out how to grasp the situation as a concept is to
learn dialectics.

Immanent critique

"We must pose this existential, concrete, present situation to the
people as a problem which challenges them."

Freire, 2011, p. 95

The dynamism that drives the Logic is contradictions that are
internal to the concept itself, rather than criticism from outside the
concept. Hegel does not counterpose to a concept, a better concept,
but rather investigates the concept itself, in its own terms, from
what is already implicit in the concept. Likewise, when we said
that the formations of consciousness in Phenomenology develop
only as a result of subjecting their own principles to criticism, it is
important to see that it is internal criticism, criticism that emerges
from the concept or form of activity itself, when it oversteps its
own limits. Attack from outside only causes a social formation to
harden up, and actually suppresses contradictions, as in the old
aphorism about the need for an external enemy to close ranks. So
criticism has to come from within the situation itself. This is why
Freire is so adamant that the activists must not go into a community to tell people what they must do.

Hegel demonstrated this method in all his works. Every concept that he deals with is developed and allowed to demonstrate its own limits, and give birth to its negation. The expression "immanent critique" was coined by the Frankfurt School, but it accurately describes both the method Hegel used in developing his own system, and the method Marx used in his work on political economy: not counterposing socialism to capitalism, but bringing out the contradictions inherent in the bourgeoisie's own theory of its own way of life. In order to emancipate ourselves, we have to bring to light the contradiction within our own situation—and no one can do it for us. Only an immanent critique reveals the truth of the situation and allows change.

So formations of consciousness have to be seen as projects, rather than seeing society as composed of different groups or categories of people. Every community is pursuing some ideal, and struggling to realize it, and it is only by such struggle that change can come about. And within any community, numerous such projects are being pursued. This is what makes up the fabric of a community. The method of problem-posing education expresses this understanding. People can only acquire a concept if they need the concept in order to solve some problem; that concept which captures the contradiction they are facing constitutes an ideal that they can struggle to realize. This concept can only arise through thoroughgoing criticism of the existing society. By focusing criticism on one artefact or one relation, along the lines pioneered by Goethe, a new vision can be developed. And in the process we learn to think philosophically.

Now I want to spend a little time on two twentieth-century currents of Hegel interpretation that, in my view, focus on certain aspects of Hegel, at the expense of missing other elements. I refer to the interpretation initiated by Kojève in France based on the master-servant dialectic, and the Pragmatist interpretation that focuses on interactions. Both interpretations highlight the concept of Recognition, but misconstrue Recognition because the idea of mediation, which is central to Hegel's thought, is overlooked.

Masters, servants, and mediation

The master-servant dialectic is a narrative that appears in every version of Hegel's system from his first effort in 1802 up to the final version of *Encyclopedia* in 1830. But it reached its fullest exposition in *Phenomenology* of *Spirit* (2011/1807), after which it became shorter and less dramatic in each successive version. It is the only instance in Hegel's work in which he uses a narrative. There are two reasons for the choice of the narrative form in this instance. The topic is the emergence of Spirit into self-consciousness, that is, how modern civilization, marked by the existence of a state and private property, emerged from the "state of nature." Hegel's story is a direct answer to the "state of nature" narratives of people like Rousseau and Hobbes who idealized the "noble savage" and saw the formation of states and private property as a kind of fall from grace. Hegel wanted to show that the state of nature means the reign of force and violence, and although the state is born in violence, it is not maintained by violence, but on the contrary, leads to freedom. The other reason for the use of narrative may be that he saw that the concepts regulating the ethical life of a state, rest on narratives like the epics of the ancient world.

The story is that two people meet in the wild; having in common no law or language, they are forced to fight to the death for the other's recognition as a person worthy of rights; one subject chooses life and is subordinated by the other and subject to that law. The master has needs, but rather than satisfying his desire, which destroys the object of desire that has to be recreated all over again, he turns his defeated foe into a servant, who labors continuously on his behalf. The irony is that the master's main desire is recognition but the only recognition that is of value is recognition by an equal, and his dilemma can only be resolved by the servant achieving freedom. Meanwhile, the servant, by laboring to meet the master's needs has created the means for their own emancipation. Thus, what begins in violence and force, leads through its own logic to the rule of law and a modern state.

The point is that the narrative deals with an occasion of unmediated interaction, which, Hegel is at pains to point out, can never happen in a modern state, where there are always customs and laws to regulate interaction. But he shows that even in this instance, interaction is possible because the two subjects may have within them the means of mediating their own interaction. This is achieved by the two subjects each splitting into two, namely the needs and the means of their satisfaction. By the servant's labor mediating between the master's needs and their satisfaction, the servant's needs are met. Thus, so long as you can produce something that another person values, then interaction is possible. This initial interaction, based on needs and labor, develops through its own internal contradictions into a political system in which every individual enjoys rights.

Hegel says at the beginning of Logic "there is nothing, nothing in Heaven, or in Nature or in Mind or anywhere else which does not equally contain both immediacy and mediation." So it is vital to see how even in this exceptional situation where two subjects, utterly alien to one another, meet, that Hegel works out how the relation can be mediated. But Kojève and all those who followed him missed this point. They saw only the unmediated confrontation, the struggle to the death (why?) ending in the enslavement of one by the other, but with the prospect of redemption through labor.

Nonetheless, the fact is that this scenario marvelously captures the situation that arises when a colonial power arrives on the land of a prospective colony. Exactly! And it is easy to see how this narrative proved an excellent way to theorize the situation of a colonized people and the rationale for their struggle for self-determination and Recognition as a nation alongside other nations. But the key thing is that the whole plot unfolds from an unmediated confrontation, which, according to Hegel, can never happen in a modern state. So why does Hegel have it in his system at all? Because, if we have a confrontation of nations, or the emergence of a new social movement, or any oppressed and excluded group struggling to achieve self-consciousness and demanding recognition for their specific ideals and form of life, then the narrative also describes this situation. But never does Hegel see the relation between individuals in terms of a fight to the death and nor does he believe that there is any kind of drive to subordinate others in the human spirit. On the contrary freedom and equality arrive only thanks to struggle.

So it is easy to see why Kojève's lectures caused such a commotion and how they came to have such an impact on the anti-colonial struggle and the women's movement, but it should also be remembered that this narrative represents such a minuscule part of Hegel's whole work, and in so many ways, the master-servant narrative is very untypical of Hegel's work as a whole.

Interactions, movements, and mediation

The master-servant narrative is often referred to as the "struggle for recognition," and this notion of recognition, has caught on more broadly, without the fight to the death and narrative drama of the master-servant dialectic; people need recognition. Indeed in Hegel's (1805) draft of his system, Recognition functioned as the key concept.

Recognition has broadly the same meaning as it has in international relations, and again it was Fichte who first introduced the idea of Recognition into philosophy. Recognition means being accepted within a larger family as a subject enjoying moral equality with others and in charge of their own affairs as part of that larger family. Indeed, Hegel's theory of education was based on a person's need to have the means for such participation in civil society and the state. For an individual, Recognition means inclusion, inclusion as a citizen in society, inclusion as an equal in some profession or a project of some kind.

In his 1805 system, Hegel saw the circulation of the products of labor on the market, as items of value, as the key form of recognition upon which a modern state could be built. The modern state itself rests on the recognition of every (adult male) as an autonomous agent or citizen. In such a state, relations between citizens were to be mediated by participation in all kinds of professional associations, local government, and so on, as well as by the rule of law. Recognition is always extended by a collective or an institution of some kind. Hegel did not intend Recognition as a means of understanding interactions between individuals, since these are always regulated by custom and law.

Modern social theory has amply demonstrated that Hegel's concept of "Recognition" has a crucial explanatory role to play in understanding social action. Anyone who has ever organized a strike will know that lack of recognition for one's work is a much more powerful motivator today than simple desire for more purchasing power.

While the concept of Recognition has proved to be a powerful idea, both for theorists and activists, it is commonly taken to be a relation existing between two subjects (be they individual persons or "social subjects") without taking account of the mediation between them. This mediation involves the stakes that are being fought over and the sources of motivation as well as the rules, customs, and language in which the dispute is fought out. These forms of mediation pre-date the struggle for recognition, and in fact form both the source of the problem and the means of its solution. It is a feature of today's liberalism that theorists imagine that a culture can exist purely and simply on the basis of interaction between independent individuals. But nothing happens in a cultural vacuum, and Hegel was above all a theorist of cultural development, and of how people create, recreate, and change the culture within which they live.

Hegel and education

Hegel was a teacher throughout his life; at first as a private tutor, then as an unpaid lecturer, then headmaster of a high school, then as a professor, lecturing to both students and the public. He had a speech impediment that made his lectures difficult to listen to and his books are almost unintelligible, but he was apparently an excellent teacher. After his death his students transformed his esoteric ideas into a popular movement.

His approach to education was geared to preparing young people for participation in civil society, rather than imparting knowledge. But he ridiculed the demand that students needed to "think for themselves." But Hegel set a very high standard for his students, demanding that they study the classic writings and understand them, so as to be ready to become autonomous contributors to the development of culture in their own right. Without first acquiring an understanding of the existing culture, such participation would be impossible.

References

de Beauvoir, S. (1972). *The Second Sex*, trans. H. M. Parshley. London, GB: Penguin.

Engels, F. (1997). "Feuerbach and the end of classical German philosophy." In L. Feuerbach, K. Marx and F. Engels (eds). *German socialist philosophy* (pp. 183–225). New York, NY: Continuum.

Fichte, J. (1796/2000). "Foundations of natural right." In F. Neuhouser (ed.). *Foundations of natural right according to the Principles of the Wissenschaftslehre* (pp. 1–133). Cambridge, U.K.: Cambridge University Press.

Freire, P. (2011/1970). *Pedagogy of the oppressed*, trans. Ramos, M. B., London, GB: Continuum.

Hegel, G. W. F. (1805). *The philosophy of spirit (Jena Lectures 1805–6)* PART II. Actual Spirit. Retrieved from: www.marxists.org/reference/archive/hegel/works/jl/ch02a.htm

— (1910/1807). *The phenomenology of mind*, translated, with an Introduction and notes by J. B. Baillie, London, UK: George Allen & Unwin.

— (1952/1821). *Hegel's philosophy of right*, translated with Notes by T. M. Knox. Oxford, UK: Oxford University Press.

— (1955). *Hegel's lectures on the history of philosophy*, trans. John Sibree. New York, NY: Dover.

— (1969/1816). *The science of logic*, trans. A. V. Miller. London GB: George Allen & Unwin.

— (1971). *Hegel's philosophy of mind. Part three of the encyclopedia of the philosophical sciences (1830)*, trans. William Wallace, together with the zusätze in Boumann's text (1845), trans. A. V. Miller, with a Foreword by J. N. Findlay. Oxford, UK: Oxford University Press.

— (1979). *System of ethical life [1802/3]) and First philosophy of spirit [1803–4]),* trans. T. M. Knox. New York, NY: State University of New York Press.

— (1984). *The letters*, trans. C. Butler and C. Seiler. Bloomington, IN: Indiana University Press.

— (2009/1830). *Hegel's logic*, trans. William Wallace, with a Foreword by Andy Blunden. Pacifica, CA: Marxists Internet Archive Publications.

— (2011/1807). *The phenomenology of spirit*, trans. Terry Pinkard. http://web.mac.com/titpaul/Site/Phenomenology_of_Spirit_page.html

Hess, M. (1964/1843). "The Philosophy of the Act." In A. Fried and R. Sanders (eds). *Socialist thought, a documentary history* (pp. 260–1). Chicago, IL: Aldine Publishing Co.

Kojève, A. (1969/1933–9). *Introduction to the reading of Hegel. Lectures on the phenomenology of spirit.* Ithaca, NY: Cornell University Press.

Lenin, V. I. (1972/1916). *Collected works*, vol. 38. London, GB: Lawrence & Wishart.

Lukács, G. (1971/1923). *History and class consciousness*, London, GB: Merlin.

— (1975/1938). *The young Hegel*, London, GB: Merlin.

Marx, K. (1975/1845). "Theses on Feuerbach." In L. Churbanov and L. Golman (eds). *Marx Engels collected works* (vol. 5, p. 3). New York, NY: International Publishers.

— (1976/1848). "Manifesto of the communist party." In L. Churbanov and L. Golman (eds). *Marx Engels collected works* (vol. 6, p. 3). New York, NY: International Publishers.

— (1986/1857). "The method of political economy." In L. Churbanov and L. Golman (eds). *Marx Engels collected works* (vol. 28, p. 37). New York, NY: International Publishers.

— (1996/1867). "Preface to the first German edition of *Capital*." In L. Churbanov and L. Golman (eds). *Marx Engels collected works* (vol. 35, p. 7). New York, NY: International Publishers.

Pinkard, T. (1996). *Hegel's phenomenology. The sociality of reason.* Cambridge, UK: Cambridge University Press.

— (2000). *Hegel. A biography.* Cambridge, UK: Cambridge University Press.

Williams, R. R. (1997). *Hegel's ethics of recognition.* Los Angeles, CA: University of California Press.

2

Freire and Marx in Dialogue

Tricia Kress and Robert Lake

In Memoriam: Paula Allman
1944–2011

"If you abstract Freire's ideas from the Marxist theoretical context, you will miss the precision of his analysis and ignore the revolutionary or transformative intent of his work."

Allman, 1999, p. 90

When we first began planning this volume, we did not intend on writing this chapter about Marx's influence on Paulo Freire's work. Neither of us is a Marxist scholar, and we knew there were folks who are much more qualified to write this piece than we are. Robert first proposed this volume to David Barker of Bloomsbury Publishers, who was interested but made it clear that acceptance was contingent on 70 percent of the volume being written by "senior scholars." Robert reached out to several senior scholars, who then put us in contact with additional senior scholars, and it was Peter Mayo who recommended that we reach out to Paula Allman for our chapter about Marx's influence on Freire. In the summer of 2011, Paula graciously agreed to write the chapter but also told us that she was very sick with lung cancer. A few months later, Paula wrote to us to share sad news that she did not have much time left and she was doubtful that she would be able to complete her contribution. She passed away shortly thereafter on November 2, 2011. We dedicate this piece to Paula Allman, social activist and brilliant scholar of Karl Marx, Paulo Freire, and Antonio Gramsci. Paula, we hope that you are resting in peace and find yourself in dialogue with these thinkers whose ideas you lived with so passionately.

"Paulo said he slept with a copy of 'Das Kapital' under his pillow. He read from it daily like one can suppose the Pope reads from the Bible. He said he was luck[y] to find a copy that was not so bulky."

Fuentes, 2010, p. 134

Freire and Marx: Influence, divergence, and evolution of thought

To understand the work of Paulo Freire, its roots as well as its relevance in the present time and in generations to come, one cannot ignore the influence of Karl Marx. As Mayo (2004) points out, "The Marxist-humanist element is all pervasive in Freire's work" (p. 5), and "Marx's early writings are constantly referred to and provide the basis for Freire's social analysis in his most celebrated work, Pedagogy of the Oppressed" (p. 2). Indeed, a number of prominent ideas that emerge in Freire's philosophy are derivations of themes in Marx's work. Like Marx, Freire underscores the significance of: ideology and consciousness; praxis as the dialectical unity between thought and action; alienation, dehumanization and the reduction of people to "thing-like" status; and liberation via social transformation as the "goal" of history. For example, Dale (2003) points out

> The dialectical social conflict Freire (1970/2000) identifies between the oppressors and the oppressed is directly indebted to Marx's (1933) theory of dialectical materialism. The achievement of conscientization, the telos of Freirean pedagogy, mirrors an escape from the Marxist condition of false consciousness. (p. 57)

Yet Freire's work, however much influenced by Marx, also departs from Marxism in significant ways, particularly around the treatment of education. Notably, Morrow and Torres (2002) explain,

> How was the working class to become self-conscious and create revolution? Marx's answer is revolutionary praxis, an activity that implies a theory of learning: the processes through which dominated consciousness might be transformed into emancipatory consciousness. But Marx's conception of historical materialism does not explicitly develop a social psychological conception of education or learning as transformation beyond metaphorical discussion of "dialectical" reversals. (pp. 23–4)

Lewis (2007) affirms that "Marx pinpoints the problem of education yet lacks a pedagogical solution to this problem" (p. 286); thus Freire's pedagogy informed by Marxism is able to take Marx's work to the next level. As a general theme, when we consider the influence of Marx on Freire's work, we begin to see that in some cases their ideas diverge sharply, and in these moments, Freire's work seems to be an evolutionary advancement on Marx.

One such point of influence, divergence, and evolution is at the notion of human agency which did not appear in Marx's writings until his later works (Dale & Hyslop-Margison, 2010). Freire and Marx both argue that "humans are necessarily exploited and dehumanized by the unequal social relations and surplus labor value embedded within capitalism" (p. 112). Freire's assertion that the oppressed would be the liberators of humanity appears to emerge from Marx's adoption of Hegel's master-slave relationship in the context of capitalist-labourer relations. As Morrow and Torres (2002) explain, "According to this model, only the worker as 'slave' is in a position to understand true freedom as equality; the resulting revolutionary consciousness then becomes the basis of a new form of society that abolishes class division" (p. 23). We see this mirrored in *Pedagogy of the Oppressed*: "It is only the oppressed who, by freeing themselves, can free their oppressors. The latter, as an oppressive class, can free neither others nor themselves" (Freire, 2000, p. 56). Still, Freire appears "far less prepared than the early Marx to accept the inexorable historical dialectic associated with the struggle for changing this relationship"

(Dale & Hyslop-Margison, 2010, p. 112). Rather, Freire's work is more consistent with Marx's evolving perspective that saw human agency as essential for social transformation. Further, he seeks to transcend this dialectic in the move from the oppressor-oppressed relationship that dehumanizes us all toward humanity's liberation. In Freire's words, "It is therefore essential that the oppressed wage the struggle to resolve the contradiction in which they are caught; and the contradiction will be resolved by the appearance of the new man: neither oppressor nor oppressed, but man in the process of liberation" (Freire, 2000, p. 56). Accordingly, while both Freire and Marx saw the endgame of history as liberation from oppression and exploitation, Marx placed more emphasis on social structure than did Freire who also emphasized the significance of individual cognition. For Freire, "Change in the form of social transformation could only occur through the reflection/recognition and action of the oppressed to free themselves from oppressive conditions" (Dale & Hyslop-Margison, 2010, p. 111).

A second example, and perhaps most prominent, is in their treatment of religion. Here, it would appear, at least at first glance, that Marx and Freire were nearly opposed to each other in their philosophies, with Marx denouncing religion and Freire integrating it. Marx's classic critique of religion was predicated on four main tenets: 1) religion is made by humans and is a project of their fears and desires; 2) psychologically, it compensates for the frustrations of everyday life; 3) it acts as a mediator between man and the world, prohibiting people from examining their worlds scientifically, thus keeping them naive; 4) it is used by power holders as a mechanism for social control (Torres, 1992). "For Marx, religion was the archetype of false consciousness since it encouraged working-class individuals to pursue posthumous gratification for suffering rather than transforming their present circumstances" (Dale & Hyslop-Margison, 2010, p. 111). Meanwhile, Freire's work is infused with religion and spirituality; his Christian faith as well as liberation theology significantly influenced his philosophy, in that, liberation of the oppressed is a moral imperative for all of mankind. Freire's work draws quite extensively from religious allusion, often making mention of "rebirth," being "born again," "redemption," and "Easter," but he does so not without critique of his own. In fact, his critique parallels Marx's rather closely, but he departs from Marx in that he does not disregard religion; instead, he sees it as a potential site of conscientization (Freire, 1985).

For example, Torres (1992) explains that for Marx,

> religion arose in particular historical circumstance; as a form of
> social consciousness it responds to a specific period of history in
> human society and will disappear when this period reaches its
> end. And since the history of human society is made by humans
> the transcending of that period and its corresponding social
> consciousness is the responsibility of human action. The critique
> of religion is no more than a first step towards the revolutionary
> transformation of social relations that nurture religion. (p. 2)

Similarly, in *The Politics of Education*, Freire (1985) says about
religion, "Churches are not abstract entities; they are institutions
involved in history. Therefore to understand their educational role
we must take into consideration the concrete situation in which
they exist" (p. 121). He refers to bourgeois religion as the "naïve
and shrewd walking hand in hand" (p. 122), and as "anesthetic
or aspirin practice, expressions of a subjectivist idealism that can
only lead to preservation of the status quo" (ibid.). However, Freire
does not accept the bourgeois church as the essence of religion, but
rather as a perversion that like the oppressor-oppressed relationship needs to be transformed along with society. Freire actually
integrates the notion of the rebirth of religion (what he refers to as
"Easter") with praxis. In his words,

> The real Easter is not commemorative rhetoric. It is praxis; it is
> historical involvement. The old Easter of rhetoric is dead—with
> no hope of resurrection. It is only in the authenticity of historical
> praxis that Easter becomes the death that makes life possible. But
> the bourgeois world view, basically necrophiliac (death loving)
> and therefore static, is unable to accept this supremely biophiliac
> (life-loving) experience of Easter. The bourgeois mentality—
> which is far more than just a convenient abstraction—kills the
> profound historical dynamism of Easter and turns it into no
> more than a date on the calendar. (Freire, 1985, p. 123)

For Freire, religion itself is not the problem, but rather the fashion-
ing of religion into a tool of domination via the necrophiliac bourgeois consciousness. As a final departure from Marx, Freire (1985)
specifically makes mention that hope lies not in walking away from
religion, but in recreating it.

Freire's and Marx's works also converge and diverge with/from each other in their intended use. Whereas both bodies of work are meant to be read and heard, Freire's work is also meant to be lived and experienced. Marx sought to teach the masses about the operations of capitalism and their resulting disadvantage (Gabriel, 2011), but for Freire liberation would not be won by talking at the oppressed. Notably, their attention to education (or lack thereof) demonstrates this point. As Morrow and Torres (2002) explain, "Marx's writings on education, women, and children amount to just a few dozen pages [. . .] these discussions are embedded in a very general premise about the intimate relationship between knowledge and social practice that is sketched in Marx's 'Theses on Feuerbach'" (p. 24). They further assert, Marx's work presupposed a learning process on the part of the workers in order to bring about revolution, but little attention was paid to how that process is actually brought about. "How does the culturally deprived, alienated worker become an active learner when the very conditions inhibit the formation of the reflective consciousness" (ibid.)? Here, Freire's work regarding education can be thought of as an extension of Marxism that is grounded in the lived realities of the people. Notably, Freire (1985) explains that the power of critical educators "lies not in their merely speaking for those who are forbidden to speak, but most important, in their side-by-side struggle with those silenced so that they can effectively speak the word by revolutionarily transforming the society that reduces them to silence" (p. 146). Liberation needs to emerge from the oppressed who by liberating themselves will liberate humanity (Freire, 2007). And yet, as Mayo (2004) explains, "Pedagogical activity is discussed not in a vacuum but in the context of an analysis of power and its structural manifestations" (p. 5). In this regard, Freire and Marx were epistemologically aligned (they espoused the same ideals, utilized a number of the same concepts, and at times even spoke the same discourse); however, ontologically, the way they went about their work was at times quite different. Broadly speaking, Freire's work can be thought of as reinforcing and extending (i.e. evolving) Marxism through education infused with a real-world sensibility that emerged from the lived experiences of workers.

Finally, Freire demonstrates an acute awareness of education as a social institution that is shaped by and shapes the sociohistorical context, and, therefore, can function as a mechanism for both reproducing the unjust social order and transforming it. He explicitly cautions against the potential for education to maintain domination, even if that education is about so-called liberating ideals. In his words, "Attempting to liberate the oppressed without their reflective participation in the act of liberation is to treat them as objects which must be saved from a burning building; it is to lead them into the populist pitfall and transform them into masses which can be manipulated" (Freire, 2000, p. 65). In this regard, Marx's notion of alienation then filters into Freire's concept of alienating and oppressive education. As learners (and teachers too) are divorced from the gnosiological process, like alienated workers, they become part of the "machine." This then leads us to Freire's notion of praxis, which, while informed by Marxism, diverges from Marx in significant ways. First, Freire's notion of praxis is not coupled with labor, which for Marx is the ontological basis of humanity. Second, Freire's notion of praxis is dialogical and not just individualistic—praxis is a relationship between subjects, and not only between subject-object. Third, "Freire gives priority to communicative relations and 'love' rather than conflict in pedagogical and social relations" (Morrow & Torres, 2002, p. 28). By engaging the oppressed in their own learning, critical pedagogy, as philosophy and practice of reflective action among people in the world (not just laborers), is informed by and has the potential to bring forth the goals of Marxism. Through the development of critical consciousness via reading the word and the world, "the oppressed find the oppressor out and become involved in the organized struggle for their liberation" (Freire, 2000, p. 65). Freire's humanistic praxis, "retains value in the context of concrete, local struggles and social movements where agents must articulate particular utopian visions from within their own unique life-histories" (Morrow & Torres, 2002, p. 29).

Freire and Marx in relationship: History as a conversation

In preparation for this chapter, we encountered a wealth of literature about both Freire and Marx, and a considerable amount about the intersections of their work. As we read numerous texts written by and about both Freire and Marx, we began to understand that the way in which Freire engaged with Marxism resembled the ways in which he engaged with the people in his life, which was also the way he intended for his work to be engaged with by others. Freire "lived" alongside Marx even though Karl Marx the man had long since passed. This was obvious in how he spoke about Marx in relation to his work and his life. Fuentes's (2010) above recollection of Paulo Freire joking that he slept with *Das Kapital* under his pillow is just one example of how Marx was present in Paulo's life even as he slept. In *We Make the Road By Walking* (Horton & Freire, 1990), Freire personified his interactions with Marxism in a similar way. He explained his foray into Marxism thusly, "the more I talked with the people, the more I learned from the people. I got the conviction that the people were sending me to Marx. The people never did say, 'Paulo, please why don't you go to read Marx?' No. The people never said that, but their reality said that to me" (Freire in Horton & Freire, 1990, p. 245). Later in this same discussion, he refers to his reading of Marx as "meetings" and he tells of how he "spoke" to Marx. We quote Freire here (in Horton & Freire, 1990) at length.

> Then I began to read Marx and to read about Marx, and the more I did that the more I became convinced that we really should become absolutely committed to a global process of transformation. But what is interesting in my case—this is not the case for all the people whose background is similar to mine—my "meetings" with Marx never suggested to me to stop "meeting" Christ. I never said to Marx: "Look, Marx, really Christ was a baby. Christ was naïve." And I also never said to Christ, "Look, Marx was a materialistic and terrible man." I always spoke to both of them in a very loving way. (p. 246)

Captured in Freire's words is a sense of being with Marx, of spending time with him, which is reminiscent of the ways that numerous scholars have written about their own in-person meetings with Paulo Freire (Wilson et al., 2010). Freire engaged with Marx's ideas as not just existing in the brain but as alive, existing in, and emerging from people's lived realities. He invited philosophers like Marx into his life and into conversation with him, which was appropriate, since for Freire, dialogue was essential to his praxis.

The way Freire spoke about and incorporated Marxism into his work is reminiscent of Oakeshott's (1962) notion of history as a conversation.

> As civilized human beings, we are the inheritors, neither of an inquiry about ourselves and the world, nor of an accumulating body of information, but of a conversation, begun in the primeval forests and extended and made more articulate in the course of centuries. It is a conversation which goes on both in public and within each of ourselves. (p. 490)

Erich Fromm sums up Marx's view of history in saying that "man gives birth to himself in the process of history" (1964, p. 15). In other words, there is no history without man; rather than history determining the fate of men, it is man who creates history through his present actions. Freire too saw history as a conversation, and he not only considered how our present ideas dialogue with and extend those of the past but also how contemporary thought and action is recursively connected to the yet unforeseen future (Horton & Freire, 1990). Freire's works contain a number of examples of dialogue in the form of intellectual conversation. It is worth pointing out that in 1987 alone, Freire coauthored three "talking books" that were written in part or whole in a dialogue format (Freire & Macedo, 1987; Shor & Freire, 1987; Horton & Freire, 1990). Thus, we regard it as quite natural to build on this tradition in the remainder of this chapter.

In the sections that follow, we demonstrate Marx's influence on Freire by bringing to life the ways in which Marx's writing is woven into Freire's work and is also a representation of historicity in praxis; that is, the historical authenticity of the influence of Marxism on Freire's work is undeniably philosophical but it is also enacted in the world. Freire himself pointed out that it is not enough to simply examine the role of our forefathers in shaping the current moment, rather, we need to carry those ideas into the present and bring them to bear on the contemporary context. In his words, "Progressive educators of the past have played their part in bringing us to this point, in unveiling practices of oppression and injustice. We still have crucial roles to play. We need to view our work with a sense of perspective and history" (Freire, 1999, p. 29). To accomplish this, we have created a dialogue between

Paulo Freire and Karl Marx. Because both philosophers' works are best understood when contextualized, we have chosen a particular contemporary context (N.E. Where University) in which to situate them and orient their conversation. We have utilized, as much as possible, direct quotes from both Freire and Marx, which we have woven together into a conversation that reflects our understanding of Freire and Marx in relationship to each other, to the past, and to the contemporary moment. This approach allows us to accomplish a number of things: First, the conversation we have constructed models Freire's praxis of dialogue and of being "in conversation with" others and the world. Second, it demonstrates how these ideas are alive as much today as they were in Marx's time and in Freire's time. Third, since critical pedagogy involves having a dialogue with people, we aim to cultivate in our readers what we hope becomes a permanent practice, that is, engaging with text in a way that it becomes the voice in their heads, not just words on a page. Dialogue enables us to meet these goals because our readers can hear the cadence of Freire's and Marx's voices; they are able to envision how these men would be in the world if they were here with us right now; and they are encouraged to join the dialogue as they read. Our readers, thus, live alongside Freire's and Marx's ideas as we overlay and infuse them into our world. In effect, this chapter pushes against the dehumanization and alienation of typical academic forms of writing by demonstrating Freire's and Marx's philosophies as coming from and being in humanity ad infinitum. By bringing their ideas into a context that is familiar enough to our intended audience, we ask our audience to also welcome Freire and Marx into their homes, to share a meal with them at their dinner tables, to learn with them in their classrooms, and to be present with them in their lives, just as Marx was present for Freire. With our readers, we too "make the road by walking" with Freire and Marx in this fictional, but easily recognizable world.

The setting: N.E. Where University

N.E. Where University is a public higher education institution that has been struggling through the global economic downturn of the early twenty-first century. Over the past several years it has suffered the onslaught of the resulting corporatization as the board of directors sought to bolster the university's financial situation via private donations and sponsorships. Students and faculty have also been feeling the brunt of the economic circumstances as class sizes and tuition fees have been increasing, online courses are proliferating, and the number of full-time faculty is decreasing while adjunct faculty is on the rise. The institution also seems to have a vibrant culture of resistance growing amid the student body.

Knowledge for sale in the Neoliberal university

Freire: (Walking past benches in the university commons, thinking out loud) "That man over there looks just like pictures I have seen of Karl Marx!" Freire sits down next to him.

Marx: It's about time you got here! I have been waiting for you for over an hour!

Freire: I apologize, I was taken by all the activity on campus. There seem to be so many contradictory messages occurring at the same time. On the one hand, you have such lively activity in the common spaces, and yet, seemingly mechanical activities in many classroom spaces, with notable exceptions, of course. We are at a public institution meant to serve the people, and yet, it seems that private interests have infiltrated much of the university, right down to the beverages that can be purchased.

Marx: I am pleased that you have so deeply grasped the concept of the dialectical nature of reality that enables us to know what needs changing. I was beginning to wonder if all of society was sinking into animal consciousness and alienation.

Freire: But do you think that is even possible? For oppression to be so complete that alienation permeates all of humanity? "I believe that [. . .] space for change, however small, is always available," but "In this process it is necessary for educators to assume a political posture that renounces the myth of pedagogical neutrality" (Freire & Macedo, 1987, p. 126).

Marx: Yes there is always possibility for change because "capital is constantly compelled to wrestle with the insubordination of the workers" (Marx, 1977, p. 490). However, there appear to be many social conditions that may contribute to anesthetizing workers' consciousness. From what you are telling me about what is happening on this campus, it seems that the "machine," in this case, is the commodification and standardization of "knowledge." This knowledge becomes a "means of domination over, and exploitation of, the producers; they mutilate the laborer into a fragment of a man, degrade him to the level of an appendage of a machine" (Marx, 1977, p. 799).

Freire: That's right, and "one cannot remake, reinvent, or reconstruct a society by means of a mechanical act" (Freire and Macedo 1987, p. 113). Just like the way you explain the self-perpetuating relationship between the capitalist and the labourer, "the forces that mold education so that it is self-perpetuating would not allow education to work against them. This is the reason any radical and profound transformation of an educational system can only take place (and even then, not automatically or mechanically) when society is also radically transformed" (Freire, 1985, p. 170).

On transformation through education

Marx: How do you propose that this radical transformation should take place? How can your view of educational praxis create the kind of world I once envisioned?

Freire: In the present neoliberal context, indeed in any context in which people are exploited at the hands of others, education must involve a critical examination of the social context, and specifically labor relations and relationships among different groups of people. For instance, "a radical and critical education has to focus on what is taking place today inside various social movements and labor unions. Feminist movements, peace movements, and other such movements that express resistance generate in their practices pedagogy of resistance. They teach us that it is impossible to think of education as strictly reduced to the school environment" (Freire & Macedo 1987, p. 61).

Marx: Right you are! The problem is still one that comes out of bourgeois education. And what of education as both institution and industry? I see posters here advertising a promise of gainful employment with the completion of the university degree, but in a capitalist system, there can be no guarantees of employment for all people. "The self-valorization of capital by means of the machine is related directly to the number of workers whose conditions of existence have been destroyed by it" (Marx, 1977, p. 557). Education tied to the production of labor can easily become a tool in this process of destruction and dehumanization. "In handicrafts and manufacture, the workman makes use of a tool; in the factory the machine makes use of him. There the movements of the instrument of labor proceed from him; here it is the movement of the machines that he must follow" (p. 548).

Freire: Absolutely! So even having a university degree may perpetuate this condition you just described, since in the capitalist system of education there are two distinct sets of curricula "one curriculum for leadership and another for [followership]" (Kliebard, 1986, p. 111). In followership you are taught to passively accept the conditions of school, work, and society and not to question, but to shift responsibility to "official" others. This is why "An educator has to question himself or herself about options that are inherently political, though often disguised as the existing structures. Thus, making choices is most important. Educators must ask themselves for whom and on whose behalf they are working" (Freire, 1985, p. 180).

Marx: Precisely! That takes us right back to questions I began asking when I was a young man about the dialectical opposition between the owner of the means of production and the workers! By the way, how did you ever become so thoroughly acquainted with my work?

On religion and false generosity

Freire: "When I was a young man, I went to the people, to the workers, the peasants, motivated really by my Christian faith. . . . I talked with the people, I learned to speak with the people-the

pronunciation, the words, the concepts. When I arrived with
the people-the misery, the concreteness, you know! But also the
beauty of the people, the openness, the ability to love which
the people have, the friendship. . . . the obstacles of this reality
sent me to [you,] Marx. I started reading and studying. It was
beautiful because I found in [your work,] Marx a lot of things
the people had told me-without being literate. Marx [, you are]
a genius. But when I met [your work] Marx, I continued to meet
Christ on the corners of the street-by meeting the people (Freire
quoted in Elias, 1994, p. 42).

Marx: I think I should clarify, my quarrel was not with spirituality
per se, but with religious/philosophical idealism and what my
friend Engels called "false generosity"; that is, the "opiate of the
people." Let me provide a hypothetical scenario here: "If in the
land of complete political emancipation we find not only that
religion exists but that it exists in a fresh and vigorous form
that proves that the existence of religion does not contradict the
perfection of the state. But since the existence of religion is a
defect, the source of this defect must be looked for in the nature
of the state itself. We no longer see religion as the basis but simply
as a phenomenon of secular narrowness" (Marx, 2002, p. 49).

Freire: Agreed, bourgeois secular religion of which you speak
is not true generosity. "True generosity lies in striving so that
these hands—whether of individuals or entire peoples—need be
extended less and less in supplication, so that more and more
they become human hands which work and, working, transform
the world" (Freire, 2000, p. 45).

Marx: You know, not too many people have heard that I once
told my wife that if "she wanted 'satisfaction of her metaphysical
needs' she should find them in the Jewish prophets rather than in
the Secular Society she sometimes attended" (cited in Eagleton,
2011, pp. 157–8). But let's get back to my quarrel with idealism…
"In direct contrast to German philosophy which descends from
heaven to earth, here we ascend from earth to heaven. That is
to say, we do not set out from what men imagine, conceive, nor
from men as narrated, thought of, or imagined, conceived, in
order to arrive at men in the flesh. We set out from real, active
men and on the basis of their real life process we demonstrate

the development of the ideological reflexes and echoes of this life process" (Marx, quoted in Fromm, 1964. p. 9).

Freire: Exactly! This brings us back to why we are here. "Today in the university we learned that objectivity requires neutrality on the part of the scientist; we learned today that knowledge is pure, universal, and unconditional and that the university is the site of knowledge. We learned today, although only tacitly, that the world is divided between those who know and those who don't (that is those who do manual work) and the university is the home of the former. We learned today that the university is a temple of pure knowledge and that it has to soar above earthly preoccupations, such as mankind's liberation" (Freire, 1985. p. 118).

On history, consciousness and language

Marx: Things have not changed at all in this regard in the last 129 years since my death. It is clear that a bourgeois view of history that views knowledge in a fixed, ahistorical, top-down manner is still in the ascendancy. "History does nothing, it 'possesses no immense wealth', it 'wages no battles'. It is man, real, living man who does all that, who possesses and fights; 'history' is not, as it were, a person apart, using man as a means to achieve its own aims; history is nothing but the activity of man pursuing his aims" (Marx, 1844/1956, n.p.).

Freire: Exactly! "History has no power. As [you] Marx [have] said, history does not command us, history is made by us. History makes us while we make it. Again, my suggestion is that we attempt to emerge from this alienating daily routine that repeats itself. Let's try to understand life, not necessarily as the daily repetition of things, but as an effort to create and recreate, and as an effort to rebel, as well. Let's take our alienation into our own hands and ask, 'Why?' 'Does it have to be this way?' I do not think so. We need to be subjects of history, even if we cannot totally stop being objects of history, and to be subjects, we need unquestionably to claim history critically. As active participants and real subjects, we can make history only when we are continually critical of our very lives" (Freire, 1985, p. 199).

Marx: And in that continual condition of critical self-reflection, what my friend Engels calls "false consciousness" might be revealed for what it is.

Freire: Yes, my work is deeply rooted in this along with your central emphatic insistence that freedom from alienation only results from critical consciousness and praxis, which I interpret as "reflection and action directed at the structures to be transformed " (Freire, 2000, p. 126). On the other hand "the praxis of domination" operates by superimposing its own language and denying the oppressed "the right to say their own word and think their own thoughts" (ibid.).

Marx: "One of the most difficult tasks confronting the philosopher is to descend from the world of thought to the actual world. Language is the immediate actuality of thought. Just as philosophers have given thought an independent existence, so they were bound to make philosophical language, in which thoughts in the form of words have their own content. The problem of descending from the world of thoughts to the actual world is turned into the problem of descending from language to life" (Marx, 1845, ch. 3, n.p.).

Freire: What you have just said describes the essence of my work in education. I start with the life experience of the learner and use that as a basis for creating agency through language. "Literacy conducted in the dominant language is alienating to subordinate students, since it denies them the fundamental tools for reflections, critical thinking, and social interaction . . . students find themselves unable to re-create their culture and history. Without the reappropriation of their cultural capital, the reconstruction of the new society envisioned by progressive educators and leaders can hardly be a reality" (Freire & Macedo, 1987, p. 159).

On the use of force for revolution

Marx: I can understand perfectly and shudder to think about the wholesale deculturalization that has taken place when the oppressed become the oppressor. It is tragic beyond words that sadistic dictators twisted my words and used them as a basis for justifying violence. When I said "Force is the midwife of every old society pregnant with a new one. It is itself an economic power" (Marx, 1977, p. 916). Never in my wildest nightmares could I envision that the most horrendous acts of genocide would be carried out under the banner of communism (see www.scaruffi. com/politics/dictat.html).

Freire: "Force is not used by those who have become weak under the preponderance of the strong, but by the strong who have emasculated them" (Freire, 2000, pp. 55–6). "I (He) never spoke, nor was I (he) ever an advocate, of violence or of the taking of power through the force of arms. I (He) was always, from a young age, reflecting on education and engaging in political action mediated by educational practice that can be transformative" (Freire & Macedo, 1998, p. 21).

Evolutionary advancement through dialogue and love

Marx: Then the very best recourse lies in the use of dialogue rather than force. I learned a great deal about the value of dialogue with Engels, but he was my friend. I appreciate the way you have turned dialectical constructs into dialogical ones. As you may know, I am critical of philosophy that is uncritical of its own relation to the world and emerges as "Criticism with a completely uncritical attitude to itself" (Marx, 1987, p. 143). I see in your dialogical approach a means toward self-criticism leading to new ways of thinking about the world.

Freire: Dialogue is essential if we truly seek social transformation. "Dialogue cannot exist, however, in the absence of a profound love for the world and for people. The naming of the world, which is an act of creation and re-creation, is not possible if it is not infused with love. Love is at the same time the foundation of dialogue and dialogue itself. It is thus necessarily the task of responsible Subjects and cannot exist in a relation of domination.

Domination reveals the pathology of love: sadism in the dominator and masochism in the dominated" (Freire, 2000, p. 90).

Marx: I did not emphasize love in my work like you have. My work was to shake the masses awake and break up the hard soil and begin removing the rocks of the feudal/capitalistic system and then plant the kind of trees that are capable of splitting rocks into pieces. This kind of work called for more courage than love because even the relations of family had been corrupted: "all family ties among the proletarians are torn asunder and their children transformed into simple articles of commerce and instruments of labor," and "The bourgeois sees in his wife a mere instrument of production" (Marx & Engels, 1987, p. 227).

Freire: But that is not love; I believe love is courageous "Because love is an act of courage, not of fear, love is commitment to others. No matter where the oppressed are found, the act of love is commitment to their cause—the cause of liberation. And this commitment, because it is loving, is dialogical. As an act of bravery, love cannot be sentimental; as an act of freedom, it must not serve as a pretext for manipulation. It must generate other acts of freedom; otherwise, it is not love. Only by abolishing the situation of oppression is it possible to restore the love which that situation made impossible. If I do not love the world—if I do not love life—if I do not love people—I cannot enter into dialogue. On the other hand, dialogue cannot exist without humility. The naming of the world, through which people constantly re-create that world, cannot be an act of arrogance" (Freire, 2000, p. 90).

Marx: This is the case in the formation of the anti-dialogical capitalist-worker relationship, which is built on the capitalist's arrogance and both of their selfishness. "The only force bringing them together and putting them into relation with each other is the selfishness, the gain and the private interest of each. Each pays heed to himself only and no one worries about the others. And precisely for that reason, either in accordance with the pre-established harmony of things, or under the auspices of an omniscient providence, they all work together to their mutual advantage, for the common weal, and in the common interest" (Marx, 1977, p. 280). However, being predicated on arrogance and selfishness, this system devolves into exploitation. "Being independent of each other, the workers are isolated. They enter into relations with the capitalist, but not with each other. Their co-operation only begins with the labor process, but by then they have ceased to belong to themselves" (p. 439). They are dehumanized and cannot engage in dialogical relationships because they have been reduced to capital. "Capital is dead labour, which, vampire-like, lives only by sucking living labour, and lives the more, the more labour it sucks" (p. 342).

Freire: And when one group reduces another to machinery, to an object that is not human, there cannot be true dialogue between them. "Dialogue, as the encounter of those addressed to the common task of learning and acting, is broken if the parties (or one of them) lack humility. How can I dialogue if I always project ignorance onto others and never perceive my own? How can I dialogue if I regard myself as a case apart from others—mere 'its' in whom I cannot recognize other 'I's? How can I dialogue if I consider myself a member of the in-group of pure men, the owners of truth and knowledge, for whom all non-members are 'these people' or 'the great unwashed'? How can I dialogue if I start from the premise that naming the world is the task of an elite and that the presence of the people in history is a sign of deterioration, thus to be avoided? How can I dialogue if I am closed to—and even offended by—the contribution of others? How can I dialogue if I am afraid of being displaced, the mere possibility causing me torment and weakness? Self-sufficiency is incompatible with dialogue. Men and women who lack humility (or have lost it) cannot come to the people, cannot be their partners in naming the world. Someone who cannot acknowledge himself to be as mortal as everyone else still has a long way to go before he can reach the point of encounter. At the point of encounter there are neither utter ignoramuses nor perfect sages; there are only people who are attempting, together, to learn more than they now know" (Freire, 2000, p. 90).

Marx: And at this point where we reach dialogue, we are able to begin to see the "richness of man's essential being is the richness of subjective human sensibility (a musical ear, an eye for beauty of form—in short, senses capable of human gratifications, senses confirming themselves as essential powers of man) either cultivated or brought into being. For not only the five senses, but the so-called mental senses—the practical senses (will, love, etc.)—in a word, human sense—the humanness of senses—come to be by virtue of its object, by virtue of humanized nature. The forming of the five senses is a labor of humanized nature. The forming of the five senses is a labor of the entire history of the world down to the present" (Marx, 1987, pp. 108–9). It is becoming quite clear in this dialogue that there is still so much that is unfinished and I certainly would not consider myself a perfect sage. "I am not [even] a Marxist" (Zinn, 1999, p. 6). Please, do go on.

Freire: I think the sensuousness you speak of gets to the heart of dialogue. Dialogue is about humanization. "Dialogue further requires an intense faith in humankind, faith in their power to make and remake, to create and re-create, faith in their vocation to be more fully human (which is not the privilege of an elite, but the birthright of all). Faith in people is an a priori requirement for dialogue; the 'dialogical man' believes in others even before he meets them face to face. His faith, however, is not naive. The 'dialogical man' is critical and knows that although it is within the power of humans to create and transform, in a concrete situation of alienation individuals may be impaired in the use of that power. Far from destroying his faith in the people, however, this possibility strikes him as a challenge to which he must respond. He is convinced that the power to create and transform, even when thwarted in concrete situations, tends to be reborn. And that rebirth can occur—not gratuitously, but in and through the struggle for liberation—in the supersedence of slave labor by emancipated labor which gives zest to life. Without this faith in people, dialogue is a farce which inevitably degenerates into paternalistic manipulation" (Freire, 2000, p. 90).

Marx: Can you get any more paternalistic than Socratic dialogue? The quest within his method is for ideal truth, not knowledge created in process with others. The configuration is still one "which descends from heaven to earth, here we ascend from earth to heaven" (Marx, cited in Fromm, 1964, p. 9). Yet, if in beginning of dialogue, we start in the real world of spontaneous human action and speech and the concreteness of labor and human desire, and that becomes the basis for conversation, then perhaps we can avoid the manipulation you speak of.

Freire: Yes, and "Founding itself upon love, humility, and faith, dialogue becomes a horizontal relationship of which mutual trust between the dialoguers is the logical consequence. It would be a contradiction in terms if dialogue—loving, humble, and full of faith—did not produce this climate of mutual trust, which leads the dialoguers into ever closer partnership in the naming of the world. Conversely, such trust is obviously absent in the anti-dialogics of the banking method of education. Whereas faith in humankind is an a priori requirement for dialogue, trust is established by dialogue. Should it founder, it will be seen that the preconditions were lacking. False love, false humility, and feeble faith in others cannot create trust. Trust is contingent on the evidence which one party provides the others of his true, concrete intentions; it cannot exist if that party's words do not coincide with their actions. To say one thing and do another—to take one's own word lightly—cannot inspire trust. To glorify democracy and to silence the people is a farce; to discourse on humanism and to negate people is a lie" (Freire, 2000, p. 90).

Marx: In truth, this democracy is not better than despotic communism. If we are to eliminate human suffering, we must seek out "the genuine resolution of the conflict between man and nature and between man and man—the true resolution of the strife between existence and essence, between objectification and self-confirmation, between freedom and necessity, between the individual and the species" (Marx, 1987, pp. 102–3). Perhaps, dialogue is the starting point for the genesis of a humanistic world that has yet to be.

On hope for the future

Freire: This looking forward to a potential future without suffering, Marx, is crucial to dialogue because it cannot "exist without hope. Hope is rooted in men's incompletion, from which they move out in constant search—a search which can be carried out only in communion with others. Hopelessness is a form of silence, of denying the world and fleeing from it. The dehumanization resulting from an unjust order is not a cause for despair but for hope, leading to the incessant pursuit of the humanity denied by injustice. Hope, however, does not consist in crossing one's arms and waiting. As long as I fight, I am moved by hope; and if I fight with hope, then I can wait" (Freire, 2000, p. 90).

Marx: Then we will fight and we will hope, in solidarity until capitalist exploitation has come to pass by "a definitive resolution of the antagonism between man and nature, and between man and man [as a] true solution of the conflict between existence and essence, between objectification and self-affirmation, between freedom and necessity, between individual and species" (Marx cited in Fromm, 1964, p. 68). "The proletarians have nothing to lose but their chains. They have a world to win" (Marx & Engels, 1987, p. 243).

References

Dale, J. (2003). Freire, Aristotle, Marx, and Sartre: A critique of the human condition. Paper presented at The Midwest Research to Practice Conference in Adult, Continuing, and Community Education, The Ohio State University, Columbus, OH.

Dale, J. and Hyslop-Margison, E. (2010). *Paulo Freire: Teaching for freedom and transformation: The philosophical influences on the work of Paulo Freire*. Dordrecht, The Netherlands: Springer.

Eagleton, T. (2011). *Why Marx was Right*. New Haven, CT: Yale University Press.

Elias, J. L. (1994). *Paulo Freire: Pedagogue of liberation*. Malabar, FL: Krieger Publishing Company.

Freire, P. (1985). *The politics of education: Culture, power, and liberation*. South Hadley, MA: Bergin & Garvey.

— (1999). "Making history and unveiling oppression," *Dulwich Centre Journal*, 3, 37–9. Retrieved from: www.freireproject.org/content/intervi ew-paulo-freire-dulwich-centre.

— (2007). *Pedagogy of the oppressed*. New York, NY: Continuum.

Freire, A. and Macedo, D. (1998). "Introduction." In A. Freire and
D. Macedo (eds). *The Paulo Freire reader* (pp. 1–44). New York, NY:
Continuum.

Freire, P. and Macedo, D. (1987). *Literacy: Reading the word and the
world.* South Hadley, MA: Bergin & Garvey.

Fromm, E. (1964). *Marx's concept of man.* New York, NY: Frederick
Ungar Publishing.

Fuentes, L. (2010). "Remembering Paulo: Stories." In T. Wilson, P. Park
and A. Colon-Muniz. *Memories of Paulo* (pp. 133–8). Rotterdam, The
Netherlands: Sense.

Gabriel, M. (2011). *Love and Capital: Karl and Jenny Marx and the birth
of a revolution.* New York, NY: Little, Brown and Company.

Horton, M. and Freire, P. (1990). *We make the road by walking:
Conversations on education and social change.* Philadelphia, PA:
Temple University Press.

Kliebard, H. (1986). *The struggle for the American curriculum: 1893–
1958.* Boston, MA: Routledge and Kegan Paul.

Lewis, T. E. (2007). "Revolutionary leadership, revolutionary pedagogy:
Reevaluating the links and disjunctions between Lukacs and Freire."
Philosophy of Education. 285–93.

Marx, K. (1844/1956). *The holy family or critique of critical criticism.
against Bruno Bauer and company.* chapter 6. Retrieved from: www.
marxists.org/archive/marx/works/1845/holy-family/ch06_2.htm

— (1845/1932*). The German ideology.* Ch. 3. Retrieved from: www.
marxists.org/archive/marx/works/1845/german-ideology/ch03p.htm

— (1977). *Capital: Volume one.* New York, NY: Vintage Books.

— (1987). *Economic and philosophic manuscripts of 1844* (pp. 203–8).
Buffalo, NY: Prometheus Books.

— (2002). *Marx on religion.* J. C. Raines (ed.) Philadelphia, PA: Temple
University Press.

Marx, K. and Engels, F. (1987). "Manifesto of the Communist party." In
K. Marx. *Economic and philosophic manuscripts of 1844.* Buffalo,
NY: Prometheus Books.

Mayo, P. (2004). *Liberating praxis: Paulo Freire's legacy for radical
education and politics.* Rotterdam, The Netherlands: Sense.

Morrow, R. A. and Torres, C. A. (2002). *Reading Freire and Habermas:
Critical pedagogy and transformative social change.* New York, NY:
Teachers College Press, pp. 203–43.

Oakeshott, M. (1962). *The voice of poetry in the conversation of
mankind. Rationalism in politics and other essays.* London, England:
Methuen, pp. 197–247.

Shor, I. and Freire, P. (1987). *A pedagogy for liberation: Dialogues on
transforming education.* Westport, CT: Bergin & Garvey.

Torres, C. A. (1992). *The church, society, and hegemony: A critical sociology of religion in Latin America*. Westport, CT: Greenwood Publishing.

Wilson, T., Park, P. and Colon-Muniz, A. (2010). *Memories of Paulo*. Rotterdam, The Netherlands: Sense.

Zinn, H. (1999). *Marx in Soho: A play on history*. Cambridge, MA: South End Press.

3

The Gramscian Influence

Peter Mayo

Paulo Freire has acknowledged Antonio Gramsci as an important influence on his thinking. This is hardly surprising given the impact that Antonio Gramsci has had on the Left in Latin America from the 1960s onward, up to today; there is a burgeoning literature on this (Aricó, 1988; Coutinho, 1995; Fernández Díaz, 1995; Melis, 1995). Furthermore, Gramsci also exerted a tremendous influence on the area that Freire inspired, notably nonformal and popular education in Latin America (La Belle, 1986; Ireland, 1987; Torres, 1990; Kane, 2001). In the mid-1980s, Gramsci was heralded as "probably the most frequently cited Marxist associated with popular education" (La Belle, 1986, p. 185).

While in exile in Chile, Freire is said to have been exposed to Marxist thinking that made its presence strongly felt in *Pedagogy of the Oppressed* (Freire, 1970), not least Marx's own dialectical manner of conceptualization re-echoed by Freire in many ways in the first three chapters of the volume. It was in Chile that, according to Morrow and Torres (1995, p. 457), Freire was exposed to Gramsci's work. Marcela Gajardo introduced him to the edited anthology of Gramsci's writings translated into Spanish by José Aricò from Letteratura e vita nazionale (Literature and National Life) (ibid.) When addressing participants at a workshop at the Institute of Education in London in the 1990s, Freire is on record as having said:

> . . . I only read Gramsci when I was in exile. I read Gramsci and I discovered that I had been greatly influenced by Gramsci long before

I had read him. It is fantastic when we discover that we had been influenced by someone's thought without even being introduced to their intellectual production. (Freire, 1995, pp. 63, 64)

Gramsci features in several writings by Freire either in formulations made by Freire himself or else in similar statements by those who collaborated with Freire on a number of books, notably persons with whom he exchanged views in his so-called talking books. The name of Chilean exile, Antonio Faundez comes to mind (Freire & Faundez, 1989). I am one of a number of persons who explored similarities and contrasts between Gramsci's and Freire's works (Mayo, 1999, 2005/2008), together with a number of other colleagues including the late Paula Allman (1999), Paul Ransome (1992), Marjorie Mayo (1997), and Margaret Ledwith (2005). Others like Diana Coben (1998) have refuted any kind of affinity in thought between the two.

Raymond Allen Morrow and Carlos Alberto Torres, who, when I was a student of theirs at Canada's University of Alberta, encouraged me to compare Freire's work with Gramsci, both make frequent references to Gramsci when engaging Freire's ideas (Morrow & Torres, 1995). For some strange reason, bringing their ideas together seems a "natural" thing to accomplish, and much has got to do with the influence that Gramsci held in the part of the world from which Freire's initial pedagogical ideas emerged. Some authors have spoken of the manner Latin Americans found affinities between their continent and the Italy of Gramsci's time. This includes Italy's Mezzogiorno (the South), to which Gramsci devoted so much attention in his writings, notably "Alcuni temi sulla quistione meridionale" (Some themes from the Southern Question) (Mayo, 2007) and his notes in Italian history in the *Quaderni del Carcere* (Prison Notebooks) (Gramsci, 1975).

The contextual similarities and contrasts have been dealt with by a number of writers, so that I need not rehearse the literature here. What I would suggest in this chapter is the open Marxism, that is to say, the rather "open" reading of Marx and Marxism, to which Gramsci helped give rise, revitalizing it as part of an analysis of a specific context, notably post-Risorgimento Italy, which must have appealed to Freire in his quest to eschew an orthodox reading of Marx (no fault of Marx himself). He sought to avoid that orthodox reading he calls a "liberating fatalism" (Freire, 1985, p. 179) and which Gramsci similarly refers to as a "theory of grace and predestination" (Gramsci, 1957, p. 75). Freire avoided such an approach to develop a revitalized view of Marxism in light of the specificities of the contexts with which he was involved: Latin America and Africa, with a European parenthesis. Given his proximity in Geneva to Italy, which he certainly visited (I am aware for instance of one visit to Partinico near Palermo in the Mezzogiorno where he connected with Danilo Dolci), this European period must have rendered Gramsci's ideas even more prominent in Freire's thinking. Gramsci was quite "big" in Italy in the turbulent 1970s and early 1980s but his star waned later on, especially after the fall of the Berlin Wall and the transmutations experienced by the party he helped found; he is nowadays much more revered outside Italy than within his own country—a case of nemo profeta in patria (Mayo, 2009, p. 601).

Gramsci on education and politics

It is common knowledge that Hegemony is the key concept one associates with Gramsci. It is not an original concept since it dates back to the ancient Greeks and was used by revolutionary political figures such as Lenin and Plekhanov before Gramsci. There are those who argue that it made its presence felt even in the linguistics debates to which Gramsci was exposed when he was a student of Philology at the University of Turin, thanks to his mentor, Matteo Bartoli (Ives, 2004, p. 47). Without providing any systematic exposition, Gramsci elaborated this concept, presenting it as the means whereby social forces, manifest throughout not only civil society but also what is conceived of as political society (the division is heuristic as they are interrelated facets of an "integral state"), and are, as Peter D. Thomas (2009) underlines, transformed into political power within the context of different class projects. I would also add to this conceptualization the view, mentioned by Thomas and certainly by Gramsci, following Marx, that the integral state has a strong relational dimension. This emerges quite clearly in Gramsci's early and later formulations concerning the relationship of the Factory Council and the Socialist State, the former "prefiguring," to use a term adopted by Paula Allman, a new form of State, through its more democratized horizontal social relations of production. This prevents us from reifying the state as a "thing," from engaging in "thingification" as Phil Corrigan (1990) would call it. It is also manifest in Gramsci's conceptualization of every relationship of hegemony being a pedagogical relationship.

The importance of this theorization for those who believe in a politically engaged education for the gradual ushering in of a different world cannot be missed. It is perhaps for this reason that Gramsci has had such a considerable influence on that area of educational theorization and empirical research known as critical pedagogy, as the works of authors such as Paula Allman, Jean Anyon, Michael Apple, Antonia Darder, Henry Giroux, Peter McLaren, Deb J. Hill, Margaret Ledwith, and David W. Livingstone so clearly indicate. Paulo Freire has been a highly influential figure in critical pedagogy. One of the field's major exponents and founding figures, Henry Giroux, heralds Freire as one of the primary exponents of a historically specific understanding of critical pedagogy.

Hegemony needs to be renegotiated and built in a manner that immerses the concepts and practices involved in popular consciousness. It involves a long and "intense labour of criticism" and essentially "educational" work before and after the conquest of the state. As Thomas (2009) underlines, Gramsci argued that different historical formations are at different levels in terms of their development of civil society. These formations differ in the quality of the relationship between state and civil society. This applies to both east and west and north and south.

The hegemonic apparatuses need to be built and consolidated to become the channels of the ruling class's life-world (lebenswelt), "the horizon within which its class project is elaborated and within which it also seeks to interpellate and integrate its antagonists" (Thomas, 2009, p. 225). Thomas rightly points out that the ascent of this vision needs to be consolidated daily, if the class project (in Gramsci's view, the proletarian class project) is to continue to assume institutional power (ibid). The implications for educational activity are enormous. Education is viewed in the broadest sense and not in the sense of simply schooling (schooling is expounded on by Gramsci in Notebooks IV and XII). It therefore incorporates all elements of the hegemonic apparatus including adult education institutions and projects (these include projects of the kind in which Gramsci was himself directly involved as teacher, student, and organizer), media institutions, etc. His major pedagogical philosophy, inferred from his overriding philosophy, would be a "pedagogy of praxis." His overriding philosophy is the "philosophy of praxis" that is meant to connect with people's common sense. Common sense contains elements of good sense that however need to be rendered more coherent, less contradictory. The philosophy of praxis must transcend "common sense" in a manner, as Thomas (2009) and others explain, that is not speculative, and that does not become doctrinaire or a definitive system of ideas. The philosophy of praxis ought to be characterized by what Thomas (2009) highlights as absolute historicism (chapter 7), which renders possible the translation of philosophical and conceptual perspectives into intellectual resources for hegemonic organization, absolute immanence (chapter 8), a moment of conceptual clarity and organization inherent in determinate social relations, and absolute humanism (chapter 9). The last mentioned refers to a conception of the subject or person as an "ensemble of historically determined social relations," a situation that also allows us to view theories and philosophies in terms of their being institutionally embedded, serving as a hegemonic apparatus and being integrated in and therefore being ideologically overdetermined by the integral state. Educators, seeking to highlight the politics of education, can draw on this insight.

Gramsci and Freire

The connections with Freire's thought should be apparent at this stage. Popular education might well be conceived of as an important element in that "intense labour of criticism" and "diffusion of culture and spread of ideas" (Gramsci, 1977, p. 12) that, Gramsci argued, should occur both before and subsequent to the change in control of the state. Freire referred to the former as "cultural action for freedom" and the latter is referred to as "cultural revolution." It is a revolution characterized by ongoing reappraisal and critique, denúncio/anúncio, as the nature of power needs to be transformed. In Freire's words one needs to "reinvent" power (Freire, 2000).

The central concept that Freire has in mind for such a process is praxis with his pedagogy being the "pedagogy of praxis," a pedagogy that enables participants to gain critical distance from the world with which they are familiar to experience it differently and, as Ira Shor (1980, 1987) puts it, extraordinarily. It constitutes the means whereby one can reflect upon one's world of action to transform it.

This connects with the entire corpus of writings that Gramsci produced in prison, in which he advances the concept of the "philosophy of praxis," praxis also being the process with which he was engaged through his separation, through incarceration, from the world of direct political action. Incarceration provided him with a critical distance from this world of action just as exile did to Freire, removing the Brazilian from an area that, he felt at the time, was roused for transformation. The pedagogical philosophy to emerge from this body of writing by Gramsci is similar to Freire's pedagogy, a pedagogy of praxis. Gramsci's "philosophy of praxis" implies a pedagogical approach given that hegemony is an ensemble of pedagogical relations—"every relationship of hegemony is a pedagogical relationship," Gramsci tells us. Gramsci's entire project is a pedagogical project since pedagogy is central to the workings of hegemony itself.

The pedagogy of praxis is the means to transcend common sense (an uncritical and fragmentary view of reality that has its elements of good sense but which lacks coherence). The quest for Gramsci is to render this common sense more coherent, the elaboration of this fragmentary philosophy into a more systematic and sound philosophy. That fragmentary philosophy again contains elements of "truth" with which any force seeking to exert its hegemony must connect. In short, any effective attempt at a "pedagogy of praxis" cannot be doctrinaire and at the furthest remove from people's experience but must connect with it in a meaningful way. This is what right wing hegemonic forces have done in building their own hegemony, as Stuart Hall indicates when discussing the rise of Thatcherism in Britain. This connects with Freire's view of the transition from naïve to critical consciousness. This view has been subject to the same accusation of elitism leveled at Gramsci's notion of converting common to good sense. As for Freire being influenced by Gramsci's thought before having been introduced to his work, this seems to be an example of what the Brazilian educator must have had in mind when making this statement at the University of London's Institute of Education.

Freire and other persons engaged in popular education seem to borrow heavily from Gramsci in their conceptualization of those persons who carry out the intellectual and pedagogical work intended to bring about the much augured collective transformations. Gramsci's notion of the organic intellectual is influential here. The intellectual is here being defined through not some immanent feature but her or his function in shaping opinions and developing and disseminating world views. In short the intellectual is analyzed in terms of the role he or she performs in either supporting/cementing the existing hegemonic arrangements or challenging them.

Transformation is a key element in Freire's conception of intellectuals. Though valorizing the function of such traditional intellectuals as those of international acclaim and academics (see his exchanges with professors from UNAM in Escobar et al., 1994), Freire often expressed views that are more on the lines of Gramsci's analysis of the role of intellectuals in society. In Freire's case, and with respect to the intellectual's task in cementing or challenging hegemonic relations, the intellectual helps problematize issues, through a problem-posing approach to dialogue, that fosters the critical consciousness necessary to help generate social change predicated on social justice (Mayo, 2011).

The closest reinvention of Gramsci's analysis of the role of intellectuals in revolutionary practice is to be found in the Letters to Guinea Bissau (Freire, 1978) and most notably in Letter 11. There, as in other writings, he tackles the issue of the colonial legacy in education, which is very elitist and restricts the attainment of qualifications to a small cadre of people who serve as urban intellectuals having close links with and supporting the colonial powers. He adopts Amilcar Cabral's notion (see Cortesão, 2012) of the elitist intellectual, in such a situation, having to commit class suicide. In doing so the elitist intellectual is "reborn" as a revolutionary worker who identifies with the aspirations of the people. This immediately recalls Gramsci's notion of the revolutionary party (the Modern Prince) and movement assimilating traditional intellectuals to render them intellectuals who are organic to the struggle for social transformation that takes the form of a lengthy "intellectual and moral reform."

The intellectuals analyzed by Gramsci, with respect to their function in Italian society and the evolution of its politics, are various, ranging from grand intellectuals who help fashion the cultural climate of the period (Benedetto Croce, Giustino Fortunato), or who, through their artistic productions, stamp their mark on the Italian cultural scene (Luigi Pirandello), to subaltern intellectuals operating in restricted spheres of influence (priests, lawyers, managers, teachers). Educators play an important role here together with other cultural workers.

The transformation of traditional intellectuals is an important revolutionary task for Gramsci. He might have seen himself, as a product of a classical though incomplete formal education, as someone who could easily have ended up fitting the traditional intellectual category. His dropping out of university, owing to his physical ailments that made him miss exams, despite his billing by Matteo Bartoli as the archangel destined to defeat the grammarians (see Mayo, 2009, p. 601), and early immersion in socialist and radical socialist politics, steered him in a different direction. He is however under no illusion regarding the task of converting traditional intellectuals to ones who are organic to the subaltern cause and the party or movement supporting it. Despite acknowledging the virtues of the classical school, he knew that the intellectual education of the middle class reinforces the class position of its recipients. As he explained with regard to the function of Southern intellectuals in Italy, also with respect to the role language plays in this process (see Ives, 2004), this education makes them "absolutize" their activity and conceive of it as being superior to that of those who did not benefit from the same opportunity. His broadening of the notion of intellectual, which can include foremen, party activists, trade union representatives, adult educators, etc., since they perform an intellectual role in influencing opinions and worldviews, allows him to believe in the role of subaltern groups in generating, from within their ranks, their own intellectuals. Like Gramsci, Freire insists, again in letter 11 of the Guinea Bissau book, that it is also necessary to generate from within the ranks of the subaltern a new type of intellectual, whose thinking and activity help generate a new weltanschauung, a new world view. The lines here could easily have been lifted verbatim from translations of Gramsci's notes on intellectuals and the organization of culture in the Quaderni. The challenge in a revolutionary setting, characterized by attempts at what Freire elsewhere calls the transformation of power, is to not create elitist intellectuals who commit class suicide but prevent their formation in the first place (Freire, 1978, p. 104). The point of departure for intellectuals working with, and not on behalf of, the people is the latter's concrete existential situation. There is a need to reach out to the people's preoccupations and quotidian experience. This is crucial for Gramsci regarding the renegotiation of hegemonic relations, for helping in creating the foundations of a new hegemony—connecting with the people's common sense, which is never 100 percent false but contains partial truths, and then moving on from there to help create a more coherent view. Likewise Freire would consider remaining at the level of one's concrete existential situation as basismo, a popular Latin American term indicating a form of populism.

The foregoing insights attest to Gramsci's influence on Freire. The influence becomes even stronger when one takes into account the influence that Gramsci wields on those who keep Freire's legacy alive. The classic example here concerns Gramsci's distinction between "organic" and "conjunctural" and its use in popular education circles. "Conjunctural Analysis" is to be distinguished from an analysis of what is "organic" and therefore "relatively permanent" (Gramsci, 1971, p. 177); it is a process from popular education in Latin America that has also been taken up in North America, for instance, in the context of the "the Moment" project at the Jesuit Centre for Social Faith and Justice in Toronto. "Naming the Moment" entails "the process of identifying key moments when the conjuncture offers unique opportunities for changing oppressive structures."

"Naming the Moment" has, at its core, a process of democratic conjunctural analysis, identifying and examining the movement of key forces (economic, political, cultural, etc.) and their impact on various structures of society. The democratic nature of the process allowed participants to advocate for various actions according to the needs of the moment and to also recruit allies. As a popular education process "Naming the Moment" drew on a wide range of means of dialogue from the common small-group discussions to the use of popular theatre, visual art, and song. And, as with popular education, it took more time and resources than more conventional processes of community organizing (popular educator, Chris Cavanagh, in Borg & Mayo, 2007, pp. 44–5).

Conclusion

In conclusion, I would argue that Antonio Gramsci saw in the education and cultural formation of adults the key toward the transformation of hegemony. Many would use the term "counter-hegemony" here, which I would avoid, given that Gramsci himself did not use it—my sense is that there is the danger that this term posits some kind of a binary opposition regarding "hegemony" and "counter-hegemony," the kind of binary opposition that Gramsci's conceptualization of the term avoids. The relationship is a dialectical one, involving internal relations between the two, relations that need to be renegotiated within the interstices of the hegemonic structures themselves. The attainment of an "intellectual and moral reform," which Gramsci regarded as necessary for such a transformation to occur, entailed a lengthy process of education characterized by what Raymond Williams would call the "long revolution." The process involved education in its many forms, formal, nonformal, and informal. Organic intellectuals engaged in this lengthy process of working for social transformation were to explore a number of sites with the potential to serve as sites of transformative learning. Gramsci was a role model with his constant, indefatigable immersion in projects and his creation of opportunities for adult learning during his years as a political activist/leader and politician and during his imprisonment, especially the time when he awaited his trial on the island of Ustica where he is believed to have left a mark among the islanders. However his major legacies are the various theoretical insights deriving from his own revolutionary praxis, insights that continue to make Gramsci a constant source of reference in political theory. As we have seen, his contribution was not lost on Freire with whom he shared political pedagogical insights and which Freire, like other many left-wing intellectuals and practitioners, took on board in his quest for an educational contribution to "the creation of a world in which it will be easier to love" (Freire, 1970, p. 24; see also Allman et al., 1998).

References

Allman, P. (1999). *Revolutionary social transformation. Democratic hopes, political possibilities and critical education.* Westport, CT and London, GB: Bergin & Garvey.

Allman, P., Mayo, P., Cavanagh, C., Lean Heng, C., and Haddad, S. (1998). Introduction. ". . . the creation of a world in which it will be easier to love." *Convergence XXI* (1 and 2), 9–16.

Aricó, J. (1988). *La Cola del Diablo. Itinerario de Gramsci en America Latina.* Caracas, Venezuela: Editorial Nueva Sociedad.

Borg, C. and Mayo, P. (2007). *Public intellectuals, radical democracy and social movements. A book of interviews.* New York, NY: Peter Lang.

Coben, D. (1998). *Radical heroes: Gramsci, Freire and the politics of adult education.* New York, NY: Garland.

Corrigan, P. R. D. (1990). *Social forms/human capacities: Essays in authority and difference.* New York, NY and London, GB: Routledge.

Cortesão, L. (2012). Paulo Freire ve Amilcar Cabral. (Paulo Freire and Amilcar Cabral) in *Eleştirel pedagoji—critical pedagogy,* Year. 4, No. 19, pp. 23–6.

Coutinho, C. N. (1995). *In Brasile' in Gramsci in Europa e in America.* A. A. Santucci (ed.). Rome and Bari: Sagittari Laterza. pp. 133–40.

Fernández Díaz, O. (1995). *In America Latina in Gramsci in Europa e in America.* A. A. Santucci (ed.). Rome and Bari: Sagittari Laterza. pp.141–57.

Freire, P. (1970). *Pedagogy of the oppressed.* New York, NY: Continuum.

— (1978). *Pedagogy in process: The Letters to Guinea Bissau.* New York, NY: Continuum.

— (1985). *The politics of education.* D. Macedo (ed. and trans.). South Hadley, MA: Bergin and Garvey.

— (1995). *Reply to discussants in Paulo Freire at the institute.* M. de Fugueiredo-Cowen and D. Gastaldo (eds). London, GB: Institute of Education, University of London. pp. 61–7.

— (2000). *Cultural action for freedom* (revised edition). Cambridge, MA: Harvard Educational Review.

Freire, P. and Faundez, A. (1989). *Learning to question: A pedagogy of liberation.* Geneva, Switzerland: World Council of Churches.

Gramsci, A. (1957). *The modern prince and other writings,* L. Marks (ed. and trans.). New York, NY: International Publishers.

— (1975). *Quaderni del carcere, edizione critica* (IV vols.). V. Gerratana (ed.). Turin, Italy: Einaudi.

— (1971). *Selections from the prison notebooks.* Q. Hoare and G. Bowell Smith (eds). New York, NY: International Publishers.

— (1977). *Antonio Gramsci: Selections from political writings (1910–1920).* Q. Hoare and J. Matthews (eds). New York, NY: International Publishers.

Ireland, T. (1987). *Antonio Gramsci and adult education: Reflections on the Brazilian experience.* Manchester, GB: Manchester University Press.

Ives, P. (2004). *Language and hegemony in Gramsci.* London, GB: Pluto Press; Halifax, Nova Scotia, Canada: Fernwood Publishing.

Kane, L. (2001). *Popular education and social change in Latin America.* London, GB: Latin American Bureau.

La Belle, T. J. (1986). *Nonformal education in Latin America and the Caribbean: Stability, reform or revolution?* New York, NY: Praeger.

Ledwith, M. (2005). *Community development: A critical approach.* Bristol, UK: Policy Press.

Mayo, M. (1997). *Imagining tomorrow: Adult education for transformation.* Leicester, UK: NIACE.

Mayo, P. (1999). *Gramsci, Freire and adult education: Possibilities for transformative education.* London, GB and New York, NY: Zed Books.

— (2005) "Antonio Gramsci and Paulo Freire some connections and contrasts." In *Encyclopaidea* No. 17, pp. 77–102; republished 2008 in C. A. Torres and P. Noguera (eds). *Social justice education for teachers: Paulo Freire and the possible dream* (pp. 51–68). Rotterdan and Taipei: Sense Publishers.

— (2007). "Gramsci, the Southern question and the Mediterranean." *Mediterranean Journal of Educational Studies*, 12 (2), 1–17.

— (2009). "Editorial: Antonio Gramsci and Educational Thought." *Educational Philosophy and Theory*, 41 (6), 601–44.

— (2010). *Intelectual/intelectuais. in dicionário Paulo Freire.* D. R. Streck, E. Redin and J. J. Zitkoski (eds). Belo Horizonte, Brasil: Autentica, pp. 227–9.

— (2011). *Learning with Adults. A Critical Pedagogical Introduction* (with L. English). Rotterdam, The Netherlands: Sense.

Melis, A. (1995). "Gramsci e l'America Latina." In G. Baratta and A. Catone (eds). *Antonio Gramsci e il progresso intelletuale di massa* (pp. 227–34). Milano, Italy: Edizioni Unicopli.

Morrow, R. A. and Torres, C. A. (1995). *Social theory and education. A critique of theories of social and cultural reproduction.* Albany, NY: State University of New York Press.

Ransome, P. (1992). *Antonio Gramsci. A new introduction.* Hemel Hempstead, Hertfordshire, UK: Harvester-Wheatsheaf.

Shor, I. (1980, 1987). *Critical teaching and everyday life.* Chicago, IL and London, GB: University of Chicago Press.

Thomas, P. D. (2009). *The Gramscian moment: Philosophy, hegemony and Marxism.* Amsterdam, The Netherlands: Brill.

Torres, C. A. (1990). *The Politics of nonformal education in Latin America.* New York, NY: Praeger.

4

Rethinking Freire's "Oppressed": A "Southern" Route to Habermas's Communicative Turn and Theory of Deliberative Democracy

Raymond Morrow

". . . those who thus classify me by drawing on certain naive phrases that can be lifted out of my works—and are today the object of my own self-criticism—must try to accompany me through the steps of my own evolution."

Freire, 1985, p. 152

"Error is a moment in the search for knowledge."

Freire, 2003, p. 65

Competing strategies for resisting the domestication of Freire

One of the most contested issues in the reception of Freire has been leftist objections to the reduction of his pedagogy to a "method": "Paulo Freire's thought and work is revolutionary, but continuously in danger of being domesticated . . . by the 'progressives' in Western cultures into mere methodology" (McLaren & Lankshear, 1994, p. 3). Though agreeing with the strategic importance of the dangers of "domesticating" Freire's contributions, the following discussion will question the contemporary usefulness of rescuing Freire as a "revolutionary," especially in a specifically Marxist sense. Instead, his approach will be viewed as a variant of critical social theory that converges with Habermas's project in implying a reconstruction of historical materialism that gives primacy to radical democratization for the realization of humanization and autonomy. The discussion thus builds upon and extends a previous collaborative effort with Carlos Alberto Torres concerning the partial convergence and potential for mutual learning between Freire and Habermas (Morrow & Torres, 2002). The present author has subsequently discussed related issues in a series of papers on their relation to development, education, and indigenous knowledge (Morrow, 2008, 2009) and whether the reception of Habermas in Latin American could be charged with Eurocentrism (Morrow, 2012/forthcoming).

A first step will be to comment on some of the limitations of two other options that have been proposed for avoiding the instrumentalization of Freire's work as simply a method: first, the defense of his engagement in Brazilian politics as not being a "retreat" from his earlier revolutionary stance because of its compatibility with a Gramscian "open Marxism"; and second, a critical postmodernist and poststructuralist reading that emphasizes his utopian concern with a pedagogy that opens up a radical discourse of the "logic of possibility" and "social remembrance."

The first option was influentially initiated by Stanley Aronowitz's interpretation of Freire's later shift from a revolutionary to a democratic discourse. He instructively defends the consistency of Freire's "radical democratic humanism" in relation to a kind of "secular liberation theology" that recognizes the contextual necessity of engaging new social movements (Aronowitz, 1993). For example, Aronowitz cites Freire's contention that revolutionary parties must respond to the challenge of new and popular social movements, drawing the following conclusion: "With these remarks, Freire distances himself from elements of his own revolutionary Marxist past, but not from a kind of open Marxism represented by Gramsci's work" (p. 22). The assumptions of Gramsci's theory of democratic transition is outlined by Aronowitz in a later article (Aronowitz, 2009). Consequently, *"any attempt to interpret Freire's recent positions as a retreat from the revolutionary pedagogy of his earlier work is entirely unjustified . . ."* (p. 23, emphasis added). Similarly, the editors of the anthology in which Aronowitz's chapter appears refer approvingly to his interpretation of the "revolutionary soundness of Freire's current emphasis on the struggle for a 'radical democracy' on the grounds that in the present historical circumstances it is not realistic to put socialism on the immediate agenda" (McLaren & Leonard, 1993, pp. 3–4). But this phrasing—consistent with Aronowitz's effort to rescue a "revolutionary" Freire—suggests that it is this longer term revolutionary "hidden agenda" that justifies the conjunctural pragmatism of democratic compromise. Another version of the effort to link Freire and Gramscian Marxism is evident in Peter McLaren's more recent disillusionment with his earlier critical postmodernist position, shifting toward a more Marxist interpretation that pairs Freire and Che Guevara (McLaren, 2000) and later gives support for Paula Allman's effort to create a synthesis of Marx, Gramsci, and Freire as "critical revolutionary educational theory" (McLaren, 2010).

Though the strategy of interpreting Freire from the perspective of a Gramscian Marxism has proved to be productive for many purposes, it has also been plagued by some significant difficulties. First, such strategies obscure the ways in which Freire's later democratic position was indeed "a retreat from the revolutionary pedagogy of his earlier work," hence cannot be easily legitimated in terms of its "revolutionary soundness." Though he does not retreat from his radical pedagogy of resistance, he does back away from its symbiotic link with Marxist theory as part of a "pedagogy of revolution." Though aspects of Freire's educational theory can be appropriated by an open Gramscian Marxism, there is no basis for concluding that his later position can be reduced to it and therefore credited with "revolutionary soundness." As Freire himself later cautions: "I do not identify myself today as democratic just because socialism cannot offer current historical opportunities. While I am a radical and substantive democratic, I am a socialist. There is no way of countering the one with the other" (Freire, 1996, p. 114). As well, efforts to link Freire with a Gramscian theory of revolution contradict Freire's explicit rejection of being "re-written" in Marxist categories (Freire, 1994, p. 181). Such a project may be legitimate from a Gramscian perspective, but it should be recognized that it does violence to Freire's expressed intentions.

Second, such efforts to defend a Gramscian Freire fail to adequately historicize and "re-invent" Gramsci in relation to the contemporary historical context or identify some of his fundamental weaknesses, for example, his celebration of "Fordism" and lack of a critique of technology; the incompleteness of the theory of the subaltern and its problematic relation to the collective subject necessary for revolution; and the lack of a well-developed democratic theory (a theme developed in the writings of the Italian social philosopher Norbert Bobbio).

In contrast, Henry Giroux and Peter McClaren (at least in his earlier work) have attempted to interpret Freire as a "critical postmodernist" and bring him into a conversation with poststructuralism and postmodernism. Nevertheless, it is acknowledged that this requires "taking some liberties" given that "Freire's theoretical formulations are not formally situated within the disciplinary trajectories of structuralism and poststructuralism" (McLaren & Silva, 1993, p. 60). The outcome in McLaren's account is a somewhat over-theorized account of Freire's theory as implicitly developing a conception of utopian social remembrance. Giroux's characterization of Freire's strategy as offering a "language of possibility" is more cautious because it refrains more from directly projecting the theorist's utopian imagination onto how workers themselves ought to think and dream within a process of transformative mobilization.

Another theme developed in this critical postmodernist reception was recognition of the "postcolonial" aspects of Freire's theory in a sense related to postcolonial literary theory. What the postcolonial discussion added to previous discussion's of Freire as a Third World theorist, especially as developed by Giroux, was a better understanding of Freire as a "border thinker," thus drawing out the cosmopolitan and global dimensions of his peripheral stand-point (Giroux, 1993).

Though instructive at the time for facilitating recognition of the affinities between Freire and critical postmodernist tendencies, several limitations of such readings are evident. First, such discussions detracted attention from the actual epistemological origins and characteristics of his postfoundationalism in German historicism and the hermeneutically grounded theories of language and power found in the Frankfurt tradition and existentialism.

Second, though Freire was sympathetic to these utopian post-structuralist readings of his work, it should be noted that they went far beyond his more humble and situated understanding of conscientization and utopian imagination, despite a flirtation with revolutionary theory in the late 1960s and 1970s. For example, after his return to Brazil, Freire cites approvingly a conversation among workers as an example of an authentic expression of "reading the world": "What we really want, they clearly said, each in turn, 'is a just society, or at least, to begin with, a less unjust society.' As one of the leaders said: 'This is a process which does not come to a halt: it is something which moves, just as history moves'"(Freire & Faundez, 1989, p. 62). Not only is such radical reformist working-class consciousness not an expression of revolutionary consciousness, its prosaic sense of justice reveals a significant gap between the "high theory" of McLaren's account of redemptive remembrance and the kinds of actual struggles that have had a significant impact on democratization.

Third, though associating Freire with postcolonial theory was constructive in many respects, such discussions in the 1990s did not address the historical specificity of the Latin American postcolonial (Moraña et al., 2008). The failure to sustain a proposed "subaltern studies" project in Latin America is indicative of these problems (Beverly, 2000).

A fourth weakness of such critical postmodernist readings is that the "deconstructive" focus of poststructuralism does not lend itself directly to a more detailed institutional theory of radical democracy and social movements, nor provide inspiration or guidance for the historical and empirical social scientific investigations necessary for the concrete understanding of the diversity of social struggles and liberation processes.

The Freire-Habermas convergence and Freire's intellectual development

The third reading of Freire approaches the implications of his radical democratic humanism from the perspective of the potential dialogue between his social and educational theory and Habermas's theories of communicative action and deliberative democracy, despite the absence of any explicit reference to Habermas's work or basis for an actual "influence" (Morrow & Torres, 2002). From this perspective, the following problematic will be addressed here: the version of radical democratic humanism that he defends with his return to Brazil was anticipated in his early embrace of Mannheim's notion of "fundamental democratization" and Fromm's socialist humanism, but does not follow automatically from either his partial awareness and selective appreciation of the early Frankfurt critical theory tradition (e.g. Marcuse) and French existentialism (e.g. Sartre), and even less so the idealized model of revolutionary dialogue outlined theoretically in *Pedagogy of the Oppressed*. Addressing the question of the evolution of his thinking thus needs to be formulated in terms of the sociology of knowledge: what were the historical and theoretical conditions of possibility of the discontinuities or subtle "breaks" in his political thinking that were evident in both his shift to—and subsequent retreat from—his revolutionary phase toward a radical democratic one? His later personal reflections and self-criticism on these issues do not attempt to track explicitly key aspects of his changed relationship to his theoretical past, aside from maintaining an argument about the overall consistency of the evolution of his thinking with respect to critical pedagogy and democracy.

As background for the discussion that follows, several of the central features of the convergence between Habermas and Freire need to be introduced. Theoretically, the convergence of their efforts as forms of communicative and dialogical critical social theory can be traced along four dimensions that, taken together, mark a break with the Marxist tradition and its theory of revolution: 1) a postfoundationalist metatheoretical framework for a philosophy of social science grounded in a theory of communication and dialogue that legitimates a critical social science concerned with liberation and emancipation; 2) a theory of the social and cultural reproduction of society and domination that identifies contradictions that create possibilities for transformation through the struggles of diverse social movements; 3) a developmental theory of the social subject that frames the relations between historical forms of domination and possibilities for critique and practice; and 4) a theory of individual and collective learning that locates education in relation to the challenges of transformative change and deliberative democracy (Morrow & Torres, 2002, pp. 14–15).

The developmental logic of the relation between Freire and Habermas's theoretical perspectives actually takes the form of paradoxical pattern of divergence-convergence. The turning points can be traced to important shifts in their thinking around 1967–71, at which point they were moving in opposite directions within the logic of their intellectual development at mid-career: Habermas began to rethink the revolutionary theory of his early Frankfurt School mentors at the very time that Freire embraced a "science of revolution."

Though Habermas began with a more neo-Marxist critical theory position indebted to his Frankfurt School mentors, by the late 1960s he began a process of transition that culminated in the paradigm shift evident in the theory of communicative action and further developed in the theory of deliberative democracy (Habermas, 1984, 1987, 1996a, b). Habermas's rethinking of classical revolutionary theory was signaled by his 1971 introduction to his essay collection on Theory and Practice (Habermas, 1973): "The vindicating superiority of those who do the enlightening over those who are to be enlightened is theoretically unavoidable, but at the same time it is fictive and requires self-correction: in a process of enlightenment there can only be participants" (p. 40). In this period Habermas stops using the notion of an "emancipated society" that alluded to Marx's theory of class revolution.

Freire's critical pedagogy only becomes ambiguously linked with revolutionary theory in the late 1960s, as the culmination of being forced into exile in 1964 and increasing awareness of the class dimensions of education and modernization. Though Freire's dialogical theory of education and the generalized version of his concept of the oppressed brought him closer to Habermas (e.g. his theories of the democratic public sphere, distorted communication, critical knowledge interests, communicative action), linking liberation with a revolutionary model of transition nevertheless led to a conjunctural parting of the ways until his reconvergence with Habermas when back in Brazil in the 1980s.

Freire's intellectual development can thus be characterized in terms of three overlapping phases: 1) until 1964 when forced into exile, his political perspective was defined by Mannheim's conception of "fundamental democratization" and resistance to the dogmatic Marxist theory he knew in Brazil, though he had already developed the foundations of his dialogical pedagogy; 2) following his exile and working in Chile, he entered a Marxist revolutionary phase that begins theoretically with *Pedagogy of the Oppressed* and continued at a practical level as a literacy consultant in diverse revolutionary situations, despite also facilitating literacy projects in nonrevolutionary democratic contexts; and 3) in returning to Brazil in 1980, he elaborated a new synthetic position involving a return to the democratic focus of his early work, but enriched with awareness of the "critically postmodern"—or more precisely, historicist—assumptions of his epistemology, the diversity and limitations of revolutionary movements, and the strategic importance of popular and "new" social movements. It is only in this third phase that his approach converges with Habermas at the political level, even though the intersubjective epistemology of his critical pedagogy actually anticipated insights parallel to Habermas's theory of communicative action. The developmental trajectory of his career can thus be viewed as an expression of the foundational commitment of his critical pedagogy to Marx's third thesis on Feuerbach, not only as a critique of revolutionary (and technocratic) elitism but also the biographical recognition that "The educator himself needs education" (Freire, 1985, p. 159).

The rest of this chapter will explore and defend an argument regarding the transitional "revolutionary moment" that sets the stage for his turn to or "re-discovery" of what Habermas calls a deliberative model of democracy (Habermas 1996a, b). The discussion that follows will explore in more detail the evolution of Freire's thinking in terms that help focus on the shift to and then away from this "revolutionary moment": 1) his radical historicism, which grounds his call for "re-invention," thus facilitating his responsiveness to changing historical circumstances; 2) his postcolonial and peripheral perspective as a "Southern theorist" (Connell, 2007), which results in a generic theory of the "pedagogy of the oppressed" that Freire momentarily mis-recognizes as consistent with an idealized Marxism-Leninism, thus diverting attention from a nonrevolutionary theory of democratic praxis; and 3), a final retreat from revolutionary theory in the name of the priority of radical democracy as a learning process and the necessary foundation of any potential socialist project grounded in ethical critique and the uncertainty of knowledge.

Radical historicism

The crucial feature of Freire's historicism—which is rooted in German historicism and close to the version proposed by Karl Mannheim—is that it attempts to steer between historicist particularism and historicist philosophies of history grounded in some form of historical determinism and teleology (e.g. Hegel and some interpretations of Marx). Nevertheless, though his ontological perspective does suggest a universalizing normative philosophy of history—the vocation of humanization, the realization of such possibilities can only be a human achievement as the outcome of struggles whose form and outcome cannot be determined in advance. As well, strategies of struggle need to be devised in relation to objective social realities whose constraints can only be evaluated practically, contextually, and experimentally as part of efforts to overcome "limit situations."

It is in relation to this contextual and pragmatic historicism that Freire's concepts of "re-invention" and "re-discovery"—and related criticism of "transplanting" ideas in heterogeneous contexts—can be understood as an appeal to the ongoing revision of theory and practice necessary for continuing the process of liberation. A representative example of this reflexivity is evident in his criticism of revolutionary factions in contemporary Brazil: "One cannot reread the world if one does not improve the old tools, if one does reinvent them . . . a new reading of my world requires a new language—that of possibility, open to hope" (Freire, 1997, p. 77). He also applied this reflexive notion of "re-reading" to his own biography. Important examples include his later admission of having neglected the question of the oppression of women and the problematic use of Portuguese for literacy training in Africa.

At this point it is necessary to turn to a more detailed analysis of the complex relations between the second and third phases—the shift toward and then away from the revolutionary option. A close examination of the origins and argument of *Pedagogy of the Oppressed* will reveal it to be a transitional and incomplete form of revolutionary "Southern theory" whose full and contradictory implications could be realized only though subsequent experience and self-criticism.

The southern route: The oppressed

As we have seen, Freire's radical historicism can be traced back to the perspectivism of German historicism, a tradition that—with the notable exception of Herder—has tended to be rather Eurocentric (and sexist) with respect to the "standpoints" that define historical locations. In the context of the origins of Freire's theory, two key aspects of his historicist approach involve an implicit critique of Eurocentric historicism, as well as classical Marxism: the need to address differences of perspective relating to North-South and center-periphery relations, including the history of colonialism and slavery in Brazil; and the imperative of broadening the Marxist critique of domination from a theory of the working class to one that embraces the peasant populations of agrarian societies, as well as other forms of oppression.

Freire's historicist critical appropriation—not a mechanistic "transplanting" as he would say—of European theory makes it possible to refer to him one of the world's most influential examples of "Southern theory" as defined by the Australian sociologist Raewyn Connell (Connell, 2007). Her approach helps avoid the limitations of both the increasingly anachronistic notion of "Third World" theory and the narrower literary and cultural implications of postcolonial theory and its focus on very different colonial traditions than found in Latin America. Though she devotes a chapter to Latin America and has a background in educational sociology, she surprisingly neglects to mention Freire, perhaps because he is not a sociological theorist in the strict sense. Nevertheless, he is certainly the most influential Latin American social theorist globally. More specifically, Freire's "Southern theory" can also be situated as part of the postoccidentalist Latin American tradition of critical social theory (Mendieta, 2007).

In the present context, two features of Freire's argument need to be briefly introduced as a prelude to considering the "revolutionary moment" of his theorizing in the next section: some of the peculiar features of the concept of the "oppressed" (and related notion of "the people") as an alternative to the Marxist concept of working class; and the implications of how the analysis of the oppressed was based on a very specific and limited theory of power.

First, it can be argued that his use of the concept of the oppressed is not only a "Southern" response to the realities of Brazil as a peripheral society with a colonial history, it also implies a critique of Marxism that was largely unconscious. But the resulting implicit critique is obscured by a concluding chapter of *Pedagogy of the Oppressed* devoted to an idealized Marxist model of revolutionary transition. At one level, Freire's reference to the oppressed could be viewed—as evident in most of his examples—as simply incorporating rural workers or peasants (complex categories whose internal differentiations are not considered) into a broader notion of the proletariat as the "oppressed classes"—themes already evident in Latin American Marxism-Leninism and Maoism. At the same time, however, his discussion of the oppressed is developed at a more general level, clearly implying a much more comprehensive, indeed universal concept embracing all possible sources for and standpoints of domination. In short, the theory of the oppressed implied a critique of class reductionism of the Marxist tradition, even though similar themes are indirectly anticipated in Gramsci's treatment of the "Southern question" in Italy and his fragmentary discussions of the "subaltern."

To turn to the second question, Freire proposed a theory of power as domination, but one of limited scope and range of application. More generally, it could be described as a critical social psychology of the origins of domination in the oppressor-oppressed relation and the potential of a critical pedagogy to cultivate processes of conscientization that facilitate critical consciousness and liberation. This theme is expressed in the focus on the oppressor-oppressed relation at a high level of generality, hence making universal claims of a quasi-ontological kind. Indeed, part of the universal narrative drama of *Pedagogy of the Oppressed* is that it provides an epic utopian story of the potential liberation of the oppressed from oppressors. As an implicit theory of power, therefore, Freire's theory works with an inter-group model of social relations that has its origins in what Max Weber called "traditional domination" originating in patriarchy and what Michel Foucault later referred to as the "sovereign power" of European monarchy. Freire's use of the metaphor of Hegel's feudal lordship-bondage model provides the philosophical basis for Freire's own analysis. Though of foundational importance as far as it goes, the obvious limitation of this model is that it is not suited for comprehending more impersonal and structural relations of power and domination. Weber's concept of "legal-rational" domination, Marcuse's "one-dimensional" society, Foucault's related concerns with "bio-power" and "governmentality," and Steven Lukes's theory of the three faces of power represent several of the more influential efforts to analyze more abstract power relations and impersonal domination that transcend more visible personal relations of domination. In short, the reduction of a theory of domination and liberation to the intergroup theory of power based on a binary opposition between oppressors and oppressed as a collective subject can be questioned from both the perspectives of critical sociological and revolutionary Marxist theory.

To summarize, Freire's shift to a revolutionary Marxist perspective involved theoretical arguments that simply could not be ultimately reconciled either with the Marxist-Leninist theory that informed his discussion or the critical pedagogy that was supposed to guarantee the authenticity of revolutionary processes. To historicize the evolution of Freire's thinking, in short, what is needed is an immanent critique of what might be called the revolutionary phase or "moment" of his intellectual trajectory. Accordingly, the following section will argue that at that time Freire mis-recognized the full implications and tensions within his own theory and its relation to the conjunctural moment. The following reinterpretation of the genesis of *Pedagogy of the Oppressed* will thus attempt to follow through on Freire's own suggestion:

> The educator must fully understand the economic, social, cultural, and historical conditions that culminated, for example, in the writing of *Pedagogy of the Oppressed*. When one thinks about the context that generated *Pedagogy of the Oppressed* and

also thinks about one's own context, one can begin to re-create *Pedagogy of the Oppressed*. (Freire & Macedo, 1987, p. 134)

The revolutionary Marxist moment and the missing fifth chapter

Ironically, despite building on the revolutionary images of a unique historical moment, *Pedagogy of the Oppressed* was not a "conjunctural book," as a friend pointed out to Freire from the beginning (Freire, 1994, pp. 190–1). The massive subsequent international reception of the book confirms that assessment, but also raises the historicist question of potential conjunctural aspects that might invite retrospective criticism and reinvention. The nonconjunctural dimension is confirmed by how, every decade thereafter, the book could have been rewrittten—hence reinvented—using the examples of the most prominent emerging struggles, as evident in his own later recognition of feminist theory and his concern with popular movements with his return to Brazil. Despite the masculinist and revolutionary focus of most of the examples, in short, his diverse readers could later readily project themselves into liberation processes from other standpoints based on gender, race, indigeneity, etc., whether in revolutionary or nonrevolutionary settings. In other words, aspects of the phenomenon of the "many Freires" that has often been noted has its origins in the ambiguity, inconsistencies, and incompletion of the argument of the book, issues that Freire only alludes to in his later self-criticisms.

The reception of *Pedagogy of the Oppressed* by diverse audiences for more than three decades can thus be explained partly by the fact that it contains both a general theory of oppression-liberation and a more specific theory of "revolutionary praxis" deemed necessary for "oppressed orders" that cannot tolerate problem-solving education (Freire, 2005, p. 86). The text was written on two levels, differentiating two forms of cultural action: revolutionary action (as carried out by urban and rural workers as representatives of "the people") both before and after a revolutionary transition, and a more generic nonrevolutionary theory of democratic mobilization. But the latter is not clearly defined or discussed in detail, though it is implied by the generality of the first three chapters on banking versus critical education and the methodology of generative themes.

Symptomatic of his own self-criticism, however, is that in his later recollection of writing the book, his focus shifts from "revolutionary" to "democratic struggle," as is evident in his emphasizing the marginalized nonrevolutionary democratizing theme and renaming it in contemporary terminology as part of a process of achieving "citizenship," hence "the various levels of engagement in the process of mobilization and organization for the struggle—for the defense of rights, for laying claim to justice" (Freire, 1994, p. 40).

The conditions of the book's production, however, do provide clues to some of the tensions between the specific revolutionary and more general democratic model. It was written in the later part of the four and a half years he spent in Chile as part of a "profound learning process" related to his rural literacy work, Chile as a haven for leftist intellectuals from all over Latin America, and global events such as student movements, the death of Che Guevara, Mao's cultural revolution, and international receptions of Marcuse and Fanon. In the process he thought that he was finally able to define theoretically the implications his earlier practice in Brazil (Freire, 1994, pp. 40–3). This conjunctural revolutionary standpoint thus relied on both Marxist-Leninist (Althusser, Che Guevara) and Maoist reference points, as well as, though less directly, liberation theology and dependency theory.

The first three of the four chapters of the book—completed in 1968 before leaving for New York in 1969—are largely nonconjunctural in the sense that they developed a more radicalized synthesis—based on the concept of the "oppressed"—of his earlier critical pedagogy: the rationale for a *Pedagogy of the Oppressed* (chapter 1); the critique of banking education (chapter 2); and the methodology of literacy training based on generative themes (chapter 3). After completing these chapters he let the text sit for two months before becoming "reacquainted" again: "I did not make many important changes in it. But I did make the basic discovery that the text was unfinished. I needed one more chapter" (Freire, 1994, p. 60). That last chapter was written mostly on the road around Santiago or "now in hotels in cities or towns further away . . . After dinner I would fairly race to my room, and seclude myself there the whole night through, writing chapter 4" (ibid.). Finally, "with the fourth chapter finally ready, I looked at the first three again and touched them up, then I handed over the whole text to a typist" and distributed copies to friends.

Some of those touch-ups in the earlier chapters likely related to the new themes stressed in the final chapter on revolutionary praxis, which begins with a quotation from Lenin. For example, in the earlier chapters the otherwise more open-ended concept of problem-posing education is discussed more generally as contributing to the "becoming" of unfinished beings. Nevertheless, probably in light of final chapter, Freire suddenly declares in concluding chapter two that "problem-posing education is revolutionary futurity" (Freire, 2005, p. 84).

Three significant features of Freire's focus on an essentializing notion of "the revolution" require further discussion: 1) the lack of a clear theoretical connection between critical literacy training, conscientization, and specifically revolutionary consciousness; 2) the assumption that revolution provides the only alternative for the transition to "transitive," critical consciousness; and 3) the reliance upon a Marxist-Leninist theory of revolution informed by the structuralist Marxism of French philosopher Louis Althusser.

With regard to the first point, chapter three on the construction of generative themes says nothing about "revolutionary futurity" or revolutionary consciousness, as opposed to the thematics as defined by the learners, but then returned to them by the teachers as problems to be solved. For example, the chapter concludes with reference to a learner's question about the meaning of nationalism. This disjuncture reappears again in the long article written after the book. Again, the discussion of adult learners (Part I) takes place at a very abstract level, concluding that conscientization "makes the transformation of their state of apathy into the utopian state of denunciation and annunciation a viable project" (Freire, 1985, p. 59). Yet neither this analysis—which concludes with a discussion of example of land reform in Chile—nor the appendix on generative codes provides any indication that the outcome of conscientization as utopian thinking would have to be revolutionary. In short, even in this period there is no assumption that "learning to question" through nonmanipulative "critical" or "transformative" literacy training necessarily or likely produces "revolutionary," as opposed to democratic or reformist, consciousness.

Regarding the second question of the necessity of revolution, in the long article published in 1970 Freire provided a more extensive rationale for a revolutionary strategy in dependent Latin American societies: "Since revolution is still a possibility in this phase, our analysis will focus on the dialectical confrontation between the revolutionary project (or, lamentably, projects) and the new regime" (p. 81). This assumption was based on his analysis of the emergence of the oppressed "masses" in Latin American societies, which "are still closed societies today" (p. 75). As he pessimistically concludes, "Latin American societies in transition are confronted with only two contradictory possibilities: revolution or coup d'état" (p. 80).

Third, in the final (fourth) chapter Freire embraces the necessity of a particular form of revolution, as indicated by the essentializing notion of "the revolution" (which curiously requires lamenting the plurality of "projects"). Consequently, at this stage he ignores the diversity of possible revolutionary processes in different contexts such as Africa or Latin America, as well as the implications of non-revolutionary democratic possibilities. Consequently, there is a tendency to conflate "cultural action for freedom" almost exclusively with "revolutionary cultural action," which in turn contributes to readings that overgeneralize his analysis: the assumption that only revolutionary action can produce critical transitive consciousness, even though this conclusion applies, strictly speaking, only to "oppressive" and "closed" societies.

Further, Freire's analysis of revolution ignores the extensive discussion of other revolutionary options in Western Marxism (e.g. anarchism's suspicions about the revolutionary state or even Gramsci), reducing the question instead to an idealized form of Marxism-Leninism. On the one hand, he analyzes revolutionary praxis as a dialogue that creates "communion" between leaders and masses, as exemplified by Che Guevara, Mao, etc. On the other, he draws upon French philosopher Louis Althusser's structuralist Marxism to justify the scientific character of revolutionary theory. Accordingly, a "scientific unveiling of reality" to expose myths and ideology is viewed as the "indispensable instrument" guiding conscientization (Freire, 1985, p. 85).

A complementary formulation in The *Pedagogy of the Oppressed* strangely conjoins an appeal to a "science of revolution" and its mission "as an act of love":

For me, the revolution, which is not possible without a theory of revolution—and therefore science—is not irreconcilable with love. On the contrary: the revolution is made by people to achieve their humanization. What, indeed, is the deeper motive which moves individuals to become revolutionaries, but the dehumanization of people? (Freire, 2005, p. 89, note 4, emphasis added)

These anomalies evident in *Pedagogy of the Oppressed* suggest several comments. First, it can be argued that he mis-recognized the degree to which his theory implicitly challenged the revolutionary Marxist movements at the time, partly because of his problematic assumption that they were as fully dialogical as he claimed. His understanding of the Maoist cultural revolution was particularly unfortunate: "In China, to be conscious is not a slogan or a ready-made idea. To be conscious is a radical way of being, a way characteristic of humanity" (Freire, 1985, p. 106). Symptomatically, despite the sympathies expressed in the text, Cuba and China steadfastly rejected his pedagogical theory. Nevertheless, though Brazilian activist Frei Betto's effort to introduce Freire in Cuba in the 1980s was rebuffed, there is now tolerance in Cuba of a small Freire influenced educational institute (Pérez Cruz, 2007).

Second, Freire clearly did not have time to properly digest the implications of Althusserian structuralism. He probably hurriedly worked through the French edition of *For Marx* (though released in 1965, a 1967 edition is cited) "in the heat of the night" on the road in Chile. In the long article published in 1970, the Spanish translation of Reading Capital (1969) is first cited and was presumably read in the United States that same year under the hectic conditions of moving and teaching. At this time, he apparently did not realize that such a "Marxist science" was fundamentally incompatible with his own democratic humanism and historicist epistemology, as evident in his appreciation of Mannheim, Fromm, Kosik, Gramsci, and the dialogical and hermeneutic philosophy of science of the Mexican philosopher Eric Nicol, who is cited in both his first book and one of his last, *Pedagogy of Hope*.

Third, Freire's text did contain reflexive loopholes that would facilitate both his eventual shift away from the revolutionary model and the book's reinvention in the hands of readers. His defense of revolution was from the beginning doubly conditional: first, the conjunctural assumption that there was no alternative in Latin America to armed revolutionary insurrection as a way of initiating a process of radical democratization; and second, the contention that revolutionary cultural action had to take a democratic dialogical form to be authentic. The first conditional proviso about the apparent necessity of revolution, however, was complemented by a general qualifying principle: "The limits of cultural action are set by the oppressive reality itself and the silence imposed by the power elite" (Freire, 1985, p. 90). So if the oppressive reality were to change—if "limits of cultural action" were to be vastly extended and opened up in a "democratic transition," then nonrevolutionary democratic action might become a viable option. The second proviso regarding dialogical authenticity, on the other hand, paradoxically set the stage for the redeployment of his analysis in a more empirically informed argument as part of a normative critique of Marxism-Leninism in practice.

Fourth, these tensions in the text can be linked to a violation of his own educational methodology as grounded in personal experience and practice. He anticipated this issue in his preface: "It is possible that some may question my right to discuss revolutionary cultural action, a subject of which I have no concrete experience" (Freire, 2005, p. 39). But the real issue is not his "right" to do so, but to be aware of the risks. Only in the subsequent decade did he get such experience, which ultimately transformed his understanding of revolution, especially by recognizing diversity of revolutionary processes (e.g. Africa versus Latin America), their limitations, and the need for democratic compromise where possible (e.g. Nicaragua, El Salvador, Brazil). The outcome was a rejection of any essentializing, unitary conception of "the revolution" that could be an object of "science" as exemplified in Althusser's structuralist theories and the revolutionary praxis of Castro, Guevara, and Mao. Though he does not appear to have ever explicitly renounced these inconsistent passages in his work, he does warn that militant political intellectuals inevitably run the risk of authoritarianism "if they are not capable of going beyond a messianic concept of social change, of revolutionary change" (Freire, 1983, p. 28).

Finally, viewed retrospectively in terms of the immanent critique sketched above, it can be argued that the text was still incomplete because of a missing fifth chapter on nonrevolutionary "radical democratic praxis" and cultural action that was needed to complement the discussion of revolutionary praxis in chapter four. Despite this conjunctural silence, however, there is a sense in which his publications after returning to Brazil constitute that final chapter as an epilogue, which is the topic of the following concluding section.

Freire's postfoundationalist and democratic (re)turn

"Therefore for me, all of these issues must be faced now must be properly addressed by the end of this century—problems like the role of social movements and the issues of power . . . I now feel that in transforming society, the important task is not to take power but to reinvent power."

Freire, 1985, p. 179

The political standpoint of the "final Freire" can be summarized as a theory of radical democratic cultural action that can be used to supplement theories of deliberative democracy. This position is most concisely stated in his foreword responding to the book *Paulo Freire: A Critical Encounter*: "Oppression must always be understood in its multiple and contradictory instances, just as liberation must be grounded in the particularity of suffering and struggle in concrete, historical experiences, without resorting to transcendental guarantees" (Freire, 1993a, p. x). Accordingly, he speaks only of "liberatory pedagogy" not "revolutionary pedagogy." Indeed, this foreword could be read as a précis of the final, fifth chapter of *Pedagogy of the Oppressed* on "democratic cultural action" that was never written.

The present analysis has drawn upon the Freire-Habermas partial convergence and complementarity thesis as part of demonstrating that Freire does indeed implicitly retreat not only from crucial aspects of the account of revolution found in *Pedagogy of the Oppressed* but also from equating his critical pedagogy with "revolutionary pedagogy" in the Gramscian sense. Such considerations suggest shifting the ground of debate away from the nostalgic question of Freire's "revolutionary" credentials as part of the Marxist tradition by recognizing the underlying continuity of his project as grounded in a processual and procedural understanding of the contribution of his critical pedagogy to democratization as the springboard of liberation. So the possibility that he may have "retreated" from his previous revolutionary position should neither be glossed over by assimilating him into Gramscian Marxism nor dogmatically attributed to "revisionism" and "opportunism" and reduced to mere "reformism."

Understanding Freire as a "Southern theorist"—more specifically, a postoccidentalist, Latin American critical social theorist— reaffirms the advantage of viewing his theory as part of a dialogue of mutual learning with Habermas. From this perspective Freire's "revolutionary" democratic pedagogy can be viewed as a form of "Southern theory" that provides a foundational pedagogical contribution to the theory of deliberative democracy. The crucial shift in his vocabulary was thus away from a simplistic, romantic model of democratic relations as a form of "communion" between masses and revolutionary leaders to one that viewed the dialogue of democratic politics in more concrete terms as part of dynamic "procedural" relations among deliberative groups, as exemplified in his administration of educational reform (Freire, 1993b, p. 24). In place of the abstract, undifferentiated understanding of the oppressed as a collective subject, his analysis shifts to the recognition of the plurality of struggling groups and their debilitating divisions: "I do not understand how, in Brazil, we can maintain feminist, black, Indian, working class groups separately struggling for a less perverse society. Each group is fighting its own battles" (Freire, 1997, p. 86). Instead, he calls for strategies that promote solidarity and "unity in diversity." From this deliberative perspective, in reflecting on the case of El Salvador, he equates the "reinvention of society" as part of consolidating a democratic lifestyle. Crucial to this democratic process is overcoming "sectarian" positions, even though "deepening" radical ones, as part of a "learning process" for both the powerful and "the crushed" (Freire, 1994, pp. 197–8). Similarly, proponents of deliberative democracy have pointed to its particular value in deeply divided societies (Dryzek, 2005).

Having questioned the rhetorical abuse of the term "revolutionary" at the outset, in concluding it may nevertheless be appropriate to suggest that deliberative democracy, as an admittedly utopian project, does have a revolutionary dimension:

> Deliberative democracy is a revolutionary political ideal. It calls for fundamental changes in the bases of political decision making, scope of those included in decision-making processes, institutions that house these processes, and thus the very character of politics itself. Deliberative democracy is also revolutionary in a second sense. It has been thought to require dramatically more egalitarian political, social, and economic conditions than exist in any contemporary society. Background inequities in resources, status, and other forms of privilege upset the communicative equality that deliberation requires. (Fung, 2005, pp. 397–8)

Not surprisingly in light of the preceding reconstruction of Freire's intellectual evolution, theories of deliberative democracy converge with his repeated call for "reinventing power" rather than "taking power" as the most important issue on the agenda of radical politics. But as he laments: "In respect to these issues, I don't think I have much of a contribution to make, and I say this, not with false modesty, but with sadness. Nonetheless, I will continue trying to contribute to a greater understanding of these issues" (Freire, 1985, p. 179). But his enduring contribution was to pose the problem as part of a reflexive effort to sustain the "coherence" of his democratic critical pedagogy. And as he always insisted—in a fully Deweyan and Habermasian critical pragmatist spirit—problemposing and learning from error are crucial foundations of collective learning.

References

Aronowitz, S. (2009). "Gramsci's concept of political organization." In J. Francese (ed.). *Perspectives on Gramsci: Politics, culture and social theory* (pp. 8–19). Abingdon, UK and New York, NY: Routledge.
— (1993). "Paulo Freire's radical democratic humanism." In P. McLaren and P. Leonard (eds). *Paulo Freire: A critical encounter* (pp. 8–24). London, GB and New York, NY: Routledge.

Beverly, J. (2000). "The dilemma of subaltern studies at Duke." *Nepantla: Views from the South*, 1, 33–44.

Connell, R. (2007). *Southern theory*. Cambridge, UK: Polity Press.

Dryzek, J. S. (2005). "Deliberative democracy in divided societies: Alternatives to agonism and analgesia." *Political Theory*, 33, 218–42.

Freire, P. (1983). *Pedagogy in process: The Letters to Guinea-Bissau*. New York, NY: Continuum.

— (1985). *The politics of education: Culture, power and liberation*. South Hadley, MA: Bergin & Garvey.

— (1993a). "Foreword." In P. McLaren and Peter Leonard (eds). *Paulo Freire: A critical encounter* (pp. ix–xii). London, GB and New York, NY: Routledge.

— (1993b). *Pedagogy of the city*. New York, NY: Continuum.

— (1994). *Pedagogy of hope: Reliving the pedagogy of the oppressed*. New York, NY: Continuum.

— (1996). *Letters to Cristina: Reflections on my life and work*. New York, NY and London, GB: Routledge.

— (1997). *Pedagogy of the heart*. New York, NY: Continuum.

— (2003). *El Grito manso*. México, D.F.: Sigle Veintiuno.

— (2005). *Pedagogy of the oppressed*. New York, NY and London, GB: Continuum.

Freire, P. and Faundez, A. (1989). *Learning to question: A pedagogy of liberation*. New York, NY: Continuum.

Freire, P. and Macedo, D. (1987). *Literacy: Reading the word and the world*. South Hadley, MA: Bergin & Garvey.

Fung, A. (2005). "Deliberation before the revolution: Toward an ethics of deliberative democracy." *Political Theory*, 33, 397–419.

Giroux, H. (1993). "Paulo Freire and the politics of postcolonialism." In P. McLaren and P. Leonard (eds). *Paulo Freire: A critical encounter* (pp. 177–88). London, GB and New York, NY: Routledge.

Habermas, J. (1973). *Theory and practice*. Boston, MA: Beacon.

— (1984). *The theory of communicative action, Vol. 1: Reason and the rationalization of society*. Boston, MA: Beacon.

— (1987). *The theory of communicative action, Vol. 2: Lifeworld and system: A critique of functionalist reason*. Boston, MA: Beacon Press.

— (1996a). *Between facts and norms: Contributions to a discourse theory of law and democracy*. Cambridge, MA and London, GB: MIT Press.

— (1996b). "Three normative models of democracy." In S. Benhabib (ed.). *Democracy and difference: Contesting the boundaries of the political* (pp. 21–30). Princeton, NJ: Princeton University Press.

McLaren, P. (2000). *Che Guevara, Paulo Freire, and the pedagogy of revolution*. Lanham, MD: Rowman & Littlefield.

— (2010). "Foreword: Challenging imperial capital and the struggle for critical consciousness: Paula Allman's revolutionary critical pedagogy." In P. Allman (ed.). *Critical Education Against Global Capitalism: Karl Marx and Revolutionary Critical Education* (pp. xvii–xxvii). Rotterdam: Sense Publishers.

McLaren, P. and Lankshear, C. (1994). "Introduction." In P. McLaren and C. Lankshear (eds). *Politics of liberation: Paths from Freire* (pp. 1–11). London, GB and New York, NY: Routledge.

McLaren, P. and Leonard, P. (eds) (1993). *Paulo Freire: A critical encounter.* London, GB and New York, NY: Routledge.

McLaren, P. and Tadeu da Silva, T. (1993). "Decentering pedagogy: Critical literacy, resistance and the politics of memory." In P. McLaren and P. Leonard (eds). *Paulo Freire: a critical encounter* (pp. 47–89). London, GB and New York, NY: Routledge.

Mendieta, E. (2007). *Global fragments: Globalizations, Latinamericanisms, and critical theory.* Albany, NY: State University of New York Press.

Moraña, M., Dussel, E., and Jáuregui, C. A. (eds) (2008). *Coloniality at large: Latin America and the postcolonial debate.* Durham, NC: Duke University Press.

Morrow, R. A. (2008). "Paulo Freire, indigenous knowledge and eurocentric critiques of development: Three perspectives." In C. A. Torres and P. Noguera (eds). *Social justice education for teachers: Paulo Freire and the possible dream* (pp. 81–100). Rotterdam, The Netherlands: Sense Publishers.

— (2009). "Habermas, eurocentrism and education: The indigenous knowledge debate." In M. Murphy and T. Fleming (eds). *Habermas, critical theory, and education* (pp. 63–77). London, GB and New York, NY: Routledge.

— (forthcoming). "Habermas, eurocentrism and Latin American social theory: The challenge of Mignolo's decolonial research program." In T. Bailey (ed.). *Global Perspectives on Habermas.* London, GB: Routledge.

Morrow, R. A. and Torres, C. A. (2002). *Reading Freire and Habermas: Critical pedagogy and Transformative change.* New York, NY: Teacher's College Press, Columbia University.

Pérez Cruz, F. J. (2007). "Paulo Freire and the Cuban revolution." In L. Servage and T. J. Fenwick (eds). *Learning in Community: Proceedings of the joint international conference of the Adult Education Research Conference* (AERC) and the *Canadian Association for the Study of Adult Education* (CASAE), June 2007 (pp. 695–700). Halifax, Nova Scotia, Canada: Mount Saint Vincent University.

5

Freire, Buber, and Care Ethics on Dialogue in Teaching

Nel Noddings

Both Paulo Freire and Martin Buber put great emphasis on dialogue in education. Indeed, Buber said, "The relation in education is one of pure dialogue" (1965, p. 98). Dialogue is also central in care ethics. How do these views differ, and how might they modify each other?

It may be helpful at the outset to understand that Freire and Buber give dialogue a somewhat technical meaning, especially in connection with teaching. By "dialogue" they do not mean simply "conversation," as suggested in dictionaries. For both, dialogue has purpose: for Freire, the purpose is a transformation of the world; for Buber, it is a "selection of the effective world." For care ethics, the purpose is to initiate or maintain caring relations and to understand what the other is feeling and thinking. Ordinary conversation can sometimes contribute positively to this purpose.

Freire

Freire identifies revolutionary education with dialogue, and the "essence" of dialogue, he writes, is the word (1970, p. 75). The word, in turn, has two dimensions: reflection and action: "There is no true word that is not at the same time a praxis [a radical inter-action of reflection and action]. Thus, to speak a true word is to transform the world" (ibid.).

True dialogue, Freire writes, requires critical thinking. Today, critical thinking is a matter of keen interest to educators all over the world, but it is rarely defined in practical terms, if it is defined at all. Freire might say that our use of the term does not express a true word. It is worth examining Freire's definition closely; for him, critical thinking is

> thinking which discerns an indivisible solidarity between the world and men and admits no dichotomy between them—thinking which perceives reality as process, as transformation, rather than as a static entity—thinking that does not separate itself from action, but constantly immerses itself in temporality without fear of the risks involved. (p. 81)

We might question the phrase "without fear" and substitute "despite fear." Freire himself devotes some space to the fear of free-dom experienced by the oppressed, and clearly that fear does not disappear instantaneously. Indeed, we might argue that a fear of freedom infects a large number of middle-class students today. In part, this fear can be traced to the arbitrariness of the prescribed curriculum. The constant press of required courses and testing leaves little room for dialogue. Many students, therefore, seem to believe that mastery of the given curriculum is the only way to suc-cess in life.

Dialogue generates critical thinking, but it also requires critical thinking. Understanding this, teachers must be patient and con-stant in encouraging dialogue, moving from relatively uncontro-versial conversation to the critical thinking that underlies true dialogue.

Freire contrasts critical thinking with naïve thinking that func-tions to maintain the status quo:

> For the naïve thinker, the important thing is accommodation to this normalized "today." For the critic, the important thing is the continuing transformation of reality, in behalf of the continuing humanization of men. (ibid.)

But accommodation to the "normal" may be necessary to attain acceptability, and acceptability may be necessary to gain listeners. I have written on his topic (Noddings, 2002) and will say more about it in the section on care ethics. We can agree with the emphasis made by Freire, but we may want to look more closely at the role of normalized life in effecting transformation.

Freire is highly critical of the "banking method" of education:

> Education thus becomes an act of depositing, in which the students are the depositories and the teacher is the depositor. Instead of communicating, the teacher issues communiqués and makes deposits which the students patiently receive, memorize, and repeat. (1970, p. 58)

This criticism has met with widespread verbal approval in the educational community but, paradoxically, the banking method has become more and more firmly entrenched. The school curriculum is more narrowly prescribed today than ever before and, despite the theoretical attractions of constructivism, Freire's recommendations for a problem-posing approach are rarely followed.

A problem-posing approach is, however, receiving some attention at the theoretical level, especially among ecologists. Those deeply concerned about ecological problems are often strong advocates because they see the need for cooperative problem-posing and solving. The biologist, E. O. Wilson, for example, recommends what amounts to a problem-posing approach in his description of top-down teaching. He advises teachers:

> Address a large question of the kind already interesting to the students and relevant to their lives, then peel off layers of causation as currently understood, and in growing technical and philosophically disputatious detail, in order to teach and provoke . . . Do not teach from the bottom up, with an introduction such as "First, we'll learn some of this, and some of that, and we'll combine the knowledge later to build the bigger picture." (Wilson, 2006, p. 131)

The assumption here is that prior dialogue has already made clear what is interesting and relevant and so, in an important sense, the problem to be explored has been cooperatively posed. Wilson, teaching at Harvard, can be sure that his students are conscious of the reality to which he points. Freire, working with the oppressed who are fearful of freedom even as they long for it, must help his students through a process of "conscientization" to "reject the oppressive consciousness which dwells in them, become aware of their situation, and find their own language" (Gutierrez, 1988, p. 57). As Gutierrez points out, this is a difficult process of changing "precritical consciousness, that is the consciousness of one who has not taken hold of the reins of one's own destiny" (p. 121). In this situation, problem-seeking must precede problem-posing.

In any case, problem-posing is a powerful pedagogical technique that can be used, after suitable preparation, at every level. A difficulty arises, however, when we take an "all or nothing" position and vow to reject banking methods entirely. We may agree heartily with Freire that exploited (oppressed) adults should not be treated as objects or containers to be filled with information they have not sought. When we take the position that we know best and they had better listen to us, we perpetuate the condition from which we would like to liberate them. But are there not appropriate intervals in which teachers might temporarily apply "banking" methods to ensure the acquisition of needed skills? We can anticipate such intervals in Wilson's top-down problem-posing method. Such intervals of direct instruction are undertaken with the tacit agreement of students who are already convinced of the need to learn certain skills in order to solve the problem posed.

The banking method, used too soon or too extensively, works against Freire's primary aim in his pedagogy of oppressed adults—a raised consciousness that will permit them to express and pursue their own liberation. But how might this apply to the schooling of children? Children have always posed a problem for political theorists concerned with freedom. For example, in laying out his theory of liberty, John Stuart Mill informs readers:

> We are not speaking of children . . . Those who are still in a state to require being taken care of by others, must be protected against their own actions as well as against external injury. (1993/1859, p. 13)

Mill then extends his argument to "barbarians" and "backward" populations who have not yet "become capable of being improved by free and equal discussion" (ibid.). This is exactly the attitude that Freire deplores and would eliminate through conscientization. For Freire, dialogue requires free and equal discussion that generates critical thinking that, in turn, promotes true dialogue. From the start, interaction must be between equal persons, recognized as equal.

If we accept Freire's argument against a form of education for oppressed adults that perpetuates the oppression, we should be led to consider an alternative to the banking approach for children. Recognizing that children do indeed require the protection mentioned by Mill, that they are not ready for adult freedom, we can ask: What sort of education will provide that protection and prepare them for a life of genuine freedom? A partial answer to that question is found in the history of holistic education. The connections and sharing at the heart of holistic education require the active engagement of children from the start (J. Miller, 2010, 2011). Dialogue is encouraged at the outset. But we do not find conclusive answers in the holistic education movement. Critics have claimed, from a Freirean perspective, that these "free" or "holistic" schools have often depended on a form of privileged, prior preparation of children that made them already familiar with dialogue (see R. Miller, 2002). Fierce arguments arose in the 1960s, for example, over the efficacy of open education for underprivileged children. If parents do not (or cannot) prepare their children for a dialogical educational experience—and there is persuasive evidence that this is so (Heath, 1983)—the elementary school must either do so or resort to the dismal banking method.

The problems here are challenging. If some children are unprepared for a dialogical approach to education, must we start them out with a more structured method? Those who argued for this approach in the 1960s did not seem to see that such a start might very well perpetuate the thinking that maintains oppression. One could plausibly argue that privileged children would gain more from a structured program because they had already learned something about its role in maintaining their privilege. It would seem better for all children to start with a program that aims at participation, dialogue, and critical thinking.

When elementary education fails to develop dialogue and an attitude of critical thinking (a failure all too common in today's schools), Freire's method becomes vitally important at the secondary level. The many teenagers who drop out of high school are very like Freire's oppressed adults who suffer from false consciousness. For these young people, the banking approach is poisonous; it finishes them off. They need the patient, respectful renewal of human dignity in dialogue.

This is not to say, however, that direct teaching toward a specified learning objective is to be rejected entirely. Some dedicated constructivists make this error, insisting that their students must "construct" all of their knowledge when, in fact, teachers might reasonably tell students much of what they need to know. Sonia Nieto, too, stresses caution on this point: "The above discussion should not be read as promoting an either/or conception of knowledge, but rather as suggesting that learning is more complex than simply providing students with facts and information" (1999, p. 5). Knowledge involves the use of facts and skills, not their simple accumulation. Dialogue, as the base of education, provides the connection between personal purposes and the pursuit of knowledge.

Buber

Martin Buber agrees with Freire that dialogue is central to education and that the spirit of inclusion characterizes the work of teachers. By "inclusion" Buber means a relational attitude that sees things from both sides. In care ethics, for example, the carer tries to understand what the cared-for is going through. In teaching, the teacher must make an effort to see and understand from the student's position. Buber puts it this way:

> Without the action of his spirit being in any way weakened he must at the same time be over there, on the surface of that other spirit which is being acted upon . . . [on] the wholly concrete spirit of this individual and unique being who is living and confronting him, and who stands with him in the common situation of "educating" and "being educated." (1965, p. 100)

These comments give rise to several questions: How does the educator "experience" things from the side of those "being educated"? Is the student passive in being acted upon, or does he, too, act, and if so, how? I shall return to these important questions in the section on care ethics.

Although there is significant mutuality in education, Buber warns that there cannot be mutuality in inclusion:

> But however intense the mutuality of giving and taking with which he is bound to his pupil, inclusion cannot be mutual . . . [The teacher] experiences the pupil's being educated, but the pupil cannot experience the educating of the educator. (1965, p. 100)

Buber draws our attention to the structural inequality of relations such as physician-patient, parent-infant, and teacher-student. In a dialogue with the psychotherapist, Carl Rogers, Buber pointed out the difference:

> A man coming to you for help . . . The essential difference between your role in this situation and his is obvious. He comes for help to you. You don't come for help to him. And not only this, but you are able, more or less to help him. (Friedman, 1964, p. 487)

The conversation between Buber and Rogers is complicated. On one level, they agree entirely—that each human being must meet another human being as a human being fully recognized as such. There is a sense, then, in which the two participants in dialogue are equal. But there is also a structural situation to be considered. Because of that structural situation, some relations are necessarily unequal, and teaching is one such relation. A power difference exists. The teacher can try to remove it—to equalize the relation, but notice: It is the teacher who can do something in this direction; the student cannot. The power difference is inherent in a structurally unequal relation. Perhaps, then it would be more honest and more effective for teachers to recognize the difference and use their power generously, with some humility. Those of us who have worked in training teachers know that many young people find it hard to accept their power as teachers. Some even ask what gives them the right to tell their students what to do. This is, for a start, the spirit that Freire and Buber would like to cultivate. They want to treat their students as fellow human beings, not as objects. But they must move on to accept the special responsibility of teaching and put that power in the service of their students. However equal they are as persons, teacher and student are not equal in the teacher-student relation; they cannot exchange positions regularly.

Buber also takes a broad view of dialogue. Dialogue, for Buber, can be expressed in silence and across spatial separation. It is a matter of feeling and understanding from the partner's side. In teaching, it begins as acceptance. Today's teachers do not select their students, and Buber argues strenuously against the classical notion of Eros for educators:

> The man who is loving in Eros chooses the beloved, the modern educator finds his pupils before him . . . the misshapen and the well-proportioned, animal faces, empty faces, and noble faces in indiscriminate confusion . . . the glance of the educator accepts and receives them all. (1965, p. 94)

However, acceptance does not imply approval or denial of a need for change. Buber distinguishes between acceptance and confirmation. In confirming another, we help him or her to take a positive direction toward the good that is already potentially in him. I have described one form of confirmation as attributing the best possible motive consonant with reality (Noddings, 1992). Getting to know the student through dialogue, the teacher can detect the good that a student may be trying to achieve through ill-chosen methods. The teacher's confirmation of that good often inspires the student to act more consistently on it.

We think of confirmation primarily in connection with moral education—for Buber, all education is "essentially education of character" (1965, p. 104)—but it is also powerful in guiding intellectual development. When students show signs of real thinking, we should seize the moment and encourage further development by participating in their thinking. We enter true dialogue and become the "co-investigators" described by Freire. As educators, we work steadily to move from the initial dialogue of acceptance to one of critical thinking, confirmation, and transformation.

The move just described is supported by trust. Students must trust their teachers if they are to follow and profit from their direction. Buber has written beautifully on this:

> Trust, trust in the world, because this human being exists—that is the most inward achievement of the relation in education.

Because this human being exists, meaninglessness, however hard pressed you are by it, cannot be the real truth. Because this human being exists, in the darkness the light lies hidden, in fear salvation, and in the callousness of one's fellow-men the great Love. (p. 98)

Buber describes an active role for the educator. "The education of men by men means the selection of the effective world by a person and in him" (p. 101). This view raises a question about Freire's claim that the oppressed must liberate themselves. Although we may agree that the oppressed must, ultimately, act to change their own lives, teachers must be involved in the process of conscientization. Freire would probably not disagree with that, but his pedagogy suggests what may be a too rapid withdrawal of the pedagogue, and it certainly does almost nothing to change the consciousness of the oppressor. Indeed, it suggests that the oppressors are so attached to their power and possessions that only revolution (albeit nonviolent) will dislodge them from their ways. Then, is it not likely that the once-oppressed will become oppressors when they are liberated? Freire did express great disappointment over this frequent result. From the perspective of care ethics, we would argue that something must be done to change the consciousness of both oppressed and oppressor.

Buber's active educator, serving as a model for what is best in the world, accepts both oppressed and oppressor, urging both toward positions that can be confirmed. But Buber recognizes that much can go wrong in this process:

If education means to let a selection of the world affect a person through the medium of another person, then the one through whom this takes place, rather, who makes it take place through himself, is caught in a strange paradox . . . The danger [is] that . . . the will to educate may degenerate into arbitrariness, and that the educator may carry out his selection and his influence from himself and his idea of the pupil, not from the pupil's own reality. (p. 100)

In the United States today, it might be argued, this degeneration and arbitrariness have reached new heights. Freire saw this danger all too clearly. Is there a way to involve both teacher and student so that the students can participate in discovering a selection of the effective world without merely receiving that selection or foreclosing the possibility for others?

Care ethics

The arbitrariness and exploitation feared by Freire and Buber are even harder to avoid today than 50 years ago, because teachers themselves have little to say about what they will teach. The curriculum is more narrowly prescribed, and the primary end of education has been defined almost entirely in terms of financial gain. Just recently an article appeared in a prestigious national newspaper reporting on the lasting effects of a good teacher. I started to read it eagerly but finished in disgust. Apparently, students who experienced one really good teacher at the K-12 level made more money in their late twenties than students who had no such experience. What, then, might we expect for students who have eight or nine really good teachers? And were these young people happier? Were they more civic-minded? More generous and loving? Did they enjoy their work more?

Care ethics agrees with Buber and Freire that students should not be treated as objects or containers. We, too, start with dialogue aimed at creating relations of care and trust. We put great emphasis on listening. We invite students to talk to us, and we listen when they talk to each other. Although we agree with Buber that teachers must somehow look at education from the perspective of students, we are a bit nervous about what he calls "experiencing the other side" (p. 96). How is one to do this? Buber describes the process:

> Its elements are, first, a relation . . . second, an event experienced by them in common, in which at least one of them actively participates, and, third, the fact that this one person, without forfeiting anything of the felt reality of his activity, at the same time lives through the common event from the standpoint of the other. (p. 97)

Care ethics responds to this by warning that we may not experience the other side by imagining how we might feel in a similar situation. Teacher and student are different individuals, and even the "situation" or "event" must be described relationally. In what looks from the outside to be one "situation," the two participants (carer and cared-for) may describe two different situations. We must hear what the other is going through. In care ethics, receptive (not projective) attention is central, and a carer must be open to "what is there" in the cared-for. Listening is essential both ethically and pedagogically. When we listen to a student's thinking, we know better what to do in teaching her. And sometimes what we hear should move us to change a potential learning objective entirely. We might decide, for example, that this child does not need to master algebra, at least not now and perhaps never. That does not mean discarding the child along with the algebra. It means making a serious, loving, dialogical effort to help the child discover what she would like to do and to do well.

Care ethics makes a distinction between assumed needs and expressed needs, the needs expressed through dialogue. Schools today are organized almost entirely to meet assumed needs. In the example above, it has been assumed that virtually all students need algebra and will learn it if properly taught—"no excuses!" The expressed needs of students can, then, justifiably be ignored. Teachers should help students to see that, in fact, they do need algebra and proceed diligently to teach it to them. We reject this position as a prime example of arbitrariness. However, it is not a simple matter that can be decided in an "always do this" manner. We should spend time with some students, showing them that—given some of the needs they have expressed—they might indeed need algebra but, for other students, that need can safely be dismissed. The decision—which may be reversible—is made dialogically.

Care ethics, with Buber, recognizes that teaching is necessarily an unequal relation. The teacher can and must do things for the student that the student cannot possibly do for the teacher. It recognizes, with Freire, that dialogical action can be neither authoritarian nor licentious. Good teachers do not ignore expressed needs, nor do they accept them without dialogical reflection and guidance.

Teaching our lost kids—those who are likely to drop out of school—requires years of carefully encouraged dialogue. Teachers, like mothers, work to promote both the growth and the acceptability of their charges (Ruddick, 1989). By promoting "acceptability,"

I mean that caring teachers must move their students in the direction of that fault-ridden "normalized" world, but they must do it thoughtfully, not with authoritarian methods. Such teachers hope that their students, as they transform their own reality, will enter that world not naively but critically. Some day, then, the teacher-student relation will give way to the equal relation of friendship, and together they may transform that world. That is the real goal.

References

Buber, M. (1965). *Between man and man.* New York, NY: Macmillan.

Freire, P. (1970). *Pedagogy of the oppressed.* Trans. Myra Bergman Ramos. New York, NY: Herder & Herder.

Friedman, M. (ed.) (1964). *The worlds of existentialism.* Chicago, IL: University of Chicago Press.

Gutierez, G. (1988). *A theology of liberation.* Maryknoll, NY: Orbis Books.

Heath, S. B. (1983). *Ways with words.* Cambridge, UK: Cambridge University Press.

Mill, J. S. (1993/1859). *On liberty and utilitarianism.* New York, NY: Bantam Books.

Miller, J. P. (2010). *Whole child education.* Toronto, Canada: University of Toronto Press.

— (2011). *Transcendental learning.* Charlotte, NC: Information Age Publishing.

Miller, R. (2002). *Free schools, free people: Education and democracy after the 1960s.* Albany, NY: SUNY Press.

Nieto, S. (1999). *The light in their eyes: Creating multicultural learning communities.* New York, NY: Teachers College Press.

Noddings, N. (1992). *The challenge to care in schools.* New York, NY: Teachers College Press.

— (2002). *Starting at home:Caring and social policy.* Berkeley, CA: University of California Press.

Ruddick, S. (1989). *Maternal thinking: Toward a politics of peace.* Boston, MA: Beacon Press.

Wilson, E. O. (2006). *The creation: An appeal to save life on earth.* New York, NY: W.W. Norton.

6

Converging Self/Other Awareness: Erich Fromm and Paulo Freire on Transcending the Fear of Freedom

Robert Lake and Vicki Dagostino

Historical encounters between Freire and Fromm

Of all of the Frankfurt School writers that have influenced Paulo Freire, there is more concurrence with the work of Erich Fromm than any of the others. Of course Freire cites or alludes to the influence of Marcuse, Habermas, and Gramsci in his work, but Freire's work more directly converges with Fromm's social vision and humanist readings of philosophy in ways that create possibilities for individual and collective release from both inward and outward oppression. Both Fromm and Freire devoted one entire book on the subject of hope (Fromm, 1968; Freire, 1994). Hope for both men was never a passive concept or wishful thinking, but always predicated on action toward freedom that leads to a humanist vision of a better world. Freire visited Fromm more than once in the late 1960s in Cuernavaca, Mexico in a meeting arranged by Ivan Illich (Funk, 2000, p. 138). Freire cites a conversation with Fromm concerning the "difficulty that the oppressed have in localizing the oppressor outside themselves" (Freire, 1994, p. 105). In this dialogue Freire says that Fromm stated with "his blue eyes flashing that 'an educational practice like that is a kind of historico-sociocultural and political psychoanalysis'" (ibid.). In this chapter we will discuss the significance of this kind of analysis as we explore some of the ways that Freire was directly influenced by Fromm's work, and suggest ways that the impact of this influence offers us a complementary and holistic view that has the potential to lift people out of outward environments of oppression and while at the same time exposing and releasing them from the oppressor within their own being. Of course Freire himself would be one of the first to recognize the dangers of heeding artificial boundaries between the fields of educational sociology (Freire) and humanist psychology (Fromm), yet as is often the case when looking at the origins or "roots" of an idea, the newly imagined and created spaces for theory and praxis often transcend categorization. Also, from the outset, we recognize that Freire was drawn to the psychology of liberation. We are sure that is the reason he cites Fromm so often either directly or indirectly in *Pedagogy of the Oppressed*. We also recognize that Fromm thought much about sociology (Fromm & Maccoby (1970)) and education in a stunning foreword that he wrote for A. S. Neill's *Summerhill* (1960). Likewise, Freire studied the psychology of language so there is much overlap between the two theorists. If we can look through the multiple lenses of their work together, we will find a richly complicated conversation that creates a dialogical dynamic that has the potential to release the oppressed from both inward chains as well as outward circumstantial effects of oppression. So, let us jump right into the conversation.

Freire (2003) refers to Fromm in chapter one of *Pedagogy of the Oppressed* when he writes about oppression and consciousness (p. 59) and also when he refers to the power of necrophilic behavior to "transform man into a thing" (pp. 59, 65). Freire cites Fromm further on this topic when he contrasts biophilia, the love of life and living things, with necrophilia, which is the root cause behind oppression as the means of absolute control.

While life is characterized by growth in a structured functional manner,

> the necrophilous person loves all that does not grow, all that is mechanical. The necrophilous person is driven by the desire to transform the organic into the inorganic, to approach life mechanically, as if all living persons were things. . . . Memory, rather than experience; having, rather than being, is what counts. The necrophilous person can relate to an object—a flower or a person—only if he possesses it; hence a threat to his possession is a threat to himself, if he loses possession he loses contact with the world. He loves control, and in the act of controlling he kills life. (Fromm cited in Freire, 2003, p. 77)

Origins of the fear of freedom in Fromm and Freire's work

Fromm's book *The Fear of Freedom* was published in England in 1942 when Nazi Germany was at the zenith of its power. The book has far-reaching implications not only for that time in history, but since it explores why people choose domination over freedom, the text remains strongly relevant for the present time as well. Freire does not directly reference Fromm in his discussion of the fear of freedom anywhere in *Pedagogy of the Oppressed*, but a thorough reading of Fromm' works demonstrates that this idea, as used by Freire, originated with Fromm's theory of the fear of freedom. The idea of the fear of freedom is integral to the development of pedagogy of freedom from oppression. Freire uses the idea of the "fear of freedom" to develop his theory of conscientization, but, falls short of developing it fully by not exploring the impact it might have on displacing the effects of the oppressor within. This omission leaves a gap in Freire's pedagogy of freedom and praxis. In this chapter we suggest that the importance of the notion of the fear of freedom is integral to Freire's pedagogy of liberation and as such needs to be drawn out and developed more fully to enhance Freire's theory. Developing this idea and attempting to incorporate it into Freire's theory of liberatory education will advance Freire's work and help individuals move toward achieving their ontological vocation of becoming more fully human.

Humanization, according to Freire, is the people's vocation but it is constantly negated in an oppressive society. Freire believes that eventually those who are oppressed will seek to overcome their oppression because the ontological vocation, or calling toward fuller humanity, will lead them to engage in the struggle for liberation at some point. A humanizing pedagogy, then, is a tool that educators can use to help the oppressed develop a critical understanding or consciousness of their oppression. It is this critical consciousness that is necessary for liberation.

According to Freire, to overcome the oppressive situation that they find themselves in, the oppressed "must first critically realize its causes so that through transforming action they can create a new situation, one which makes possible the pursuit of a fuller humanity" (2003, p. 47), but often they are afraid of running the risk associated with liberating themselves, and convincing others to do so, because of the fear of freedom. Freire acknowledges that the presence of this kind of fear creates a difficult choice for the oppressed.

> The oppressed suffered from the duality which has established itself in their innermost being. They discover that without freedom they cannot exist authentically. Yet although they desire authentic existence, they fear it. They are at one and the same time themselves and the oppressor whose consciousness they have internalized. The conflict lies in the choice between being wholly themselves or being divided; between following prescriptions or having choices; between being spectators or actors; between acting or having the illusion of acting through the action of the oppressors; between speaking out or being silent, castrated in their power to create and recreate, in their power to transform the world. This is the tragic dilemma of the oppressed which their education must take into account. (Freire, 2003, p. 48)

Freire goes on to say that pedagogy for the oppressed is one that "makes oppression and its causes objects of reflection by the oppressed, and from that reflection will come their necessary engagement in the struggle for their liberation." A pedagogy of the oppressed will help them to recognize the duality of their existence as oppressed beings desiring liberation and that this consciousness-raising, problem-posing education they will come to see themselves as no longer oppressed or oppressor, "but humans in the process of achieving freedom" (p. 49).

In this same chapter, Freire references Fromm, but he does not point to Fromm as the originator of the idea of the "fear of freedom." We suggest, however, that this idea originated with or was based in Fromm's writings in several books, but especially *Escape from Freedom*. As we have already seen in this chapter, Freire certainly read Fromm, and many of his ideas come directly from him, so it would not be a stretch to say that the fear of freedom is closely related to, and possibly directly tied to, Fromm's theory of the fear of freedom. Moreover, this notion needs to be fully explained as Fromm theorized it. Although Freire sees this fear of freedom as the tragic dilemma that pedagogy of the oppressed must take into consideration, we suggest that this work would be greatly enhanced by focusing on the psychological component that blocks people from truly becoming liberated from oppression. This psychological component is an integral part of the process of conscientization.

While the fear of freedom is acknowledged as being a factor that keeps people mired in an inauthentic life because it keeps them from becoming beings for themselves, it is not adequately addressed from a perspective of the psychology of the individual. Because Freire takes a structural view of society and the individual, in which the individual only exists in dialogical relationship with the societal, he neglects to pay adequate attention to the psychological phenomena that he himself identifies as an important barrier to liberation. By focusing for the most part on one's ontological vocation in relation to others, Freire's work needs the further development of a pedagogical strategy that addresses the psychological fears and attachments of the individual subject. As with many theories, just because people *do* have an ontological drive toward full humanization (an idea that is founded on Freire's spiritual life) this does not mean that they will know how to go about achieving fuller humanity.[1]

Freire's educational paradigm, which strives to raise people's awareness about oppression and its causes from a very political/social perspective, would be more complete and would better help move learners toward liberation if it also strove to raise people's awareness of self and the internal/psychological dynamics that often compel them to behave in oppressive rather than liberating ways. Also, Fromm's insight into the interrelatedness of the individual and society, and his unusual grasp of the nature of contemporary, industrial, capitalistic society and its impact on modern man's[2] striving for freedom are further compelling reasons for summoning Fromm into this conversation. We can glean insight from Fromm that will contribute to a more comprehensive pedagogical strategy for liberatory education.

Inward and outward freedom

Because Freire insisted upon the subjectivity of the individual in his educational paradigm, it would stand to reason that he would not object to an assessment that there is subjectivity within each individual oppressed person, and hence that subjectivity must be nurtured through education. Although he did not see the individual as self-liberating, but believed that the individual was only self-liberating in dialectical relationship with others. We propose that subjectivity itself implies an internal depth, hence there is an "I" and an internal subjectivity of that "I" and that that internal subjectivity demands attention and is worthy of reflection.

Freirean critical pedagogy aspires to create a liberated, democratic society, a goal premised on the freedom of its individual members. The pedagogical method Freire suggests using toward this end is "problem-posing" education. Problem-posing education is the means of achieving critical consciousness and becoming a being of praxis, one who reflects *and acts* on the world in order to transform the situation of oppression. Problem-posing education is the alternative to "banking education" that Freire says treats students as empty receptacles sitting by passively and taking in information given to them from the all-knowing "teacher" without questioning or critically assessing it. Banking education, for Freire, is oppressive. It does not allow for human agency. It is objectifying and dehumanizing and does not allow for individuals to become agents in their own learning, nor agents in the world around them. Problem-posing education, on the other hand, creates subjective agents who attempt to read the world as they learn to read the word (Freire & Macedo 1987). The connection to becoming liberated is obvious, critical thinking and reading the world is part and parcel of critical literacy.

This kind of problem-posing education is important according to Freire because it is the oppressed themselves who are in the best position to liberate both themselves and the oppressor since only they have the knowledge and unique experience of having been oppressed, which allows them alone to best understand oppression and hence the need for liberation. Freire states,

> Who are better prepared than the oppressed to understand the terrible significance of an oppressive society? Who suffer the effects of oppression more than the oppressed? Who can better understand the necessity of liberation? They will not gain this liberation by chance but through the praxis of their quest for it, through their recognition of the necessity to fight for it. (2003, p. 45)

However this does not seem to be enough, even for Freire, for individuals to transform the situation of oppression. Freire admits,

> But almost always, during the initial stage of the struggle, the oppressed, instead of striving for liberation, tend themselves to become oppressors, or "sub-oppressors." The very structure of their thought has been conditioned by the contradictions of the concrete, existential situation by which they were shaped. Their ideal is to be men; but for them, to be men is to be oppressors. This is their model of humanity. (ibid.)

Freire goes on to describe how what happens to oppressed beings is that they "adopt an attitude of 'adhesion' to the oppressor" (ibid.). Their way of being, their understanding of oppression is their worldview. It shapes their thoughts. It has taken over their psyche. They recognize that they are oppressed, but they do not know any other way of being than to be oppressed. Hence, one important element toward becoming a truly liberated being of praxis is to break the psychological chains that keep them bound to the oppressor and to oppressive thinking. "Because of their identification with the oppressor, they have no consciousness of themselves as persons or as members of an oppressed class . . . It is a rare peasant who, once 'promoted' to overseer, does not become more of a tyrant towards his former comrades than the owner himself" (p. 46).

Another aspect of this connection to the oppressor, according to Freire, is the oppressed's "fear of freedom," which must be overcome in order to become truly liberated from the physical as well as psychological bonds to the oppressor. Freire states, "The fear of freedom which afflicts the oppressed, a fear which may equally well lead them to desire the role of oppressor or bind them to the role of oppressed, should be examined" (ibid.). Having internalized the prescriptions and image of the oppressor, the oppressed are fearful of freedom because it would "require them to reject this image and replace it with autonomy and responsibility" (p. 47).

There is a clear concern about becoming truly liberated from the oppressor (in psychological terms) that Freire plainly recognizes and discusses and rightly mentions in his quest toward pedagogy of freedom from oppression. It is at this point that Fromm's work becomes a vital complement to critical pedagogy that is by its very nature an ongoing and incomplete project. In this case the intellectual root stock of Erich Fromm has much more to contribute to Freire's work through Fromm's emphasis on the depth of the psychic internalization of oppression. Through individual self-reflection on the fear of freedom that exists within the individual psyche, a person might be enabled to discover the extent to which she is truly free to act according to her own will once she acknowledges that she has internalized the oppressor's mindset. Perhaps this level of exploration of the unconscious was beyond the realm of Freire's understanding of psychology. We know from reading Freire's body of his work, that he always wrote on those things that enabled him to speak "his own word" (p. 33). Who knows what that word might have been if he had lived longer? Nevertheless, the fear of freedom is, as Freire states, "*the* (emphasis added) tragic dilemma of the oppressed which their education must take into account" (p. 48).

Finding convergence in Freire and Fromm

The next part of this chapter will attempt to show how Fromm's explanation of the fear of freedom seems to be the same as the one espoused by Freire. It will also attempt to show the depth of the fear of freedom, how it arises in individuals, and how it can keep them from authentic existence, that is, freedom in Freire's terms. However, since it is *the* tragic dilemma that the education of oppressed persons must take into account, it should be fully examined and incorporated into Freire's pedagogy of freedom from oppression. Indeed, one cannot fully be liberated from oppression until this fear of freedom is resolved because it impedes action and liberation.

Freire's educational paradigm, which strives to raise people's awareness about oppression and its causes from a very political/social perspective, will be more complete and perhaps more fully help move learners toward liberation if it also strove to raise people's awareness of self and the internal/psychological dynamics that often compel them to behave in oppressive rather than liberating ways. Moreover, Fromm's social psychological understanding of the interplay of the individual and society, as well as his understandings of contemporary, industrial, capitalistic society and its impact on modern man's[2] striving for freedom are further compelling reasons for drawing Fromm into the ongoing conversation of critical pedagogy.

Because Freire insisted upon the subjectivity of the individual in his educational paradigm, it would stand to reason that he would not object to an assessment that there is subjectivity within each individual oppressed person, and hence that subjectivity must be nurtured through education. Although he did not see the individual as self-liberating, but believed that the individual was only self-liberating in dialectical relationship with others, we maintain that subjectivity itself implies an internal depth, hence there is an "I" and an internal subjectivity of that "I" and that that internal subjectivity demands attention and is worthy of reflection.

Fromm's social-psychoanalytic insight into the nature of humans provides a compelling and complementary contribution to Freire's theory and also helps us to understand the direction in which education must move if it is to create individuals capable of the action component of the praxis equation.

Freirean critical pedagogy aspires to create a liberated, democratic society, a goal premised on the freedom of its individual members. Erich Fromm defines freedom as the ability to make decisions according to one's desires. In *Escape from Freedom,* Fromm states, "[Man] would be free to act according to his own will, if he knew what he wanted, thought, and felt" (quoted in Freire, 1998, p. 6). Freire's freedom, which comes about through the achievement of critical consciousness, does not necessarily lead to freedom in Fromm's terms because it does not necessarily cause one to recognize her own will, thoughts, fears, and desires, upon which rest her decision-making power. This recognition is an internal state that comes from self-realization and from a psychological understanding of one's desires, thoughts, and drives and what motivates those drives. Freire himself recognizes that we are most human when we are free and most free when we can choose (Collins, 1977, p. 28), and that "choice is illusory to the degree it represents the expectations of others" (Freire, 1998, p. 7). However, often the choices that people make are not made from *true* choice. Often, though one may believe she is making a choice based on her own convictions, she is really making a choice that is not necessarily based on her own convictions, but on the convictions of the oppressor that she is unaware of. Having a dominated consciousness, which she has been socialized into through all of the social institutions of her society, she has incorporated the dominant ideology of the oppressor. From this we can extrapolate that the choices one makes are not truly authentic, in terms of being chosen freely according to one's own moral and ethical principles, because those principles really are not her own.

So, because freedom comes from true or authentic choice, one must become aware of dominated consciousness, but more importantly, she must become attuned to and begin to develop her own values and beliefs. She must understand how they have developed and decide if they are truly her own or are merely based on the conventions of the society that she has been socialized into. This requires autonomy and responsibility, which must be developed through thoughtful reflection on the self. Unless one is truly choosing freely from her own conscience, she is not making the most authentic choices. Authentic choice comes from self-understanding, self-reflection, and constant awareness of one's self and one's moral foundation. These aspects of critical, self-reflective praxis need to be addressed and cultivated in any true expression of liberatory education.

Freire recognizes that freedom comes from authentic choice, and suggests that once the oppressed recognize that they have adopted the oppressor's consciousness they will expel that consciousness and embrace freedom. For Freire, once freed from the chains of oppression, through recognition of that oppression, people will act to liberate themselves. However, as Erich Fromm (1992) asserts, "Man can be a slave without chains" (p. 7). Often, according to Fromm:

> The outer chains have simply been put inside of man. The desires and thoughts that the suggestive apparatus of society fills him with, chain him more thoroughly than outer chains. This is so because man can at least be aware of outer chains but be unaware of inner chains, carrying them with the illusion that he is free. He can try to overthrow the outer chains, but how can he rid himself of chains of whose existence he is unaware. (ibid.)

Fromm (1941, 1947, 1955) explains the fundamental psychological problem that keeps people from embracing freedom. "Freedom from" external oppression causes a separation from nature and from other human beings, which leads to feelings of loneliness and isolation, and what people fear most is isolation. When people feel isolated and alone, they often seek security outside of themselves and often end up resubmitting to external authority or exerting their own authority upon others, and in turn relinquish authentic existence and freedom, albeit unwittingly. Freedom entails autonomy and responsibility, and Fromm contends that the isolation that is caused by becoming aware of one's own autonomy and responsibility is what leads them directly back into becoming oppressors themselves or submitting to another's oppression because they are looking for answers.

Freire, like Marx, by whom he was heavily influenced, speaks to uncovering conflicts in the sociohistorical and political context. Fromm, who was also heavily influenced by Marx, also recognized these influences but at the same time attempted to uncover internal conflicts within the individual psyche. Fromm suggests that once one is freed from external oppression, he can still be enslaved, by his own internal discord. This perspective is vitally important because without looking at internal conflicts, it is easy to fall into naïve thinking that, once freed from external chains; one is automatically free to become more fully human.

Liberation for Freire comes about through awareness of external and politically systemic oppression. Liberation for Fromm is more concerned with awareness of our psychological fears of freedom, isolation, and separation from man and nature. Fromm looks at the conflicting tendencies in man more from the lens of psychology while Freire's lens is more or less focused on emerging sociological patterns of oppression. Fromm (1992) states that man's thinking and being are not identical, nor are man's thinking and actions. This goes deeper than Freire's notion that once an oppressed person recognizes her oppression she will behave in a nonoppressive way herself.

Fromm asserts,

> A person who has not been completely alienated, who has remained sensitive and able to feel, who has not lost the sense of dignity, who is not yet "for-sale," who can still suffer over the suffering of others, who has not acquired fully the having mode of existence—briefly, a person who has remained a person and not become a thing—cannot help feeling lonely, powerless, isolated in present-day society. He cannot help doubting his self and his own convictions, if not his sanity. (1992, p. 65)

Fromm is suggesting that even the person who is most fully human, suffers from this lonely, isolated, and powerless existence. So, although one may be free from oppression, she still suffers. She fears the freedom that she has gained. Others may not oppress her, but she is still oppressed.

Liberation for Fromm entails more than becoming aware of and acting against the oppressor. Of course as Freire states, it entails becoming free from false consciousness and a dominated ideology, but it *also* entails liberation from the internal conflicts that keep us engaging in behaviors that enslave us. Hence, freedom "from" external (political or social) oppression is *not a sufficient condition* for the achievement of freedom, and unless people progress to a positive freedom, a productive life in Fromm's terms, escaping from negative freedom will only produce psychological disturbances in the individuals that will thwart her or his pursuit of freedom, and since psychological factors impact the quest for freedom, an educational program that desires to help people fulfill their quest for freedom *must* address internal factors of cognition and emotion as much as the external factor of social injustice.

People engage in destructive, oppressive behavior because they fear the isolation, aloneness, and separation from man and nature that comes along with the freedom from dominating authority. Fromm contends that the uncertainty of life, the fear of isolation that comes with becoming a being for oneself, and the fear of the autonomy and responsibility that comes with freedom, are what lead people back into oppressive relationships and so must be addressed in one's education.

Necrophilia and the fear of freedom

Because freedom is so frightening, according to Fromm, people tend to respond in one of three ways. They attempt to escape from freedom by 1) looking for security outside of themselves again, in terms of looking for an authoritative person, belief system, or other external power source, to relieve them of the responsibility of being free (masochism), or 2) seeking to become the authority over others so that they do not feel so alone (sadism), or 3) falling into mindless (automoton) conformity. Fromm states, "In our effort to escape from aloneness and powerlessness, we are ready to get rid of our individual self either by submission to new forms of authority or by a compulsive conforming to accepted patterns" (1941, p. 134). Looked at it in this light, being freed from an oppressor will not necessarily lead to nonconformity, and/or healthy nonoppressive relationships. In another section of the same book (1941) Fromm states that what will lead to healthy/nonoppressive relationships is the spontaneity of love and productive work:

> That man, the more he gains freedom in the sense of emerging from the original oneness with man and nature and the more he becomes an "individual," has no choice but to unite himself with the world in the spontaneity of love and productive work or else to seek a kind of security by such ties with the world as destroy his freedom and the integrity of the individual self. (p. 21)

So, before we go any further, we will discuss examples of these choices as expressions of Fromm and Freire's use of necrophilia and biophilia as they relate to the praxis of critical pedagogy that leads to inner liberation. First let's think about ways that the fear of freedom results in necrophilic behavior. Remember in the beginning of the chapter that Fromm used necrophilia to describe the love of control to the degree that the oppressed are reduced to passive objects? The above mentioned three aspects of escape from freedom into necrophilious behavior are just as relevant today as they were when Fromm first wrote about them during the rise of Nazi Germany and Fascist Italy.

One has only to remember that the Patriot Act that was signed into law in the United States, less than two months after the September 11, 2001 attacks on targets in New York and Washington DC is an expression of Fromm's first type of response. People have submitted to a masochistic system of one-sided surveillance for the sake of feeling "protected" from terrorism by a higher authority, in this case the government. We will leave it to you the reader to decide if the price of this "protection" is too great.

Sadism is the next aspect he mentions. This phenomenon may take many forms ranging from a military dictatorship to a male chauvinist or more likely, someone who just has to be in control in order to feel validated and when they are not in charge of things, they often sink into pouting or depression. In some ways, sadism parallels Freire's notion of the "banking model of education" wherein the teacher expects the student to give back only the knowledge that has been "deposited" into them by the passive receiving of "knowledge." The teacher maintains one-sided unquestioning authority in this model. However we must also remember that the "banking model" can occur with all the chairs in a classroom arranged in a circle, and the topic being discussed may be about critical pedagogy. Even in this environment there may be a "bully" sadist present who intimidates the others into outward acceptance of their opinion or procedure with the others deferring to this person just to "keep the peace."

The third aspect of the fear of freedom is mindless "automaton conformity." Once again fear of economic loss is played upon to maintain the mindless automaton/necrophilliac power relationship. This is often the case when teacher performance pay is tied to achieving passing scores on standardized tests. The result is that teaching has been reduced to the role of "clerks of the empire" (Giroux, 2010). In the same article Giroux describes the deskilling of teachers in a way that we are certain that both Fromm and Freire would affirm.

As the space of public schooling is reduced to a mindless infatuation with the metrics of endless modes of testing and increasingly enforces this deadening experience with disciplinary measures reminiscent of prison culture, teachers are increasingly removed from dealing with children as part of a broader historical, social and cultural context. As the school is militarized, student behavior becomes an issue that either the police or security forces handle. Removed from the normative and pedagogical framing of classroom life, teachers no longer have the option to think outside of the box, to experiment, be poetic or inspire joy in their students. School has become a form of dead time, designed to kill the imagination of both teachers and students. (Giroux, 2010, n.p.)

These problems in education all clearly point to a system that is rife with necrophilic oppression and compel us to look for biophilic liberatory education in both Freire and Fromm's terms.

Biophilia and inward freedom

Biophilia is a word that Fromm uses in his famous humanist credo. In the following passage, he uses biophilia to holistically describe love for life in nature, humanity, and self, resulting in freedom.

I believe that the man choosing progress can find a new unity through the development of all his human forces, which are produced in three orientations. These can be presented separately or together: biophilia, love for humanity and nature, and independence and freedom. (1999/1994, p. 101)

As we have already seen, Freire used necrophilia to describe the banking model of education, and uses the term biophilia in much the same way, to describe the praxis of liberatory education. Freire describes his vision of education as "biophiliac" (1985, p. 82) and credits Fromm with giving him the term. Biophilia is indeed one of the strongest points of convergence between Fromm and Freire's work. Here are a few examples of biophilic praxis leading to inward freedom. Our first one expresses biophilic pedagogy as the ability to engage in curriculum as conversation.

One of the central themes in all of Freire's work is that the way unjust power is maintained is through seeing others as "object" (2003). This is certainly true in education as well as in the thousands of criminal acts that are committed against others every day!

The ability to listen to people comes out of biophilia because, by it, we are opened to the polyphonic aspect of meaning, not just the narrow sounds of cliché or the kind of inward thoughts that cause knee-jerk reactions to what we hear. Necrophilious persons are only in tune with themselves. Curriculum as conversation "is a matter of attunement, an auditory rather than visual conception, in which the sound of music (for Aoki, jazz specifically) being improvised is an apt example" (Pinar, 2004, p. 189). Curriculum as conversation can serve to tune the ear to participate, to resonate with the voice of others. This is no scripted endeavor, but like the jazz analogy, there is a certain aspect of the spontaneous that is welcomed. In the shared dimensions of spontaneous dialogue, there is a fuller experience of knowing. Freire is very strong on dialogue as a shared way of knowing: "I engage in dialogue because I recognize the social and not merely the individualistic character of the process of knowing" (1995, p. 379). Genuine dialogue is not the product of preformulated questions and responses. In Freire's view (1970), dialogue must be open-ended in ways that enable us to reach beyond our own thoughts and patterns of thinking.

Sidorkin (2002) offers further insight into the nature of curriculum as conversation by saying that relations cannot be described by one person's perspective. He states that "relation in general is possible only in the presence of difference. Totally identical entities cannot relate to each other. Relations result from plurality, from some tension born of difference" (p. 98). This difference is not something that needs to be overcome by a "fifty/fifty split." Every voice needs to be heard, not lowered to the least common denominator!

Sidorkin goes on to say that one of the greatest needs in schools is the cultivation of curriculum as conversation by focusing on the:

ability to "read" relationships to reflect on these cases, to talk and write about relationships. The key skill here is the ability to reconstruct the other voice. A teacher must develop this ability to hear what has not been said, to formulate what his students are not able to articulate, to engage in a dialogue when the other party may not be willing or ready to engage. The ability to understand human relations relies heavily on the heightened ability to hear and respond without preconceived notions of truth. (p. 100)

This ability to read relationships will carry over into all content areas. In fact, our praxis becomes more relevant, and potent, to the degree that we are in tune with the voice of others. Biophilia can open our being in ways that provide insight into the ways language is *perceived or received* by others and creates connections that Fromm states is integral to a productive and biophilic life.

Our next example of biophilic praxis emerges out of a love of nature that can produce inward freedom and wholeness of self. Richard Louv is one of the primary voices for a growing movement called *No Child Left Inside*. In his wonderful book, *Last Child in the Woods* Louv (2008) masterfully describes a condition he calls "nature deficit disorder" (p. 10) as one of the primary causes of attention deficit disorder (think necrophilic education here). Later in the book he cites a story from *San Francisco* magazine that serves as a powerful case study for Freire's problem-posing education and the love of nature.

> The back page of an October issue of *San Francisco* magazine displays a vivid photograph of a small boy, eyes wide with excitement and joy, leaping and running on a great expanse of California beach, storm clouds and towering waves behind him. A short article explains that the boy was hyperactive, he had been kicked out of his school, and his parents had not known what to do with him—but they had observed how nature engaged and soothed him. So for years they took their son to beaches, forests, dunes, and rivers to let nature do its work. The photograph was taken in 1907. The boy was Ansel Adams. (cited in Louv, 2008, pp. 102–3)

Our last example expresses biophilic pedagogy that displaces the fear of freedom by identification with another. In a program called *The Roots of Empathy*, a curriculum that originated in Canada in 1996, a baby and mother visit a classroom once a month for the first year of the child's life. This relationship was chosen because as founder Mary Gordon believes it "is the best example of emotional attunement there is which is why I chose it as a model of empathy for children to experience" (Gordon, 2010, n.p.).

In Roots of Empathy, students explore the inner consciousness of a baby as they observe and describe what the baby is feeling and how the parent is paying attention to the baby's needs. The students then extend these observations outwardly as they identify and reflect on their own thoughts and feelings and those of others. Ten years of data show a significant decrease in aggression, and increase in emotional understanding and care (Schonert-Reichl, 2009). One of the most dramatic stories comes from Gordon's book.

> Darren was the oldest child I ever saw in Roots of Empathy class. He was in Grade 8 and had been held back twice. He was two years older than everyone else and already starting to grow a beard. I knew his story: his mother had been murdered in front of his eyes when he was four years old, and he had lived in a succession of foster homes ever since. Darren looked menacing because he wanted us to know he was tough: his head was shaved except for a ponytail at the top and he had a tattoo on the back of his head. The instructor of the Roots of Empathy program was explaining to the class about differences in temperament that day. She invited the young mother who was visiting the class with Evan, her six-month-old baby, to share her thoughts about her baby's temperament. Joining in the discussion, the mother told the class how Evan liked to face outwards when he was in the Snugli and didn't want to cuddle into her, and how she would have preferred to have a more cuddly baby. As the class ended, the mother asked if anyone wanted to try on the Snugli, which was green and trimmed with pink brocade. To everyone's surprise, Darren offered to try it, and as the other students scrambled to get ready for lunch, he strapped it on. Then he asked if he could put Evan in. The mother was a little apprehensive, but she handed him the baby, and he put Evan in, facing towards his chest. That wise little baby snuggled right in, and Darren took him into a quiet corner and rocked back and forth with the baby in his arms for several minutes. Finally, he came back to where the mother and the Roots of Empathy instructor were waiting and he asked: "If nobody has ever loved you, do you think you could still be a good father?" (Gordon, 2009, pp. 5–6)

Through this experience, Darren began to imagine himself differently and perhaps he experienced a small shift in his sense of personal agency and inward freedom. Fromm recognizes that "freedom" is possible only to the extent that a person's psychological need for attachment and relatedness to others is met. He believes that there are other psychological needs that correspond to the need for freedom that must be met if people are to maintain nonoppressive relationship. Fromm sees freedom as resulting only when one's psychological needs for security, love, productive work, and relatedness to the world have been met. In Darren's case as well as our own, we often find that these needs are met not as we receive them for ourselves but as we give them to others. Biophilia comes out of "being" not "having." Biophilia increases when we align with the replenishing power of nature in dynamic, selfless love. Fromm states that we are:

> prone to think that the problem of freedom is exclusively that of gaining still *more* freedom of the kind we have gained in the course of modern history, and to believe that the defense of freedom against such powers that deny such freedom is all that is necessary. We forget that, although each of the liberties which have been won must be defended with utmost vigor, the problem of freedom is not only a quantitative one, but a qualitative one; that we not only have to preserve and increase the traditional freedom, but that we have to gain a new kind of freedom, one which enables us to realize our own individual self, to have faith in this self and in life. (1941, pp. 105–6)

Freedom is in being, not having

Capitalism, according to Fromm, has freed man further spiritually, mentally, socially, politically, and economically. Man, under the capitalist system learned to "rely on himself, to make responsible decisions, to give up both soothing and terrifying superstitions . . . [he] became free from mystifying elements; [he] began to see himself objectively and with fewer and fewer illusions" (i.e. to become critically conscious), and hence he became increasingly free from traditional bonds, he became free to become more. As this freedom "from" grew, "positive" freedom (the growth of an active, critical, responsible self) advanced as well. *However,* capitalism also had other effects on the process of growing freedom as well. "It made the individual more alone and isolated and imbued him with a feeling of insignificance and powerlessness" (p. 108). It also increased doubt and skepticism, and all of these factors made man more anxious about freedom.

The principle of individualist activity characteristic of a capitalistic economy put the individual on his own feet. Whereas under the feudal system of the Middle Ages, everyone had a fixed place in an ordered and transparent social system under capitalism; if one was unable to stand on his own two feet, he failed, and it was entirely his own affair. Obviously this is not productive work that leads to freedom and biophilia but rather it is oppressive and necrophilious.

> That this principle furthered the process of individualization is obvious and is always mentioned as an important item on the credit side of modern culture. But in furthering "freedom from," this principle helped to sever all ties between one individual and the other and thereby isolated and separated the individual from his fellow men. (pp. 105–6)

The results of Capitalism in terms of increasing freedom "from" and the strength of the individual character that it built, have lead people to assume that modern man "has become the center and purpose of all activity, that what he does he does for himself, that the principle of self-interest and egotism are the all-powerful motivations of human activity" (p. 109). "Yet, much of what seemed to him to be *his* purpose was not his" (ibid.). Rather, the capital that he earned and created no longer served him—he served it. "Man became a cog in the vast economic machine . . . to serve a purpose outside of himself" (p. 110). Man became a servant to the very machines he built, which gave him a feeling of personal insignificance and powerlessness. Those who did not have capital and had to sell their labor to earn a living suffered similar psychological effects, according to Fromm, because they too were merely cogs in the great economic machine, and hence instruments of "suprapersonal economic factors."

Modern man believed that he was freeing himself, but was really submitting to aims that were not his own. As such, he became untrue to himself. He did not work for himself, his happiness, or his freedom, rather, his work was done either to serve more powerful others or to acquire capital. This further isolated and alienated him from himself and his fellow man. But why did this happen? Paulo Freire theorizes that once one becomes more critically conscious of oppression, one will act to liberate themselves and others. Yet Fromm suggests that as modern man becomes more conscious of and works toward freedom from oppressive bonds, he also becomes more alienated and isolated, and he begins to feel insignificant. Fromm attributes this to the fact that negative freedom was never fully developed into positive freedom. While it did create positive freedom in some ways, that is, by providing humans with economic and political freedom, the opportunity for individual initiative, and growing rational enlightenment (p. 121) it did not provide people with a means to realize all aspects of positive freedom including productive work, love of others, and independence and inward liberation.

Positive freedom, according to Fromm's definition, is the capacity for "spontaneous relationship to man and nature, a relationship that connects the individual with the world without eliminating his individuality" (p. 29). The foremost expression of which, according to Fromm, are "love and productive work because they are rooted in the integration and strength of the total personality" (ibid.). So according to Fromm, positive freedom equals wholeness of the personality, that is, integration. But, because relations between people have also become alienating in the modern capitalistic world, human relationships assume the character of relations between things rather than between beings, further creating a sense of isolation. Fromm states:

> But perhaps the most important and the most devastating instance of this spirit of instrumentality and alienation is the individual's relationship to his own self. Man does not only sell commodities, he sells himself and feels himself to be a commodity [and] if there is no use for the qualities a person offers, he *has* none; just as an unsalable commodity is valueless though it might have its use value. Thus the self-confidence, the "feeling of self," is merely an indication of what

others think of the person . . . If he is sought after, he is somebody; if he is not popular, he is simply nobody. (p. 119)

Fromm believes that "the need to be related to the world outside oneself, the need to avoid aloneness" is as imperative to man as is the physiologically conditioned needs (like hunger, the need for sleep, etc.) "To feel completely alone and isolated leads to mental disintegration just as physical starvation leads to death" (p. 17). The mode of capitalistic production, because it has made man an instrument for suprapersonal economic purposes and increased his sense of individual insignificance, has also increased his feeling of isolation and powerlessness.

Likewise, human relationships have suffered because they have assumed a spirit of manipulation and instrumentality and have lost their sense of connectedness and relatedness. There is no sense of solidarity in modern society. Human relationships under Capitalism have ceased to be relationships between people who have an interest in one another as fellow human beings, and have become relationships based on mutual usefulness. The instrumentality of relationships is clearly seen in relationships at all levels, from employer/employee, to businessperson/customer; to one's relationship with one's own self. As such humans have became "bewildered and insecure" (p. 120) rather than strong and secure beings who are capable of loving and liberating both themselves and others.

So it appears that man in modern times has won a freedom that has not made him any happier, but only more fearful. Freire's theory supposes that freedom *from* oppression leads to authentic existence, the freedom to become more fully human—happier, more fulfilled, more able to love one another in a non-oppressive manner. It also assumes that people will act in solidarity with one another once they are conscious of oppression. In a complementary way, Fromm's focus on positive freedom takes into account that people need more than economic independence in order to overcome alienation, isolation, a sense of powerlessness, and fear so they do not themselves become oppressors or look for someone to oppress them (after overcoming alienation, isolation, a sense of powerlessness, and fear).

Fromm maintains that this fear is an illness of the mind that people want to liberate themselves from at any cost. The fear that results from isolation and alienation is unbearable to people, hence they will seek to escape the psychological toll of fear. The way to transcend this fear of freedom is to take steps toward positive freedom. Fromm writes that this occurs when people seek to:

> Relate spontaneously to the world in love and work, in the genuine expression of emotional, sensuous, and intellectual capacities; and thus become one again with man, nature, and themselves, without giving up the independence and integrity of their own individual self. The other course open to him is to fall back, to give up his freedom, and to try to overcome his aloneness by eliminating the gap that has arisen between their individual self and the world. (p. 139)

These efforts can create a worse condition than the previous state because the person "never reunites them with the world in a way he related to it before he emerged as an 'individual'" (ibid.). The resulting condition may be one that is characterized by "complete surrender of individuality and integrity of the self" (p. 140). Obviously this course is "not a solution which leads to happiness and positive freedom . . . it assuages an unbearable anxiety and makes life possible by avoiding panic; yet it does not solve the underlying problem and is paid for by a kind of life that often consists only of automatic or compulsive activities" (ibid.). The unproductive means by which people attempt to relieve themselves of such anxiety, Fromm terms "mechanisms of escape," that is, sadist, masochist, automaton conformity.

The individual in a sick society sacrifices genuine freedom and happiness for the security of fitting in with the rest of mankind, that is, for the security of feeling a sense of belonging and connectedness with other humans. It is even possible that "his very defect may have been raised to a virtue by his culture, and thus may enhance feeling of achievement" (ibid.). In US culture today, for instance, ambition for fame, and greed for money and possessions are defects that have become so accepted that they are no longer even considered defects.

In the United States today, the fear of freedom has manifested itself in an overwhelming desire to have. In fact, Fromm says that a "having orientation" predominates among those in the western world today. Those with a having orientation tend to focus on obtaining, possessing, and consuming, and they are defined by what they have. According to Fromm, one form of having, consuming, is perhaps the most important one for today's affluent industrial societies. He states that "Consuming has ambiguous qualities: It relieves anxiety, because what one has cannot be taken away; but it also requires one to consume ever more, because previous consumption soon loses its satisfactory character" (1976, p. 15). The modern consumer identifies his or herself by the formula: *I am = what I have and what I consume* (ibid.). The attitude inherent in a having orientation is that of incorporating something so that in a sense, one is incorporating its power. By incorporating power from an external source, one in essence believes they possess its strength. Individuals who believe themselves to be powerless, then, gain a sense of power and strength that they are lacking. A society centered around things rather than people, as Western industrial society is, creates individuals with a need to have in order to feel important, since "To acquire, to own, and to make a profit are the sacred and unalienable rights of the individual in the industrial society" (p. 57).

Having-oriented people focus on consuming, obtaining, and possessing because they are defined by what they have. However, Fromm contends that "I have it" tends to become "it has me," and people become driven by their possessions. Spiritual traditions have described this behavior in various ways. For example, "The Buddha has described this method of behavior as craving, the Jewish and Christian religions as coveting; it transforms everybody and everything into something dead and subject to another's power" (p. 64).

While it is necessary to have in order to live in the world, placing too much emphasis on having (to the neglect of being) causes us to suffer. Our psychological need for belonging and relatedness, therefore, cannot be attained through having because a having orientation leads to further alienation and objectivity rather than to rootedness and transcendence (which Fromm maintains are the distinctive human needs that need to be fulfilled in order to move people toward a reunion with one another and with the natural world, that is, to move toward productive, positive freedom) because it separates us from ourselves and from those around us.

Freire maintains that the oppressed have so fully incorporated the image of the oppressor into their very existence that rejecting that image and replacing it with autonomy and responsibility is far too frightening, and hence is what keeps the oppressed from becoming free and existing authentically. This is why education must address the individual as a subjective being who has deeply internalized the oppressive mindset of the oppressor. Education must help people to understand the psychological hold that oppression has on their psyche, and it must also help them to develop the ego, strength, and wisdom to break that hold and to replace it with care for the self and hence for others, while raising critical consciousness about oppressive forces in society. Such an education will go further in allowing individuals to resolve the fear of freedom and move toward a productive life.

Notes

1 Achieving fuller humanity, a notion that will be discussed more fully later, means (for Freire) becoming humanized (as opposed to being dehumanized as in oppressive relationships).
2 The use of "man" in this paper is the consequence of quoting Freire and Fromm, both of whom referred to all of humanity as such. We make no excuses for either theorist's failure to recognize the importance of using gender free writing techniques, and we recognize the problems associated with the lack of use of gender free writing. As a result, we attempt to use both pronouns "she" and "he" and/or "her" and "him" whenever we are not referencing a statement made by Freire or Fromm.

References

Collins, Denis E. (1977). *Paulo Freire, his life, works, and thought.* New York, NY: Paulist Press.
Freire, P. (1985). *The politics of education: Culture, power and liberation.* Boston, MA : Bergin & Garvey Publishers.
— (1994). *Pedagogy of hope: Reliving pedagogy of the oppressed.* New York, NY: Continuum.
— (1998). *Education for critical consciousness.* New York, NY: Continuum.
— (2003). *Pedagogy of the oppressed.* New York, NY: Continuum.

Fromm, E. (1941). *Escape from freedom*. New York, NY: Henry Holt and Co.

— (1947). *Man for himself*. New York City, NY: Henry Holt .

— (1955). *The sane society*. New York, NY: Henry Holt and Co.

— (1976). *To have or to be?* New York, NY: Bantam.

— (1968). *The revolution of hope: toward a humanized technology.* New York, NY: Bantam.

— (1992). *The art of being*. New York, NY: Continuum.

— (1999/1994).*On being human*. New York, NY: Continuum.

Freire, P. and Macedo, D. (1987). *Literacy: Reading the Word and the World* :Westport, CN: Bergin & Garvey.

Fromm, E. and Maccoby, M. (1970). *Social Character in a Mexican Village*. Englewood Cliffs, NJ: Prentice-Hall.

Funk, R. (2000). *Erich Fromm—His Life and Ideas: An Illustrated Biography*. New York, NY: Continuum.

Giroux, H. (2010). In Defense of Public School Teachers in a Time of Crisis. *Truthout*. April 14, 2010. Retrieved from: http://archive. truthout.org/in- defense-public-school-teachers-a-time- crisis58567

Gordon, M. (2009). *The roots of empathy: Changing the world child by child*. New York, NY: The Experiment Publishers.

Louv, R. (2008). *Last child in the woods: Saving our children from nature deficit disorder*. Chapel Hill, NC: Algonquin Books of Chapel Hill.

Neil, A. S. (1960). *Summerhill: A radical approach to child rearing* (Preface by E. Fromm) New York, NY: Hart Publishing Co.

Pinar, W. F. (2004). *What is curriculum theory?* Mahwah, NJ: Lawrence Erlbaum.

Schonert-Reichl, K. A. (2009). Research Report. *Roots of Empathy*. Retrieved from: www.rootsofempathy.org/documents/content/ROE_ Report_Research_E_2009.pdf

Sidorkin, A. M. (2002). *Learning relations: Impure education, deschooled schools & dialogue with evil*. New York, NY: Peter Lang.

7

Liberation Theology and Paulo Freire: On the Side of the Poor

William M. Reynolds

"Existence is not despair, but risk, If I don't exist dangerously, I cannot be."

Freire, 1987, p. 130

Introduction of contrast

It is most appropriate to discuss Paulo Freire and his intellectual as well as spiritual interconnectedness with liberation theology in the second decade of the twenty-first century. It is a time when religion, particularly Christianity, in the United States has been hijacked by the far right and has become a religion of ressentiment. The far right, then, uses that ressentiment as a Civic Gospel (Reynolds & Webber, 2009). It is a vision of spirituality that constrains rather than liberates. It is a civic gospel that ironically promotes hatred instead of peace. This becomes problematic because all forms of Christianity and Christian Theology become linked with this right wing civic gospel. Recent proclamations by ministers of the Civic Gospel are examples of the agenda of these Christocrats (see ibid.).

When we discuss the agenda of the Christocrats there is a long list of their causes that are relevant. Overshadowing those causes, however, is the ressentiment discussed in the introduction. For the Christocrats there must be a public enemy. The enemy must be demonized and continually mobilized in media discourse to provide objects for followers to rally against. The main goal is to articulate an "us" against "them" strategy (p. 45). One of enemies that is targeted for continual vociferous attacks from the Christocrats is the lesbian, gay, bisexual, and transgender (LGBT) community. Two recent examples provide evidence of this agenda.

The first example is that of pastor, Curtis Knapp of the New Hope Baptist Church in Seneca, Kansas. In a sermon entitled, "The Curse of Homosexuality" Knapp declared that LGBTs should be put to death. He stated his views in a one hour sermon given in May 2012.

> "They should be put to death," Knapp told congregants. "That's what happened in Israel. That's why homosexuality wouldn't have grown in Israel. It tends to limit conversions. It tends to limit people coming out of the closet. Oh, so you're saying that we should go out and start killing them? No, I'm saying the government should. They won't, but they should. (Edwards, 2012, n.p.)

Knapp's sermon followed close on the heels of the more infamous sermon delivered on May 17, 2012 by North Carolina pastor, Charles Worley. Rather than killing LGBT people outright, Worley's plan was closer to a concentration camp agenda.

> I figured a way out, a way to get rid of all the lesbians and queers but I couldn't get it past the Congress—build a great big large fence, fifty or a hundred mile long. Put all the lesbians in there, fly over and drop some food. Do the same thing with the queers and the homosexuals. And have that fence electrified so they can't get out. And you know what? In a few years they will die out. You know why? They can't reproduce. If a man ever has a young'un, praise God he will be the first. (Eng, 2012, n.p.)

These are just two examples of a widespread Christocratic agenda to put LGBT people within the context of the enemy and continually attack them. This community is only one of the enemies of this religion of ressentiment. It is appropriate to distinguish this Ressentiment Christianity with its dominion theology, which promotes the basic belief that Christians (Christocrats) are meant to take over secular institutions and create in the United States a Christian Nation. Of course, it is a Christian Nation under their theology of ressentiment.

Ressentiment is a state of repressed feeling and desire, which becomes generative of values. The condition of ressentiment is complex both in its internal structure and in its relations to various dimensions of human existence. While it infects the heart of the individual, it is rooted in our relatedness with others. On the one hand, ressentiment is a dark, personal secret, which most of us would never reveal to others even if we could acknowledge it in ourselves. On the other hand, ressentiment has an undeniably public face. It can be creative of social practices, mores, and fashions; of scholarly attitudes, academic polices, and educational initiatives; of political ideologies, institutions, and revolutions; of forms of religiosity and ascetic practices (Morrelli, 1999, p. 1).

Ressentiment Christianity can be contrasted with the social gospel and liberation theology.

Personal retrospective of the social gospel

This ressentiment Christianity contrasts sharply with my personal experience of being raised in the United Methodist Church. A church I left many years ago. In the late 1960s the social gospel, as I heard it, was about helping the poor and improving their circumstances. This was seen as the work of the church. In 1969 as part of a United Methodist Youth Fellowship project my group traveled to Scott's Run Settlement House near Morgantown, West Virginia, to help out-of-work coal miners repair their houses and rebuild some of the Settlement House itself. I remember reconstructing some of the homes of the workers and patching mortar on the walls of the Settlement House (see Reynolds & Webber, 2009). This was not steeped in liberation theology but it was concerned with assisting the poor. But it was not based in the notions of helping the poor come to a sense of conscientization or critical consciousness. The minister who led the group told us that this was the work of the church in America. For me the Civic Gospel is far from either the social gospel agenda or the tenets of liberation theology. Certainly it is far from the notions that Freire had of radical love, critical pedagogy, and hope. Again, the civic gospel is a gospel of ressentiment. And, the social gospel was more an interventionist strategy and not grounded in the notions of liberation generated by individuals developing a critical consciousness. The social gospel although a socially concerned theology can suffer from what Freire, in *Pedagogy of the Oppressed* (2006/1971), called malefic generosity. The work of the social gospel did not necessarily work to change an unjust social order. In fact, in many cases it maintained that order.

Accordingly these adherents to the people's cause constantly run the risk of falling into a type of generosity as malefic as that of the oppressors. The generosity of the oppressors is nourished by an unjust order, which must be maintained in order to justify that generosity (Freire, 2006, p. 60). Liberation theology puts trust in the people and works with them in a process in which they themselves become a presence capable of articulating and working toward their liberation and social justice.

Liberation Theology—
The presence of the absent

Those who were for so long 'absent' in our society and in the Church have made themselves—and are continuing to make themselves—present. It is not a matter of physical absence: we are talking of those who have had scant or no significance, and who therefore have not felt (and in many cases still do not feel) in a position to make plain their suffering, their aspirations and their hopes. But this is what has started to change.

Gutierrez, 1999, p. 20

The first step in understanding the traces of liberation theology in the work of Paulo Freire is to discuss a brief history of liberation theology and an analysis of its basic tenets. First, a brief look at the historical roots of liberation theology.

Although liberation theology can trace its roots back to the sixteenth century, most scholars who discuss liberation theology (Gutierrez, 1988; Rowland, 1999; Allen, 2000) center its origins with Vatican II's recognition of a "world church" in the 1960s and more specifically with the Conference of Latin American Bishops held in Medellin, Columbia, in 1968. The bishops who attended the meeting committed to the concept that the Catholic Church in Latin America should have a "preferential option for the poor" (Allen, 2000, p. 1). The "movement" became known as liberation theology with the publication of Peruvian priest Gustavo Gutierrez's book, *A Theology of Liberation* (1988) (see Allen, 2000). There were other theological scholars involved with the development and spread of liberation theology. Leonard Boff initially a Franciscan priest who was silenced by the Church in 1985 for his book, *Church: Charism and Power* (2011/1985). Jon Sobrino of El Salvador, a Jesuit priest, was also influential in the movement and authored numerous books three of which were, *Jesus the Liberator* (1994/1971), *The True Church and the Poor* (2004/1985), and *Christ the Liberator* (2001/1999). A third priest/scholar involved in the movement was Juan Luis Segundo of Uruguay, a physician and Jesuit priest. His contribution to the literature was the important text, *The Liberation of Theology* (2002/1976). The influence of liberation theology was strong, according to scholars, until it was criticized by the Vatican Congregation for the Doctrines of the Faith (1984/1986). At these meetings liberation theology was criticized for stressing the importance of the sins of the system over the importance of individual sin (this will be discussed in the next section). This criticism followed the general critique that liberation theology was using Marxist concepts in its elaborations concerning the questions of oppression and social injustice. It became known as Christianized Marxism. Mainstream historical research claims the influence of liberation theology decreased after the criticism and actions taken against liberation theology priests by the Congregation for the Doctrines of the Faith and the charges of the influences of Marxism. Interestingly enough, Pope Benedict XVI, the current head of the Catholic Church spent most of his early career battling liberation theology. He believed that it turned Jesus' concern for the poor into a call for rebellion.

An analysis of the phenomenon of liberation theology reveals that it constitutes a fundamental threat to the faith of the Church. At the same time it must be borne in mind that no error could persist unless it contained a grain of truth. Indeed, an error is all the more dangerous, the greater that grain of truth is, for then the temptation it exerts is all the greater (Ratzinger, 1984, p. 1).

The Pope, however, appointed Bishop Gerhard Ludwig Muller in 2012 to head the Vatican's office in charge of doctrinal affairs. This office is one of Roman Catholicism's most powerful posts. Muller, a conservative theologian, was involved in liberation theology and is a student and friend of Gustavo Gutierrez. They coauthored a book in 2004 *An der Seite der Armen* (On the Side of the Poor). The traces of liberation theology are still within the Catholic Church, despite its currently more conservative attitude. It is not surprising that liberation theology has also become much more multifaceted. Other manifestations of liberation theology emerged in the years following its inception and at present there are numerous areas connected with liberation theology. Latin American, North American, Feminist theology, Black Liberation theology, South African, Hispanic, African, Asian, and economics and liberation theology (Rowland, 1999, pp. 253–6). In order to understand liberation theology in more depth, a brief analysis of its basic tenets is necessary. This is only a basic look at some of its major principles.

Basic tenets of liberation theology

"The Spirit of the Lord God is upon me, because the Lord has anointed me to bring good news to the poor; [a] he has sent me to bind up the brokenhearted, to proclaim liberty to the captives, and the opening of the prison to those who are bound; [b] 2 to proclaim the year of the Lord's favor, and the day of vengeance of our God; to comfort all who mourn; 3 to grant to those who mourn in Zion—to give them a beautiful headdress instead of ashes, the oil of gladness instead of mourning, the garment of praise instead of a faint spirit; that they may be called oaks of righteousness, the planting of the Lord, that he may be glorified. [c] 4 They shall build up the ancient ruins; they shall raise up the former devastations; they shall repair the ruined cities, the devastations of many generations . . . 8 'For I, the Lord, love justice; I hate robbery and wrongdoing. In my faithfulness I will reward my people and make an everlasting covenant with them.'"

New International Version, Isaiah 61.1–4, 8

In general, liberation theology stressed social analysis. These theologians, who developed liberation theology, understood that social injustice was/is an issue that needed to be addressed, particularly in Latin America. "To remedy social injustice, they believed, one must first understand the social mechanisms that produce it" (Allen, 2000, p. 2). They were concerned with this social analysis and were drawn to Marxist analysis. As mentioned above, this connection to Marxist analysis resulted in major criticisms of the movement. The criticism centered on the charge that you cannot separate Marxist analysis from its connections to atheism in particular and other issues as well.

Allen (2000) elaborates on four basic principles of liberation theology. His analysis gives a good general outline of the major suppositions underlying liberation theology. They are the ideas that are central to the movement. The four concepts are "The preferential option for the poor, institutional violence, structural sin, and Orthopraxis" (p. 1). Each of these principles requires further explanation.

The poor

"Dominated peoples, 'exploited social classes,' 'despised races,' and 'marginalized cultures' were formulas often used in speaking (there was repeated reference also to discrimination against women). The point of these formulas was to make it clear that the poor have a social dimension of the poor in the context of liberation theology."

Gutierrez, 1988, p. xxi

As a result of the Conference of Latin American Bishops held in Medellin, Columbia, in 1968, perhaps the most important concept for liberation theology emerged—"the preferential option for the poor." This tenet was explicated by the liberation theologians as siding with the poor in their efforts to achieve social justice. Liberation theologians discussed the church's historical complicity in creating the social order that divided rich from poor—"Catholic missionaries served as evangelizers for European conquerors, and church leaders sided with the elites for 400 years" (Allen, 2000, p. 2). It was a consensus on the part of the bishops that it was time to switch sides. Liberation theologians discussed the necessity of commitment to the poor. In the final analysis, poverty means death: lack of food and housing, the inability to attend properly to health and education needs, the exploitation of workers, permanent unemployment, the lack of respect for one's human dignity, and unjust limitations placed on personal freedoms in the areas of self-expression, politics, and religion (Gutierrez, 1988, p. xxi).

Siding with the poor meant an analysis of the historical and contemporary conditions that underlie the causes and the maintenance of poverty. The opulence of cathedrals, iconic statues, and church vestments in the midst of such bleak poverty in Latin American countries was visible evidence of the complicity of the church with the conquerors.

Institutional violence

As for the bishops' vision of reality, they describe the misery and exploitation in Latin America as a "situation of injustice that can be called institutionalized violence," and responsible for the death of thousands of innocent victims (Peruvian Bishops Commission in Gutierrez, 1988, p. 64).

The liberationists also were outspoken on the question of the hidden violence of institutions that supported social arrangements that maintained poverty. The questioning of these social arrangements was to lead to the criticism that these liberationists were supporting revolutionary violence. Few were. They believed that since the church had supported the status quo, it was complicitous with a system that exercised violence on millions of people (Allen, 2000, p. 16).

Structural sin

In general structural sin(s) are oppressive and degrading actions taken against others. The social actions that lead to stark divisions between rich and poor are examples of structural sin. There is a sense in structural sin of collective responsibility. The emphasis on this notion of collective responsibility (structural sin) as more crucial than individual responsibility (sin) was threatening to the Church. People dealing with the intricacies of personal sin and guilt were unlikely to focus on structural sin. And the focus on structural sin questioned the exclusive authority of the Church.

Liberation theologians argued that there is a social dimension that is more than the sum of individual acts. Examples frequently cited include neocolonialism and the feudal nature of the relationship between the Latin American oligarchy and the peasants. By extension, the redemption from sin won by Christ must be more than the redemption of individual souls. It must redeem and transform the social realities of human life (Allen, 2000, p. 16).

Orthopraxis

Orthopraxis (correct action) was a term that the liberationists originated to set in contradistinction to the century's long emphasis on developing orthodoxy or correct belief and rituals. Reflective action is crucial to challenging social injustice. But, according to the liberationists, orthopraxis and belief must coexist.

For all these reasons, a principal task of "reflection on praxis in the light of faith" will be to strengthen the necessary and fruitful links between orthopraxis and orthodoxy. The necessity of this circular relationship between the two is a point frequently underscored in liberation theology; as is always the case in dealing with essential dimensions of one and the same reality it is not possible to accept one and belittle the other (Gutierrez, 1988, p. 34).

The logical consequence of a liberating theology is to pursue action with faith: action that addresses the conditions of the poor and on the structures that perpetuate those conditions. After discussing these four major points in liberation theology, we can turn our attention to their traces in the work and intellectual development of Paulo Freire.

Traces of liberation theology in the work of Paulo Freire

This new apprenticeship will violently break down the elitist concept of existence they had absorbed while being ideologized. The sine qua non the apprenticeship demands is that, first of all, they really experience their own Easter, that they die as elitists so as to be resurrected on the side of the oppressed, and that they be born again with the beings who were not allowed to be. Such a process implies a renunciation of myths that are dear to them: the myth of their superiority, of their purity of soul, of their virtues, their wisdom; the myth that they save the poor, the myth of neutrality of the church, of theology, education, science, and technology; and the myth of their own impartiality. From these grow the other myths: of the inferiority of other people, of their spiritual and physical impurity, and the absolute ignorance of the oppressed (Freire, 1987, pp. 122–3).

Gutierrez's demand of the "right of the poor to think" not only profoundly influenced Freire but also resonates with modern critical theorists in their pursuit of just forms of existence (Roberto, 2010).

Paulo Freire (1921–97) was not only instrumental in creating, but was also involved in the zeitgeist of the 1960s and 1970s in Latin America. Part of that zeitgeist was that portions of the Latin American Catholic Church's clergy developed liberation theology. The final portion of this chapter will explore the interconnections between Paulo Freire's intellectual development and liberation theology.

> His [Freire's] approach was more closely associated with the tradition of Marxist humanism, which he combined with elements of Christian humanism, emphasizing concepts like full human development, agency, subjectivity, ethics, and democracy. (Schugurensky, 2011, p. 44)

There are, of course, numerous interconnections between Freire and liberation theology. This section, however, will focus on three of them. First the interconnectedness of the concept of the culture of silence will be discussed. Second the crucial concept of conscientization or critical consciousness will be explored. Third, Freire's philosophy of hope and struggle will be analyzed.

The culture of silence

One of the most important concepts within Freire's notions of the oppressed and pedagogy is the concept of the culture of silence. Freire expressed the idea that the oppressed were "submerged" in circumstances that kept them from developing a critical consciousness and voicing their opposition to the status quo. Since, they were submerged they had little chance of breaking free. Freire felt that the educational system and the Catholic Church were instruments in maintaining this culture of silence. In terms of the church he postulated that if it does not become involved in history it nevertheless remains involved in history.

> In fact, those who preach that the church is outside history contradict themselves in practice, because they automatically place themselves at the side of those who refuse to allow the oppressed classes to be. (Freire, 2002, p. 127)

This coincides with liberation theologians who discussed the fact that the "orthodox" church had for hundreds of years served to perpetuate the divisions between the rich and poor and give legitimacy to the status quo. "Is the church fulfilling a purely religious role when by its silence and friendly relationships it lends legitimacy to a dictatorial and oppressive government?" (Gutierrez, 1988, p. 40). Freire elaborated on this basic relationship between the oppressor and the oppressed to demonstrate the ways in which institutions within the system worked to perpetuate the culture of silence. He called one of the techniques prescription. In *Pedagogy of the Oppressed* (2006/1971) he describes the element of prescription.

> Every prescription represents the imposition of one individual's choice upon another, transforming the consciousness of the person prescribed to into one that conforms with the prescriber's consciousness. Thus, the behavior of the oppressed is a prescribed behavior, following as it does the guidelines of the oppressor. (Freire, 2006/1971, p. 47)

There is no doubt that the church as well as the education system is awash in prescriptions and rituals and perpetuates hegemony. The culture of silence wrapped/wraps the oppressed in feelings of inadequacy. They are dehumanized. Their voices are silenced and for the most part have become resigned to it. They have internalized the role the oppressor has set for them. Hence the need for critical consciousness.

Conscientization

"According to him [Freire] consciousness is determined by the socio-economic and political context, and also by cultural conditioning through one's upbringing, education and religion. In other words, it is an inter-change between economic and cultural structures."

Fritz, 2010, p. 2

One of the initial requirements of developing a voice and taking action by the oppressed is developing a critical consciousness or conscientization. And that development must be accompanied by political action/praxis. Of course, there are no prescriptions for critical consciousness.

Hence conscientization whether or not associated with literacy training, must be a critical attempt to reveal reality, not just alienating small talk. It must, that is, be related to political involvement. There is no conscientization if the result is not the conscious action of the oppressed as an exploited social class struggling for liberation. What is more, no one conscientizes anyone else. The educator and the people conscientize themselves, thanks to the dialectic movement that relates critical reflection on past action to the continuing struggle. (Freire, 1987, p. 125)

This is the process that both Freire and the liberation theologians discussed as crucial to education and the development of liberation theology (as discussed previously). Liberation theologians discussed the necessity of overcoming the oppressive structures of society and the church must by means of a "profound revision" (Gutierrez, 1988, p. 68) change its presence in Latin America.

Freire discussed three levels of conscious (Fritz, 2010, p. 2) that people move through as they progress toward critical consciousness. The first level is that of magical consciousness or thinking. In this state people are silent and docile and live in the taken-for-granted. Events are explained by way of some superior, mystical, or magical force (ibid.). It is beyond their ability to remedy so they accept. Of course, religion plays a part in perpetuating this type of consciousness and was one of the objects that a conscienticizing evangelization was trying to change. Whether Freire influenced this movement or whether this movement influenced Freire concerning magical thinking is difficult to determine. The next stage in this development of a critical conscious is naïve consciousness (ibid.). In this stage people become aware of problems but the notion of changing those problems becomes individualized, not put into a larger sociopolitical context. In this stage, for example, in education, teachers might blame an individual administrator or fellow teacher for their problems or students blame an individual teacher for how awful the schooling experience has become. In terms of the church a member of the congregation might blame an individual priest for the problem of poverty or the sad state of things. The result, of course, is that the very system that causes the problems is never questioned and remains in place. Many get stuck in this stage of consciousness. The final stage is critical consciousness (ibid.) in this stage people start to see issues as systemic problems. They begin to see their positionality in terms of class, gender, race, etc. They also become conscious of repressive social structures and arrangements. As Freire cautions, however, critical conscious must be a collective process not a top-down interventionist strategy. It also needs to move beyond interesting debates about this or that theoretical perspective or building castles in the air. It must result in praxis or action on particular sites of oppression. In terms of the liberation theologians, it was orthopraxis.

A critical consciousness is not magical or naïve. It is aware of injustice and works to understand the causes of that injustice and then acts on those causes. It is not a state that one arrives at in perpetuity. It is a permanent struggle to demystify, assume responsibilities and work (Gutierrez, 1988). Again, the interconnections between Freire's notions of consciousness and the liberation theologians analysis of the problems of the church in Latin America are apparent.

One example of this praxis as a connection with Freire and liberation theology is Freire's idea of reading. Freire discusses reading in *Literacy, Reading the Word and the World* (1987).

> Reading the world always precedes reading the word, and reading the word implies continually reading the world. As suggested earlier, this movement from word to the world is always present; even the spoken word flows from our reading of the world. In a way, however, we can go further and say that reading the word is not preceded merely by reading the world, but by a certain form of writing it or rewriting it, that is, of transforming it by means of conscious practical work. For me, this dynamic movement is central to the literacy process. (Freire & Macedo, 1987, p. 35)

As Freire used his notions of literacy with the Brazilian poor, the liberation theologians and practitioners used those same ideas with their parishioners while reading the Bible. Literacy was/is crucial to the process of liberation. This is another connection between the ideas of Freire and the liberation theologians.

Hope and struggle

> "Freire's attack against all forms of oppression, his call to link ideological critique with collective action, and the prophetic vision central to his politics are heavily indebted to the spirit and ideological dynamics that have both informed and characterized the theologies of liberation that have emerged primarily from Latin American since the 1970s. In truly dialectic fashion, Freire has criticized and rescued the radical underside of revolutionary Christianity."

> Giroux, 1985, p. xvii

Gutierrez's notion (1988) that the poor had the "right to think" "not only profoundly influenced Freire but also resonates with modern critical theorists in their pursuit of just forms of existence" (Roberto, 2010, p. 1). The struggle for liberation and freedom whether within the church or any other social sphere is the constant concern of critical pedagogues, critical theorists, liberation theologians, and other cultural workers. But the struggle is filled with hope, which is the lasting legacy in Freire's work with liberation theology. Freire's *Pedagogy of Hope: Reliving Pedagogy of the Oppressed* (1999) is one example of how hope permeates all of his work. It is also imbued in the work of the liberation theologians. Freire's language is "fueled with hope and possibility" (Schugurensky, 2010, p. 44). This connection of hope can be understood if we look at passages from Gutierrez and Freire. This is not an exhaustive look, but indicative of the connections. It must be stated that this is not a type of naïve hope—the hope that we will be fine tomorrow—but a hope with deep commitment. It is consistent with Marxian and Christian utopianism (Marsden, 1991). It is hope that looks to the future but is anchored in an understanding of history and a watchfulness on the present.

> To hope does not mean to know the future, but rather to be open, in an attitude of spiritual childhood, to accepting it as a gift. But this gift is accepted in the negation of injustice, in the protest against trampled human rights, and in the struggle for peace and fellowship. Thus hope fulfills a mobilizing and liberating function in history. Its function is not very obvious, but real and deep. (Gutierrez, 1988, p. 125)

Freire discusses hope, but also gives a cautious reminder to us about hopelessness. In the present moment of cruelty and punishment it is good to remember Freire's words on hopelessness. Hopelessness leads to despair, Freire reminds us—"Hopelessness and despair are both the consequence and the cause of inaction and immobilism" (Freire, 1997, p. 9). On the other hand, for Freire hope is crucial in the struggle for a just world.

> One of the tasks of the progressive educator, through a serious, correct political analysis, is to unveil opportunities for hope, no matter what the obstacles might be. After all, without hope there is little we can do. It will be hard to struggle on, and when we fight as hopeless or despairing persons, our struggle will be suicidal. (Freire, 1999, p. 9)

So, it is in struggle and hope that we have further evidence of the connections between liberation theory and the work of Paulo Freire. Perhaps, this is the strongest link.

Freire's intellectual roots

It has been an interesting endeavor to draw the connections between Freire and liberation theology. There are not many extensive studies of this linkage. But, I do believe that it was an important part of Freire's intellectual development. I was listening to an interview of Freire entitled, "Paulo Freire: Liberation Theology and Marx." It was posted on You Tube in 2007. It is not very well translated, but you can hear the passion in his voice as he speaks about liberation theology, Marx, and Christ.

> At that instant the European journalists 1970 hadn't understood my affirmation. It's that how much more I read Marx, more and more I found a type of objective basis . . . to continue Christ's comrade. So the reading that I did of Marx . . . Of Marx's prolongations . . . Never suggested to me that I leave to find Christ in the corner of their own slums. I stayed with Marx in the worldliness, looking for Christ in the transcendentally [sic]. (Suicidealuguel, 2007)

Freire is important to many critical scholars and his legacy will endure with strength and yes, hope.

References

Abel, L. and Kieser, E. (Producers), and Duigan, J. (Director) (1989). *Romero* [Motion Picture]. United States: Lions Gate.

Allen, J. L. Jr. (2000). Key principles of liberation theology. *National Catholic Reporter*. June 2, 2000, 36 (31), 16, 1p.

Boff, L. (2011/1985). *Church, charism and power: Liberation theology and the institutional church*. Norwich, UK: SCM Press.

Edwards, D. (2012). Kansas pastor calls on U.S. government to kill LGBT people, May 30, 2012. Retrieved from: www.rawstory.com/rs/2012/05/30/kansas-pastor-calls-on-u-sGovernment-to-kill-lgbt-people/

Elias, J. L. (1994). *Paulo Freire: Pedagogue of liberation*. Malabar, FL: Krieger Publishing Company.

Eng, J. (May 22, 2012). Charles Worley, North Carolina pastor, faces backlash, outrage over call for gays to be put behind electric fence.

Retrieved from: http://usnews.msnbc.msn.com/_news/2012/05/2
2/11813973-charles-worley-north-carolinapastor-faces-backlas
h-outrage-over-call-for-gays-to-be-put-behind-electric-fence?

Freire, P. (1987). *The politics of education: Culture, Power, and liberation.*
Grandby, MA: Bergin and Garvey.

— (1997). *Mentoring the mentor: A critical dialogue with Paulo Freire.*
New York, NY: Peter Lang.

— (2002). *Education for critical consciousness.* New York, NY:
Continuum.

— (2006/1971). *Pedagogy of the oppressed.* New York, NY: Continuum.

Freire, P. and Macedo, D. (1987). *Literacy: reading the word and the
world.* Grandby, MA: Bergin and Garvey.

Fritz, C. (2010). The theory of Paulo Freire. Retrieved from: www.
stclares.ca/pdfs/The%20Theory%20of%20Paulo%20Freire.pdf

Giroux, H. A. (1985). "Introduction." In P. Freire. *The politics of
education: Culture, power, and liberation* (pp. xi–xxvii). Grandby, MA:
Bergin and Garvey.

Gutierrez, G. (1988). *A theology of liberation: History, politics and
salvation,* trans. Sister C. Inda and J. Eagleson. Maryknoll, NY: Orbis
Books (Original work published, 1971).

— (1999). "The task and content of liberation theology," trans. J. Condor.
In Rowland, C. (ed.). *A Cambridge companion to liberation theology*
(pp. 19–38). Cambridge, MA: Cambridge University Press.

Marsden, J. J. (1991). *Marxian and Christian utopianism: Toward a
socialist political theology.* New York, NY: Monthly Review Press.

Morrelli, E. M. (1999). "Ressentiment and rationality." *Philosophical
Anthropology.* Retrieved from: www.bu.edu/wcp/Papers/Anth/
AnthMore.htm

Muller, G. L. and Gutierrez, G. (2004). *An der seite der armen.* Augsburg,
Germany: Sankt Ulrich Verlag.

Peruvian Bishops Commission. (1969). *Between honesty and hope,* trans.
John Drury. Maryknoll, NY: Orbis Books.

Ratzinger, J. (1984). Liberation theology. Retrieved from: www.
christendomawake.org/pages/Ratzinger/liberationtheol.htm

Reynolds, W. and Webber, J. A. (2009). *The civic gospel: A political
cartography of Christianity.* New York, NY: Sense Publishers.

Roberto (2010). Religion and politics: A thanksgiving special [Web log
comment], October 12, 2010. Retrieved from www.freireproject.org/
blogs/religion-and-politics%3A-thanksgivingSpecial

Romero, O. (1988). *The violence of love: The pastoral wisdom of
archbishop Oscar Romero.* Trans. James R. Brockman. New York, NY:
Harper and Row.

Rowland, C. (ed.) (1999). *The Cambridge companion to liberation theology.* Cambridge, MA: Cambridge University Press.

Schugurensky, D. (2011). *Continuum library of educational thought: Paulo Freire.* New York, NY: Continuum.

Segundo, J.-L. (2002/1976). *The liberation of theology.* Eugene, OR: Wipf & Stock Publishers.

Sobrino, J. (1994/1971). *Jesus the liberator: A historical theological reading of Jesus of Nazareth.* New York, NY: Burns & Oates/ Continuum.

— (2001/1999). *Christ the liberator: A view from the victims.* Maryknoll, NY: Orbis Books.

— (2004/1985). *The true church and the poor.* Eugene, OR: Wipf & Stock Publishers.

Suicidealuguel (2007). *Paulo Freire: Liberation theology and Marx.* Retrieved from: www.youtube.com/watch?v=1Wz5y2V1af0

8

Living with/in the Tensions: Freire's Praxis in a High-Stakes World

Melissa Winchell and Tricia Kress

"I think that one of the best ways for us to work as human beings is not only to know that we are uncompleted human beings but to assume uncompleteness . . . We are not complete. We have to become inserted in a permanent process of searching. Without this we would die in life."

Freire in Horton & Freire, 1990, p. 11

A call for praxis: Grinding the gears of instrumental rationality

"Standards," "accountability," "input-output measurement," data-driven instruction," "best practices": these buzzwords satu- rate contemporary rhetoric (popular, political, professional, and academic) about teaching and learning in the United States; the saturation is so complete that these ideas have become common- sensical and hegemonic. We (Melissa and Tricia) are US-based

critical educators who live in this dangerously commonsensical
world of education; we are kept dancing with our feet to the fires of
high-stakes testing and punitive policy. Further, we find ourselves
increasingly disturbed because, as Giroux (2010) notes:

> By espousing empirically based standards as a fix for educational
> problems, advocates of these measures do more than oversimplify
> complex issues, they also remove the classroom from larger social,
> political and economic forces and offer up anti-intellectual and
> ethically debased technical and punitive solutions to school and
> classroom problems. (n.p.)

While this technocratic, bureaucratic education is most commonly
associated with K-12 public schools, higher education institutions,
particularly colleges of education, are feeling these pressures, too,
as teacher education is being filtered through the machine metaphors of Cartesianism (Kincheloe, 2003b).

For critical educators, K-12 and higher education alike, working
in this climate is precarious. On the one hand, we seek to educate
our students to think critically about their lives and the world in
order to change oppressive social structures, alleviate human suffering, and rediscover ways to live in harmony with the living world.
On the other hand, this high-stakes climate of accountability envi-
sions teachers as cogs in a machine; teachers are easily replaceable
if they begin to "malfunction" and grind the gears of the system
in which students are seen as the objects of education (i.e. teaching
and learning is done to them). In this system, knowledge is finite
and measurable, answers are singular and known (Freire, 1985).
Moreover, the climate is high stakes in more ways than one, as in a
number of states (e.g. Florida, Louisiana, and Minnesota to name
just a few), teachers' job security has become more and more tied to
accountability measures (Isensee & Butrymowicz, 2011; Deslatte,
2011; McGuire, 2012). When one's teaching career is based on a
standardized definition of student "growth" and the pressure to
keep one's job is uncertain, there is a degree of "safety" (perhaps
real, perhaps illusory) that comes with keeping one's eyes closed to
(and thereby perpetuating) a dehumanizing education. Particularly
in tenuous economic times like these, revolutionary ideas threaten
power structures, and praxis, as Freire conceived of it, can be dangerous. We need only consider the recent removal of *Pedagogy of*

the Oppressed from Tucson, Arizona's public schools to see how power reacts when threatened (Planas, 2012). Yet at the same time, it is precisely in times like these – in which practice becomes automated, reactionary, doing-without-thinking for survival – that praxis is so very necessary. We need praxis not just to survive, but to thrive; we need praxis to further the kinds of student and teacher growth that are meaningful, human, and revolutionary.

In this chapter, we are issuing a call to praxis. Our goal is to provide new perspectives for embodying praxis in our collective work as educators. To accomplish this, we aim to theorize Freire's praxis while also taking heed of Freire's (1985) caution:

> What we must not do is overdefine the concept or the theme or even take what it involves as a given fact, nor should we simply describe it or explain it. To the contrary, we should assume a committed attitude toward our theme, an attitude of one who does not want merely to describe what goes on as it happens. We want, above all, to transform the real world of our theme so that whatever might be happening now can be changed later. (p. 112)

We understand praxis as something lived; praxis can only be experienced in practice. Thus, we find it necessary to commit ourselves to embodying praxis within the narrative form of this chapter. Moreover, if praxis is lived, then praxis can be experienced differently by different people, and also differently by the same people within different contexts – there is no "one way" to engage in praxis. We see praxis not as developing sameness (as in adopting "best practices"), but rather as an orientation toward humanizing the world, ourselves, and our work with others.

In our writing of this chapter, we intend to model praxis in a number of ways. First, we are coauthoring (which necessitates dialogue, a central component of praxis), but we are providing space for our individual voices as well, so that we can allow for and demonstrate points of divergence in how we experience praxis. Second, after contextualizing and theorizing Freire's notion of praxis, we present specific moments in which Freire demonstrates his praxis, and we interject comments connecting to our understandings of praxis, in order to work within and through the theory-practice, subject-object, reflection-action tensions that Freire (1985) identifies. Third, we conclude by looking ahead toward where we see praxis and Freire's ideas taking us in the future. As we open ourselves to praxis in writing this chapter, we ask that our readers, too, open themselves to praxis as they read. Freire (1985) explains that in writing about real world phenomena, "writers must assume a gnosiological attitude [and] . . . Readers should not be simple clients of the gnosiological act of the writer" (p. 112). Like praxis, both reading and writing are processes in which readers and writers engage in knowledge work. We encourage our readers to live praxis as they share in our evolving knowledge of praxis that we capture here in words.

Praxis and the scholar-practitioner tension

We (Melissa and Tricia) are at present working together in a teacher-learner relationship; Melissa is a doctoral candidate and Tricia is her dissertation advisor. Each of us had more than a decade of experience as practitioners in K-12 and higher education settings prior to engaging in our own doctoral studies about education, so we also share a collegiality as it pertains to our teaching practice. During our predoctoral years as practitioners, neither of us had ever heard the term "praxis." For Tricia, the concept of praxis was introduced in a philosophy of research course in a rather rudimentary way as "theory put into practice," which was easy to digest, but rang hollow as a connection to the real world. In that class, there was no space created to reflect on what this actually meant in the day-to-day reality of our classrooms. There was no conversation about what theory even is or how, in fact, we apply theory in our practice all the time, even (and perhaps especially) when we are not conscious of it. Praxis was abstract; it seemed to be something that more enlightened scholars knew how to do and practitioners like Tricia did not yet know how to do. Melissa first heard the word "praxis" in one of Tricia's doctoral courses. At first, she thought that Tricia was mispronouncing the word "practice." Only much later did it occur to her that praxis was an ongoing practice. This incomplete sense of work was a concept she had not encountered in any of her years of teaching or teacher training. In her predoctoral experience, learning to teach was presented as a set of skills to be mastered (indeed the concept of a "master teacher" had been lauded as an alluring goal) and not an emerging, demanding, and open process.

Given our years as practitioners, we find it odd that the notion of praxis was absent from our experiences. It seemed to be the exclusive domain of university scholars, even though we both could probably identify many moments in our practice that we would now classify as examples of praxis. In the scholarly world "praxis" has a long, rich history. Many scholars (e.g. Arendt, 1958; Gold, 1977; Belfiore, 1984; Bernstein, 1999) address its Ancient Greek roots, paying particular attention to Aristotle's use of the concept in his writings such as *Poetics* and *Nichomachean Ethics*. Blanchette (1979) explains, "For the Greeks, praxis meant the political activity of free men" (p. 257), and it is important to note here that "free men" meant men who were part of the aristocracy and were therefore free from labor. As it applied to the education of a citizenry, in Ancient Greece education was (at least for aristocrats) not simply about utility (Gold, 1977). Education was about culture, reason, and virtue, which "was opposed to a kind of education that was merely technical training" (p. 106). This paideia had a moral dimension that the ancient Greeks saw as an expression of the "cultural ideal of the humanity of man" (ibid.) and was captured in Aristotle's writings about ethics. Gold explains, "Praxis refers to a kind of life – a way of being – which a free [Ancient Greek] citizen was engaged in and strove for" (p. 107). We see in this Greek tradition early efforts to resist technocratic education. Yet, while the idea of praxis has always been about humanizing education, it was spawned in an unequal society – praxis was meant to be humanizing for the social elite, but it was not meant for the laboring class of Ancient Greece (Blanchette, 1979). This division between thinkers (scholars) and laborers (practitioners) was not necessarily foundational to the concept of praxis itself, but it was implied via the existing class divisions of Ancient Greek society.

Among contemporary scholars, discussions about praxis are abundant and cut across disciplines such as philosophy, education, sociology, and political science. We also see praxis cutting across disparate movements within disciplines as well. For example, Bernstein (1999) points out, "the concern with man as an agent has been the focal point of" Marxism, existentialism, prag-matism, and analytic philosophy (p. 1). So too, in the research lit-erature about education, discussions of praxis proliferate and are engaged in by scholars who identify as feminists, Marxists, prag-matists, critical theorists, and many other genres of scholarship; yet, praxis does not necessarily enter into the common discourse within teacher education programs (Korthagen & Kessels, 1999), particularly given the present standards-based climate (Sleeter, 2008). Moreover, with the trend toward alternative routes to teacher certification, a practitioner in K-12 education could fea-sibly become a teacher without ever having taken a course about pedagogy; simply having a degree indicating knowledge of one's content area is in many cases sufficient for certification (ibid.). It is worth noting that this scholar-practitioner divide has a well-documented history. Various US scholars have attributed this division to a number of causes including European Enlightenment thinking, particularly Cartesianism and the mind-body split (Kincheloe, 2003b); deprofessionalization of teaching (Labaree, 2006); the discipline of Education being viewed as a "lesser" science (Lagemann, 2000); anti-intellectualism (Macedo, 1994) and the resulting reduction of the act of teaching to a "methods fetish" (Bartolome, 1994); and the feminization of the teaching force that resulted in the teaching profession being seen as infe-rior to male-dominated professions (Perlman & Margo, 2001). While we do not discount any of these social phenomena, clearly, the privileging of mind over body, thought over labor, and schol-arship over practice has a history that stretches back over a thou-sand years. Class relations foster this division and undergird all of the aforementioned contemporary trends. Over a millennium later, our experiences of being introduced to praxis only in the academy and not as practitioners indicate that this dichotomy still resonates today.

As scholar-practitioners, we connect with Freire's notion of praxis because we believe it aims to remedy rather than reinforce social inequalities. Indeed, for Freire, a praxis that maintains oppressive relationships by upholding the knowledge hierarchies between teacher and student or scholar and practitioner, is not praxis at all; rather it is a display of power. As he explains,

Only those who have power can decide what constitutes intellectualism. Once the intellectual parameters are set, those who want to be considered intellectuals must meet the requirements of the profile dictated by the elite class. To be intellectual, one must do exactly what those with the power to define intellectualism do. (Freire in Freire & Macedo, 1987, p. 122)

He specifically critiques education as an essential mechanism of oppression and dehumanization, and he calls out the hypocritical tendencies of intellectuals who speak about freeing the masses from oppression and then infantilize them and treat them as unknowing objects upon which to impart their own superior thought. In his words,

> Sometimes educators forget to recognize that no gets from one side of the road to the other without crossing it. One can only reach the other side by starting from the opposite side. The level of my knowledge is the other side to my students. I have to begin from the opposite side, that of the students. My knowledge is my reality, not theirs. So I have to begin from their reality to bring them into my reality. (Freire, 1985, p. 189)

This does not, however, imply that the professor's knowledge is superior to the students' knowledge, simply that their knowledges have emerged in different contexts and they see the world from different vantage points. Thus, we must all be learners of each other to facilitate dialogue and catalyze conscientization (self|other|world awareness) and social change. This type of praxis requires the teacher to also be a learner because "the revolutionary party that refuses to learn with the masses of people (and by so refusing breaks the dialectical unity between 'teach' and 'learn') is not revolutionary. It has become elitist" (p. 159). In the contemporary moment in which teachers are objectified and dehumanized by educrats and students are objectified and dehumanized by teachers, praxis that has the expressed purpose of breaking down hierarchies in education and society, starting with the hierarchies within our own practice, is sorely needed. Furthermore, as our praxis is tied to conscientization and vice versa, the more we engage in working through the tensions of praxis, the more we reveal opportunities to chip away at the hegemonic structures that keep us mired in oppressive social relationships.

Freire's praxis of "uncompleteness"

Embracing this type of praxis means a radical reorientation of who we are as teachers, a reorientation that is rooted in our becoming as social beings in relationship with others and the world around us. We understand praxis as a lifelong process of learning and change, which is reflected in Freire's repeated reference to teachers as "uncomplete" (Horton & Freire, 1990). The very practice of teaching, then, can be thought of as teaching-learning. This reinforces our uncompleteness, because it implies the active participation of learners, whom we do not know, in our own education. Because we have been trained to think of ourselves as knowledgeable, as having answers, as smarter than our students, Freire's idea that we should learn with and from students is a radical departure from the teacher-student hierarchies that persist in our education systems (Freire, 2000). Yet we have only to consider the realities of our students, and the ways in which those realities diverge from ours, to understand how little we know: "To try to know the reality that our students live is a task that the educational practice imposes on us: Without this, we have no access to the way they think, so only with great difficulty can we perceive what and how they know" (Freire, 1998b, p. 58). This is an uncompleteness that persists as we teach-learn, a coming-to-know that is refreshed with each encounter we have with each student.

We are also uncomplete in the sense that we are constantly coming to know ourselves, and to embrace our limitations and foibles. Freire did not "think that educators need to be perfect saints. It is exactly as human beings, with their virtues and faults, that they should bear witness to the struggle for sobriety, for freedom, for the creation of the indispensable discipline of study . . ." (Freire, 1998b, p. 59). In praxis, we constantly engage in this process of coming to know ourselves – and this includes a knowledge of our weaknesses. Uncompleteness thus has power to increase our solidarity with our students; we know we are learners, we know we are not complete, we know we do not know. Thinking of ourselves as teacher-learners, as human people having diverse human experiences even in, and especially in, the classroom, highlights a weakness with which we in academia are not usually comfortable.

Praxis sees students and professors as co-subjects, acting on an object (which Freire defines as reality) for a greater, liberatory good (Freire, 1998a). This is revolutionary in academia, in which teachers are usually the subjects of the practice, and students the objects of the "doing" of the teacher.

Praxis exposes this oppressed-oppressor relationship and marries the teaching-learning, subject-object split that is pervasive in academia:

> The more we live critically, the more we internalize a radical and critical practice of education and the more we discover the impossibility of separating teaching and learning. The very practice of teaching involves learning on the part of those we are teaching, as well as, learning, or relearning, on the part of those who teach. (Freire, 1985, p. 177)

This co-learning positionality of praxis is not made easily operational; Freire is clear that it is a tension in which we must live, but

> For this to happen it is necessary that we transcend the monotonous, arrogant, and elitist traditionalism where the teacher knows all and the student does not know anything. Obviously, we also have to underscore that while we recognize that we have to learn from our students (whether peasants, urban workers, or graduate students), this does not mean that teachers and students are the same . . . The difference between the educator and the student is a phenomenon involving a certain permanent tension, which is, after all, the same tension that exists between theory and practice, between authority and freedom, and perhaps between yesterday and today. (ibid.)

In praxis, the teacher becomes a teacher-learner by engaging with these tensions, growing more comfortable with divergence, diversity, difference, and conflict. This is a necessary part of living and a necessary part of our praxis because as Freire explains:

> We cannot exist outside an interplay of tensions. Even those who live passively cannot escape some measure of tensions. Frequently, there is an ongoing denial of tensions, but these tensions should be understood. I believe, in fact, that one task of

radical pedagogy is to clarify the nature of tensions and how best to cope with them. (Freire in Freire & Macedo, 1987, p. 49)

The tensions of teaching-learning imply a greater love, and greater tolerance, for that which is outside our experience; teaching-learning provides us an opportunity to witness and experience that which we otherwise would not have. Praxis thus opens us to the variety of experiences of life – diverse, complex, and rife with tension – that our students and we construct.

We were taken by Freire's use of birthing imagery to describe this radical reorientation; here we see Freire returning to the idea that praxis is life. Using biblical imagery, he writes that teacher-learners "must die to their old selves as sexists, racists, and elitists and be reborn as true progressives, enlisted in the struggle for the reinvention of the world" (Freire, 1996, p. 163). We are thus born again – not to a religious dogma, but to a revolutionary love for others and an identity as a teacher-learner. He calls this experience a "conversion to the people" (Freire, 2000, p. 61). We understand Freire to mean that we experience praxis not as a one-time conversion to an ideology or dogma, but as an evolution from our old self and into our new self, furthered by increasing depths of self-criticality and experiences with our students and the world. In this way the old person and the new person are not opposites, but dialecticals – each is necessary to the other. Freire's idea of praxis, then, is a rebirthing of a new life. In fact, without uncompleteness, without an evolution toward conscientization, Freire would argue that one does not actually live because living is a process of growth and change.

We are taken with the organic descriptions Freire uses throughout his work, his attention to life itself, as evidence that Freire believed that praxis is not something that we execute, but something we are as we are with one another; it is being-doing in and with the world and those around us. Indeed, Freire was often mystified by professionals who thought that education was anything other than our experiences with one another, a dialogic encounter that is "an existential necessity" (p. 88). Our professional lives are thus reimagined as ontological learning encounters that happen within human experience, an ongoing dialogue that transforms us from teachers to teacher-learners.

"Doing" praxis: Dialoguing with Freire in Recife

If praxis is lived in dialogue with others, then there is only so much decontextualized theorizing that can be done before praxis loses its potency to abstraction. To understand praxis in a more holistic way, we must examine it as it is lived. For this reason, we turn our attention now to examples of praxis as they appear in Freire's work. In 1947, Freire began working at Service Social de l'industrie (SESI), Brazil, in what he describes as a "reencounter with working-class reality" (1996, p. 81), a return to interactions with the lower social classes that had also been formative in his growing up years. SESI, he explains, was a social service agency established by the "paternalistic leadership to further its contradictory relationship with the working class" (p. 82). For Freire, SESI represented an attempt by the dominant class to subdue the lower classes with hand-outs in the hopes that the tensions between classes, which had been rising in Brazil during that time, would de-escalate. As such, SESI was not interested in participatory, democratic forms of service; it tried to suffocate critical education with the guise of politically free, value-neutral training. Nevertheless, Freire was determined to enact democratic forms of education within that context, and it was a life-changing experience for him that directly informed his praxis. He explains, "[Teaching near Recife with the workers] was a beautiful experience. I learned how to discuss with people. I learned how to respect their knowledge, their beliefs, their fears, their hopes, their expectations, their language. It took time and many meetings" (p. 65). He spends many pages discussing the different democratic measures he undertook as a director then superintendent in the SESI, and he specifically notes that it was through his mistakes that he learned to respect the people with whom he worked, including all stakeholders in the educational process, especially those who were typically left out of conversations about education.

In writing about his time at SESI with such care, Freire opens up his teaching/learning space for others to consider and critique, and he models for us a way of opening up our practice of educating (both teaching and administering education) to the people with whom we work. In this way, the entirety of his practice was fodder for an open dialogue that necessitated multiple interpretations and perspectives from others as well as an unwavering humility from Freire. It is important to note here that humility was not just about allowing for multiple points of view, it was also about allowing others to exercise their power as Freire ceded his own. Thus, in this section, it feels appropriate for us to enter into conversation with Freire around praxis. What follows are two of Freire's accounts from his work at SESI, with our reflections and comments on praxis within them. We have used text boxes to "interject" our separate voices so as to: 1) analyze and comment on how those experiences embody the kind of praxis Freire has taught us, and 2) show how this informs our understanding of praxis as the life of the teacher-learner that is at the heart of this article. Our goal in approaching Freire's praxis (and our praxis) in this way is to create openings for furthering our praxis in the future, as we reflect on our practice and open and humble ourselves as teacher-learners engaging in the perpetual tensions of teaching-learning.

First account: Contradictions in practice

In this account, Freire writes about his work as director of SESI's Division of Education and Culture. At the prompting of several parents, Freire and his coworkers reimagined their meetings with parents, other teachers, and the community, using participant-chosen themes to guide discussions and to generate dialogue and debate. What follows is an excerpt in which Freire explains how and why these changes were made.

Melisssa: I like Freire's honesty about their mistakes because it speaks to the ways we can be evolving in praxis – we can be thinking critically, but not yet doing critically. This describes me still in so many areas of my teaching and learning, and I feel hopeful that Freire is so honest not just about making a mistake, but making it for a long period of time. We see here that he is a teacher-learner, albeit in imperfect and unfolding ways. He

. . . We learned a great deal from our initial mistakes, both in the preparation of teachers and in our work with parents. In both cases we were is patient with his process; we talk a lot about the openness we need with others in praxis, but here we see that openness for Freire is also something he gives himself. He is open to his own mistakes; he both expects himself to make them and expects himself to change.

absolutely correct in the objectives of our practice and wrong in the method we used to achieve our objectives. We contradicted ourselves. We opted for an education that called for the development of critical postures that favored choices and decision making, and relied on rigorous analysis of facts. We contradicted ourselves, first, by not listening to the people with whom we were working concerning what they would like to discuss and, second, by choosing ourselves the lecture themes . . .

Tricia: It is easy to espouse a critical stance without being radical in our practice. I think here about trust and respect; we must trust in and respect our and our students' knowledges in the classroom. As critical educators, we can speak about social justice and educating for democracy, but it is much harder to teach democratically and in socially just ways. I think this has to do with the comfort of the teacher-learner relationship that has been passed down to us culturally: teacher is knowledgable and power holder; student is not knowledgable and powerless. And we work in hierarchical educational systems; teachers may have more power than students, but this does not mean they are empowered. Curriculum is provided, evaluations are administered; teachers are dehumanized too. Venturing into unknown territory, breaking these norms, is scary. How do we know without the crutch of authoritarian relationships, standards, and assessment tools that learning is happening?

Melissa: I'm really struck here by the impact of another person's voice to bring about learning. Freire is saying something profound here – that we learn in social interaction, in with-ness with

While trying to overcome our mistakes and errors, we heard a mild, almost one another, in a radical listening (Tobin, 2009) to another. He's also saying, I think, that these learnings – earlier he called this existential learning, when we learn from people – are those that we remember best. I see here that even a quiet voice has potential to transform our work, if we are humble enough to listen to quiet voices, to see them as different from ours and pregnant with alternative perspectives and possibilities for change.

polite, criticism of our work from a parent of one of our students. This criticism had an extraordinary impact on my colleagues at SESI in Recife and me.

At a meeting we had finished talking about the duty of the school to respect the knowledge that students bring to school. Seated in the front row was a young father who, uninhibited, got up and said, "If you ask me if I like this meeting, I am not going to say no because I learned some things from the professor's words. But if you ask me if this is what I wanted to learn today, I would say no. What I wanted to learn today is how to discipline, since my wife and I are having problems with the kids at home and we don't know how to solve them."

The same thing would happen at teacher training sessions. We would discuss the same themes debated in the circles for parents and teachers. The themes were not arbitrarily chosen by other persons in the group or me; they would emerge from our visits to the social nucleus of SESI, the schools, and talks

Tricia: This section also speaks to me because of the intention. He points out that the themes they chose came directly from visits to schools and their talks with teachers, but what they identified to use as themes still were not necessarily relevant to those they worked with. This hints at questions regarding the nature of "democratic practice." Is soliciting input democratic practice? Is taking into consideration the needs of others democratic practice? Perhaps, democratic practice is more than this; it necessitates more than the educator's design and implementation of the learning activity. We must allow those whom we work with to lead us, in the moment. Yet, I also hear my doctoral students' voices in my head as I write this, "But with teachers. But, the fact remained that it was only coincidence when the theme we talked about

I have to cover the standards. I will be held accountable. The students still need to know how to do multiplication and use correct grammar." I wonder, how do we develop trust in the process of teaching and learning with students?

coincided with the expectations of the participants.

Melissa: As a former professional developer for a large school district, I find painful resonance with Freire's comment that meeting participants' expectations is arbitrary at best. I think about how much time I spent "teaching" material that for many teachers didn't seem relevant to them; I think about how much time we spent trying to convince them it was relevant, or that they would need it "someday." For me, Freire's comment speaks to ways we could contextualize and localize professional knowledge as knowledge within the teachers, what they know, what they want to know, and how they come to know. Like you, Tricia, I wonder how this is done within a system that is mandating particular skill sets for teachers, particular kinds of professional development taught at particular times. I think we must seek out ways that humanize teacher education; how else can we expect ourselves to teach democratically, if we are not being developed and grown in such a way? It is asynchronous for teachers to be trained within a banking model of professional development, and then to be teaching our own students democratically. We can do better.

From that night on, we understood that we would have to deepen our democratic experience. We began to ask the participants, teachers and parents, what fundamental themes should make up the agenda for the next meeting . . .

. . . With greater participation of parents encouraged by the ability to suggest themes for the meetings and prepare for these meetings and with the critical involvement of teachers and students, circle attendance by both parents and teachers rose substantially. We also began to observe marked differences in the students' behaviors in school.

Schools and parents began to understand each other better because they knew each other more, which diminished their mutual lack of trust. (Freire, 1996, pp. 90–2)

Second account: Praxis in the workplace

Later, Freire's role at SESI changed from the director of a division of education to that of superintendent. There, too, Freire continued his efforts to democratize the organization, this time facilitating dialogue between all departments, and all the levels of the hierarchy, of SESI staff. Freire suggested Saturday morning meetings; the meetings were organized to include a presentation from a particular person within the organization. This person would describe his/her daily practices at SESI and then the group would talk about the presentation. Friere reported that the debates and rich dialogue during these meetings did much to improve relationships among SESI staff. What follows is an excerpt regarding the fourth of these Saturday morning meetings.

At the fourth meeting, Francisco, the janitor with the most seniority, was chosen to lead the discussion. He was to talk about his work, his day-to-day routine, the positive or negative aspects of his work, and how the directors, in general, related to him. . .

Melissa: I am noticing Freire's emphasis in this narrative on relationships. It's interesting to note here that the work of praxis – theory/practice to transform – happens in the context of relationships, and that relationships must have particular characteristics in order to further praxis: trust, mutual respect, and openness.

The relationships among personnel became so much better that during the meetings we advanced to analyzing our practices. These relationships enhanced our work so much that we unveiled the theory embedded in our practice . . .

. . . It is worth describing the emotion and self-assurance with which Francisco, the senior janitor, spoke and the impact that his words had on everyone. He began by saying that, "I don't have much to say about my day's work in D.R. [the regional office of SESI]. I am only a janitor doing my job, cleaning rooms and desks, buying cigarettes for the professors, serving their coffee, taking documents from one office to another. Only when I found out that I was to speak to all these people today, either by ad-libbing or by reading, did I begin to ask what it is that I do during a day at work and in life.

"I do a lot of things. First, by adding one day to another, I create a month during which I earned, with much sweat, my family's sustenance. Second, I work because I don't know how to live without work. My day is like those of millions of Brazilians and better than those millions of others who don't even have the little I have.

Melissa: I really admire the way Francisco begins his critical reflections; they are rooted in his own confusion, his own curiosity, his own re-imaginings of how things could be different. The humility with which he expresses his imagination, his emphasis on improving his own understanding (here we see praxis as evolution again), is beautiful.

"I am happy with my day-to-day life. I am humble. But there are some things that I don't understand and should mention to all of you. For example, when I enter a director's office with the coffee tray and he is in a meeting with other

---

Tricia: As someone who has worked service jobs, whose husband works a service job, and is the daughter of parents who worked service jobs, the dehumanization in the coffee incident is very real to me. Servers are often rendered invisible. I see this too in the university where people who are supposedly progressive educators interested in social justice, scarcely make eye contact with secretaries and facilities staff. I feel guilty by association, knowing that I am among the ranks of often self-absorbed academics. I hear my

professors, no one looks at me or answers when I say good morning to them.

> father's voice instructing me to treat everyone with respect, to call them by name, to greet them and thank them. Praxis cannot cease when we leave our classrooms; if it does, we are not critical, we are hypocritical.

They only grab their coffee cups and never once say, even to be different, thank-you. Sometimes I am called in by a director and he gives me money to buy him a pack of cigarettes. I go, I go down the stairs if the elevator is taking too long, I cross the street, I buy the cigarettes, I return, I give the cigarettes to the director. 'Here,' another director will tell me, giving me some change, 'bring me some matches.' Why don't they discuss what they want so I can take care of it in one trip? Why go up and down, down and up, just to buy a little bit each time?

"I think these meetings are going to help make things better. I understand much more about the work of a lot of people. I did not know what many of them did.

"I hope that those who never said good morning or thank-you don't become angry with a humble janitor. I told these stories because they are part of my day-to-day routine as janitor here in D.R."

> **Melissa:** Francisco uses the word "humble" twice. At first, I understood this as a public recognition of his social status – he is informing the group that he knows he is not a power-holder, that he knows his position as a janitor is not as powerful as theirs. But also, as we think about what humility means for us teacher-learners who are evolving in praxis, there is something more here. We see in Francisco a thoughtfulness about his practices, and an openness to other's perceptions of his input. I find this noteworthy. Francisco seems to understand (maybe because of his marginalized status, he has more experience with this; it is the powerful who are more accustomed to knowing/hearing only their own powerful perspectives) that there are other perceptions of reality other than his in the world. Still, and this is what I find the most powerful of all, he believes that his

experience, perception, and recommendations for change, are worthwhile. I love this version of humility – aware of power structures, open to others, and convinced that the input of all stakeholders matters.

One could sense in the silence, in the fidgeting of bodies on chairs, the discomfort that Francisco's comments had caused those who had never said good morning to him or thanked him for his services. His social claims are as relevant today as they were yesterday. . . . Our elitism does not allow us to perceive the lack of coherence between our liberatory discourse and our indifferent attitude toward people, who have been reduced to almost thing-like status. This is not a minor problem. (Freire, 1996, p. 95–7)

> Tricia: I see discomfort as a necessary part of change, and praxis. I consider discomfort to be a healthy indicator that something within us is being dislodged. In this case, Francisco revealed the tendency of academics to be elitist. Francisco was blatantly shown on a daily basis that the professors saw him as "thing-like"; revealing this to them made them physically uncomfortable. As a professor, I have been confronted with discomfort, usually when I least expect it, and often when my presuppositions have been exposed to me through others' eyes. The key to discomfort as a catalyst for praxis, I believe, lies in our openness to being made uncomfortable by others, which requires a fair amount of humility.

Living within the tensions of praxis

"After all, cynicism is not the weapon that will rebuild the world."

Freire, 1996, p. 161

As we think together about what we have learned from dialoguing with Freire vis-a-vis his experiences, I (Melissa) am reminded of a telling remark made to me by a colleague a few weeks ago. Together we were creating a new writing course within the English department of our community college; in the spirit of brainstorming, I began to talk about ways we could model for the students the writers and researchers we want them to be. My colleague stopped me short with these words: "Melissa, you are assuming that our students want to be like us." I felt immediately as if Freire were speaking to me, and was immediately interested in my assumptions and how I came to believe that I was the embodiment of what my students should want to become in any way. I began to think about my training as a writing teacher, and how much of it was in fact grounded in this idea that I want students to imitate me in writing, in research, and in academic habit. The comment was sobering, of course, but it also delighted me, because it was so immediately obvious to me that I am still evolving in praxis, still working at this identity of teacher-learner, and I find that process to be a compelling and fruitful one.

In reflecting on our above dialogue with Freire and the comment made by Melissa's colleague, I (Tricia) think about how easy it is to reach for sameness and familiarity, to hold deep down the desire to bring others into our worlds without reaching enough toward theirs, and to exert our power as educators to do so. In my own practice, it feels as if I wrestle with this tension constantly: how can I encourage the co-construction of dialogic learning spaces in which my students and I feel free to think and be different? How do I not use my power as an educator to enforce a new "critical" hegemonic discourse when it is so easy to fall back on talking at students about criticality and not engaging in the world critically with them? How can we forge spaces within the teacher-learner tensions where we can feel at ease with disagreeing about what teaching and learning should look and feel like, and we recognize that we can and should experience these things differently? How easy it is to overlay my preconceptions onto others in order to support my own worldview before making the difficult attempt to understand others on their own terms and challenge what I know as truth. The tensions of praxis invite me to be a teacher-learner in these moments if I am open to listening.

In the Eleventh Letter in Letters to Cristina, Freire recalls "the hat incident" that he noted was "an exemplary case for [him]." As he explains, an administrative director came to him to say he was going to "standardize the janitors' hats at SESI." In fact, the order for the hats had already been placed, but without ever consulting the janitors about whether they wanted hats at all and if so, if these hats were acceptable. Freire recommended the director ask the janitors' opinions first, because "The fact is that a hat alters a person's face and we don't have the right to change anybody's face without his or her consent." So the following week, the director called a meeting with the janitors and learned that nobody wanted hats. Freire asks: "How many hats have been imposed on us without our consent and in the name of our self-interest and welfare?" (Freire, 1996, p. 107). And in turn, how many hats have we ourselves imposed upon others in an attempt to change them? Our reflections remind us of Freire's admonition:

> The radical has to be an active presence in the educational practice. But the educators should never allow his or her active and curious presence to transform learners' presences into shadows of the educator's presence. Neither can the educator be the shadow of the learners. The educator has to stimulate learners to live a critically conscious presence in the pedagogical and historical process. (Freire in Freire & Macedo, 1987, p. 14)

In the current climate of education in the United States, unfortunately, there seems to be a lot of "shadowing" going on, whether it is teachers in the shadows of curriculum "experts" and policy-makers, or students in the shadow of teachers; we are all in the shadow of the mythical beast of "accountability." If learning is too strictly standardized, "success" in education can mean little else than sameness, and we fall into a necrophilic education that threatens to suck the life out of teaching and learning.

There is a danger, in embracing praxis, of holding too firmly to the ways in which we come to know, and what we come to know. When we do so in ways that exclude our students from engaging in their own praxis, we have not learned at all. Thus, praxis is both a humble process, and an open one. We are open to new ideas, new people, new faces, new interpretations of reality, new understandings of praxis, new criticisms of our work. If praxis is life, then it cannot be concretized. Instead, it is organic, fluid, unpredictable, and wild. Freire (1985) reminds educators like us to "each day be open to the world, be ready to think; each day be ready not to accept what is said just because it is said, be predisposed to reread what is read; each day investigate, question, and doubt. I think it is most necessary to doubt. I feel it is always necessary not to be sure, that is, to be overly sure of 'certainties'" (p. 181). We want to doubt and learn again what praxis means; dialoguing with Freire has shown us that we can and must return, again and again, to our praxis; that in practice, as in life, we are always uncomplete, and should feel free to be so, completely and without inhibition. For Freire, this was perhaps the biggest lesson to take away regarding praxis: "For me the fundamental thing in life is to work in life to create an existence overflowing from life, a life that is well thought-out, a created and re-created life, a life that is touched and made and remade in this existence. The more I do something, the more I exist. And I exist immensely" (p. 195). With/in the tensions of praxis, we learn and relearn the immenseness of our wonderfully diverse lives.

References

Arendt, H. (1958). *The human condition.* Chicago, IL: University of Chicago Press.

Bartolome, L. (1994). "Beyond the methods fetish: Toward a humanizing pedagogy." *Harvard Educational Review*, 64 (2), 173–94.

Belfiore, E. (1984). "Aristotle's concept of praxis in The Poetics." *The Classical Journal*, 79 (2), 110–24.

Bernstein, R. (1999). *Praxis and action: Contemporary philosophies of human activity.* Philadelphia, PA: University of Pennsylvania Press.

Blanchett, O. (1979). "Praxis and labor in Hegel." *Studies in Soviet Thought*, 20, 257–69.

Deslatte, M. (2011). BESE approves teacher evaluation standards. *The Times-Picayne.* Retrieved from www.nola.com/education/index. ssf/2011/12/bese_approves_teacher_Evaluati.html

Freire, P. (1985). *The Politics of education: Culture, power, and liberation.* South Hadley, MA: Bergin & Garvey.

— (1996). *Letters to Cristina: Reflections on my life and work*, trans. D. Macedo, Q. Macedo, and A. Oliveira. New York, NY: Routledge.

— (1998a). *Education for critical consciousness*, trans. M. B. Ramos. New York, NY: Continuum (Original work published 1969).

— (1998b). *Teachers as cultural workers: Letters to those who dare to teach*, trans. D. Macedo, D. Koike, and A. Oliveira. Boulder, CO: Westview Press.

— (2000). *Pedagogy of the oppressed*, trans. M. B. Ramos. New York, NY: Continuum (Original work published 1970).

Freire, P. and Macedo, D. (1987). *Literacy: Reading the word and the world*. South Hadley, MA: Bergin & Garvey.

Giroux, H. (2010). *Dumbing down teachers: Attacking colleges of education in the name of reform*. ZNet. Retrieved from www. zcommunications.org/dumbing-down-teachers-by-henry-giroux

Gold, H. B. (1977). "Praxis: Its conceptual development in Aristotle's Nichomachean Ethics." *Graduate Faculty Philosophy Journal*, 6 (1), 106–30.

Horton, M. and Freire, P. (1990). *We make the road by walking: Conversations on education and social change*. B. Bell, J. Gaventa, and J. Peters (eds). Philadelphia, PA: Temple University Press.

Isensee, L. and Butrymowicz, S. (2011). "Florida teacher evaluations tied to student test scores." *The Huffington Post*. Retrieved from www. huffingtonpost.com/2011/11/07/florida-teacher-evaluatio_n_1079758. html

Kincheloe, J. L. (2003a). "Critical ontology: Visions of selfhood and curriculum." *Journal of Curriculum Theorizing*, 19 (1), 47–64.

— (2003b). *Teachers as researchers: Qualitative inquiry as a path to empowerment* (2nd edn). New York, NY: Routledge.

Korthagen, F. A. J. and Kessels, J. P. A. M. (1999). "Linking theory to practice: Changing the pedagogy of teacher education." *Educational Researcher*, 28 (4), 4–17.

Labaree, D. (2006). *The Trouble with Ed. Schools*. New Haven, CT: Yale University Press.

Lagemann, E. C. (2000). *An Elusive Science: The Troubling History of Educational Research*. Chicago, IL: University of Chicago Press.

Macedo, D. (1994). "Preface." In P. McLaren and C. Lankshear (eds). *Conscientization and resistance* (pp. 1–8). New York, NY: Routledge.

McGuire, K. (2012). "Like never before, teachers under scrutiny." *St. Paul Star Tribune*. Retrieved from www.startribune.com/local/ stpaul/144099296.html

Perlman, J. and Maro, R. A. (2001). *Women's work?: American schoolteachers, 1650–1920*. Chicago, IL: University of Chicago Press.

Planas, R. (2012). "Neither banned nor allowed: Mexican American studies in limbo in Arizona." *Fox News Latino*. Retrieved from http:// latino.foxnews.com/latino/news/2012/04/19/neither-banned-nor-allow ed-mexican-american-studies-in-limbo-in-arizona/

Sleeter, C. (2008). "Equity, democracy, and neoliberal assaults on teacher education." *Teaching and Teacher Education*, 24 (8), 1947–57.

Tobin, K. (2009). "Tuning into others' voices: Radical listening, learning from difference, and escaping oppression." *Cultural Studies of Science Education*, 4, 505–11.

9

Paulo Freire's Concept of Conscientização

Ana L. Cruz

Introduction

Paulo Freire (1921–97), born in Brazil, is considered a major theorist, philosopher and educator of international stature. On April 13, 2012, per Law 12.612, he was declared the "Patron of Education," by the Brazilian government. Paulo Freire commenced his work in education in the northeastern state of Pernambuco until imprisoned and subsequently exiled in the wake of a military coup d'état in 1964 that subjugated Brazil under a military dictatorship for 20 years. Freire, thereafter, worked in different countries, including a long spell with the World Council of Churches based in Geneva, Switzerland. These professional commitments allowed Freire to travel and lecture internationally, to work on international education projects, and to write. Freire longed to return to his native country and he finally moved back to Brazil in 1980, after 15¹/₂ years in exile. Freire's return to Brazil was a very emotional event, as he recounts "My first contact with Brazil, with the people, with the smell of the land, my contact with the curves of the streets, with the Portuguese language" (1984, p. 513). Freire and his family settled in São Paulo where he continued his academic career, interrupted by two years as secretary of education in São Paulo (for the PT—Partido dos Trabalhadores—which at the time was leading the government in São Paulo), the largest municipality in Brazil, where he was in charge of the school system.

Freire was a prolific writer and his publications are numerous, often translated into other languages from the Brazilian Portuguese. Freire's bibliography can be a difficult thicket to penetrate; publications by Gerhardt (1993), A. M. Freire (also called Nita) (2006), and Anonymous (n.d.), however, can provide a good access to it.

Paulo Freire's educational philosophy is commonly associated with concepts such as theory and practice, praxis, the banking model of education/problem-posing model of education, the political nature of education, culture circles, dialogue, and *conscientização* (e.g. Schugurensky, 1998). This chapter will focus on the latter, trying to provide the reader with an understanding of this rather complex and evolving concept.

To fully understand Paulo Freire's work, some salient points are worth pondering. First, Paulo Freire's love for conversation and dialogue is evident in many of his books. His writing often seems to follow a conversational style, where he appears to meander between topics and thoughts, only to return to topics and thoughts already addressed earlier but further elaborating on them. Paulo Freire also always seems to have a "story" to tell, interjecting it into the narrative, based on his practical teaching experiences, for the purpose of illustrating complex concepts. Paulo Freire's writing style reflects an emphasis on oral communication and conversation often encountered in Brazil. Second, to fully appreciate the work, one needs to be cognizant of Paulo Freire's situatedness in time and history. Freire's publication history spans 39 years (not considering the works published posthumously), with each publication marked by the geographical and social-political-economical situation at that time. More importantly, the history of Brazil—from precolonial, colonial, to modern Brazil—is reflected in Paulo's work; therefore, to fully understand Paulo Freire's work it is imperative to know Brazilian history and world events that shaped that history. Third, Paulo Freire published in Brazilian Portuguese with an added emphasis on literary quality. Freire's language is precise and often very poetic; it certainly conveys optimism and hope. Despite the valiant efforts of Freire's translators (most notably Donaldo Macedo)—considering here translation into English—it is very difficult to convey the "real" Paulo Freire in translation. Macedo (1985) addresses this issue succinctly. To read the "real" Paulo

Freire is to read his work in the original, there always is something missing in translation (e.g. Borg & Mayo, 2000). Fourth, Paulo Freire's books were translated into many languages, but these different-language editions do not always coincide with respect to content. In other words, the "same" books might not only have different prefaces, introductions, postscripts, etc., but sections of the original text might have been deleted and/or additional material in the form of extra chapters might appear. Fifth, Paulo Freire's work evolved with time. This means, not only are new topics and issues added with time, broadening Freire's scholarly ouevre, but the same concept, once introduced and discussed, may be revisited later, re-elaborated (Borg & Mayo, 2000) and amended in unison with the evolving thoughts of Freire, all within the changing context of geography and time. Paulo Freire's thirst for learning never waned, he aged but the spirit of curiosity and intellectual adventure remained with him; it allowed him to "stay young" even as he physically grew older. Sixth, Paulo Freire' was very strongly shaped by Catholicism; it left a very strong impression on him and his work based on his early education and the strong influence of his catholic mother (Freire, 1972; Elias, 1976; Walker, 1981; Schipani, 1984; Kirylo, 2011). Some of this impression is reflected in many of his publications by his choice of words and use of metaphors.

Origin of the word *Conscientização*

The word *conscientização* comes from Brazilian Portuguese. The etymological roots are in the Latin *conscientia*, which means joint knowledge, consciousness, feeling, or sense. In Portuguese the noun is consciência, and also the verb conscientizar exists, meaning to raise somebody's awareness. The word *conscientização* was formed by adding the suffix –ção to the verb conscientizar, thus creating a new noun; –ção refers to process and, therefore, *conscientização* can be literally translated as the *process* used to raise somebody's awareness. The common English translation of *conscientização* is conscientization. *Conscientização* has a very specific meaning and significance in Paulo Freire's work and it will be used in its original Portuguese instead of its English "translation" throughout this chapter; as a matter of fact, it is appropriate to concur with Freire (1971, 1972) who believed that the word should be adopted unchanged into English.

Paulo Freire, however, was not the one to coin the word *conscientização* (Freire, 1971, 1972). Concerning this matter Freire (2001a) elaborates

> It is believed that I am the author of this strange term conscientização because it is the core concept of my ideas about education. In reality, it was created by a group of professors from the Instituto Superior de Estudos Brasileiros [Higher Institute of Brazilian Studies] around 1964. Among them, it can be mentioned, the names of the philosopher Álvaro [Vieira] Pinto and professor [Alberto] Guerreiro [Ramos]. As I heard the word conscientização for the first time, I immediately realized its profound meaning, because I am absolutely convinced that education, as practice for liberty, is an act of knowing, a critical move toward reality.[1] (p. 29)

He continues

> Since then, this word became part of my vocabulary. However, it was Hélder Câmara who took the lead in diffusing and translating it into English and French.[2] (ibid.)

Paulo Freire's concept of *Conscientização*

The concept of *conscientização* is at the heart of Paulo Freire's pedagogy and was introduced and particularly addressed by Freire (1970, 1992, 1994, 2005). *Conscientização* was defined in Freire (1970) as

> [. . .] the process in which men, not as recipients, but as knowing subjects, achieve a deepening awareness both of the sociocultural reality that shapes their lives and of their capacity to transform that reality. (p. 519)

Conscientização, therefore, is the active process through which a critical understanding of the social-political-economical circumstances is gained that enables one to actively change oppressive circumstances. To consider the concept of *conscientização* as a process merely to increase awareness is inaccurate; *conscientização* always will include the next step, to actively transform the circumstances that cause oppression (Freire, 1994). According to Freire (1972)

> Conscientization [*conscientização*] implies, then, that when I realize that I am oppressed, I also know I can liberate myself if I transform the concrete situation where I find myself oppressed. Obviously, I can't transform it in my head: that would be to fall into the philosophical error of thinking that awareness "creates" reality, I would be decreeing that I am free, by my mind. And yet, the structures would continue to be the same as ever—so that I wouldn't be free. No, conscientization [*conscientização*] implies a critical insertion into a process, it implies a historical commitment to make changes. (p. 5)

And, Freire continues

> Conscientization [*conscientização*], then, is the most critical approach conceivable to reality, stripping it down so as to get to know it and know the myths that deceive and perpetuate the dominating structure. (p. 6)

Conscientização also involves two other Freirean concepts: the concept of praxis, that is, the continuing dialectic relationship of action and reflection; and the concept of dialogue (Freire, 1994). To be discussed as part of *conscientização* are different levels of consciousness (Freire, 1992, 2005): (magical) semi-intransitive consciousness, naïve transitive consciousness, and critical transitive consciousness. Freire (2005) characterizes semi-intransitive consciousness as

> [. . .] his [her] sphere of perception is limited, that he [she] is impermeable to challenges situated outside the sphere of biological necessity. [. . .] represents a near disengagement between men [women] and their existence. [. . .] Men [women]

confuse their perceptions of the objects and challenges of the
environment, and fall prey to magical explanations because they
cannot apprehend true causality. (p. 13)

Naïve transitive consciousness, in contrast, is characterized by
Freire

> by an over-simplification of problems; by nostalgia for the past;
> by underestimation of the common man; by a strong tendency to
> gregariousness; by a lack of interest in investigation, accompanied
> by an accentuated taste for fanciful explanations; by fragility
> of argument; by a strongly emotional style; by the practice of
> polemics rather than dialogue; by magical explanations. (p. 14)

According to Freire (2005), there is also the danger that naïve
transitive consciousness can develop into fanaticism through
sectarian irrationality. Critical transitive consciousness, then, is
characterized

> by depth in the interpretation of problems; by the substitution
> of causal principles for magical explanations; by the testing of
> one's "findings" and by openness to revisions; by the attempt
> to avoid distortion when perceiving problems and to avoid
> preconceived notions when analyzing them; by refusing to transfer
> responsibility; by rejecting passive positions; by soundness of
> argumentation; by the practice of dialogue rather than polemics;
> by receptivity to the new for reasons beyond mere novelty and
> by the good sense not to reject the old just because it is old—by
> accepting what is valid in both old and new. (ibid.)

Conscientização is often viewed as leading from magical consciousness eventually to critical consciousness, with the different
levels of consciousness neatly separated (Wilson, 2008). This view
of *conscientização* is referred to as the stage model (Roberts, 2010).
However, Roberts (2010) argues that, closer to Freire's view, the
boundaries between the different levels of consciousness are not as
rigid, that there can be a certain amount of overlap. In addition,
Roberts (2010) contends that an individual can exhibit characteristics of different levels of consciousness, different with respect to
"the sphere of that person's life under examination" (p. 153).

Because Freire felt that the concept of *conscientização* was much misunderstood, he quit using the word in 1974 (Freire, 1984). He was often portrayed as an idealist, believing that by raising critical consciousness and recognizing oppressive circumstances alone, these oppressive circumstances would be overcome (e.g. Freire, 1998); this reading of Freire is unfounded because it overlooks the facet of *conscientização* that demands action to overcome oppressive circumstances after they are recognized. Paulo Freire, however, never gave up on the concept (Freire & Vittoria, 2007) and returned to writing about and using the word again in the early 1990s.

Some philosophical influences

Paulo Freire's work was influenced by a broad and eclectic set of philosophers and social scientists. Freire was an ardent reader who never lost his sense of curiosity. Nita Freire, in her book *Paulo Freire—Uma História da Vida* (2006), listed the authors who were referenced in each of the numerous books written by Paulo Freire. Mackie (1981) offers an introduction to the intellectual roots of Paulo Freire's work, the individuals who influenced his thinking and the resulting pedagogy. With respect to political philosophy (Mackie, 1981; Gerhardt, 1993), Freire's early work (from his doctoral thesis *Educação Atualidade Brasileira* (1959; published in 2001) to *Educação como Práctica da Liberdade* (1992)) was framed by a liberal democratic political philosophy that changed to a more radical political philosophy with *Pedagogy of the Oppressed* (manuscript 1968, published 1970), "[c]ultural integration changed into political revolution" (Gerhardt, 1993, p. 8). This change in political philosophy also affected Freire's concept of *conscientização*. According to Gerhardt (1993), praxis, the continuing dialectical relationship of action and reflection, at the heart of the concept of *conscientização*, "[. . .] became a more revolutionary praxis, and a greater emphasis was placed on the subject of commitment for and with the oppressed" (p. 9). Gerhardt, citing Simpfendörfer, continues

In his letter of acceptance to the World Council of Churches, Freire, in line with his new thinking stated emphatically: "You must know that I have taken a decision. My case is the case of the wretched of the earth. You should know that I opted for revolution." (ibid.)

This change in political philosophy coincided with the military coup d'état in 1964 (Mackie, 1981), the political developments on the South American continent, and the experiences of Freire during his Chilean years of exile. Once again it is important to emphasize that Freire's work is always immersed in the context of the time and grounded on the present social-political-economical circumstances.

Educação como Práctica da Liberdade (Freire, 1992), the book that laid the foundation for Freire's concept of *conscientização*, provides references to works by 45 different authors (as documented by Nita Freire, 2006). This book drew from liberal democratic sources and Freire was heavily influenced at that time by the writings of John Dewey, Karl Popper, Karl Mannheim, Seymour Lipset, and Alfred Whitehead (Mackie, 1981). In addition, Freire also drew from the work of Brazilian thinkers, such as Álvaro Vieira Pinto, Guerreiro Ramos, Anísio Teixeira, Gilberto Freyre, and Fernando de Azevedo, among others. The Brazilian context is, of course, especially important. The rural and poor Brazilian Northeast is Paulo Freire's homeland, the geographic and cultural place where he grew up, studied, and worked as an educator. The distribution of wealth in Brazil in general was particularly skewed toward the few at the expense of the broader population, with a democratic system that prohibited illiterate people—the vast majority of people of voting age—from voting. The left-of-center federal government continued to pursue agrarian reforms that would lead to redistribution of land, a policy opposed by conservative groups, their wealthy supporters, and the military. This time in Brazilian history was also marked by a growing Brazilian national consciousness, an understanding by segments of the Brazilian society to create a genuine culture rooted in Brazil (ibid.), and not blindly adopting the way of North American and European cultures/societies. Of special importance in this respect was the Instituto Superior de Estudos Brasileiros (ISEB; Higher Institute of Brazilian Studies), which was created by the federal government in 1955 and existed until the military coup d'état in 1964. ISEB brought together intellectuals who "took Brazilian reality as their project, seeking to identify themselves with the country as it really was rather than continuing to perceive it through European eyes" (p. 94), intellectuals viewed as "defenders of an authentic developmental model for the country" (Gerhardt, 1993, p. 3). The influence of ISEB's work on the history of Brazil, cultural mimicry (Ramos, 1957), and development of a Brazilian cultural consciousness is clearly discernible in *Educação como Práctica da Liberdade*, where Freire addresses Brazilian history extensively and uses timeframes in Brazilian history to "illustrate" the different stages of consciousness. The origin of the word *conscientização*, Freire (2001a) clearly ascribes to the work within ISEB, going even so far as to give Álvaro Vieira Pinto and Alberto Guerreiro Ramos direct credit. Paulo Freire (2001b) makes clear the intellectual link and exchange between himself and ISEB researchers; in a footnote he explains

[. . .] the problem of the naïve consciousness and critical consciousness has been debated by a group of Brazilian professors. Professor Vieira Pinto, Guerreiro Ramos, Roland Corbisier, among others. From the first [Vieira Pinto] very soon will become available a detailed study in which he discusses this theme thoroughly. I had, however, already written this chapter when, in conversation with this master, I was informed of his study.[3] (pp. 33, 34)

Álvaro Vieira Pinto was the head of ISEB's Philosophy Department and later became head of ISEB, following Corbisier, until the dissolution of ISEB in the wake of the military coup d'état. In 1960 Vieira Pinto published the two-volume *Consciência e Realidade Nacional* (Pinto, 1960). In the aforementioned footnote, Paulo Freire (2001b) also addresses some published work by Guerreiro Ramos regarding critical consciousness, the way in which he disagrees in part with Guerreiro Ramos' findings, how he reached his own conclusions, and proposed new ways of looking at critical consciousness. Paulo Freire was clearly aware of the work of the ISEBeans (i.e. ISEB intellectuals) including their ongoing discussions of yet unpublished work. ISEBeans and Freire thought about different levels of consciousness but disagreed on details. Freire stressed that critical consciousness needed to be reached through a process involving education and that critical consciousness was not reached by gaining a certain level in historical development (e.g.

the industrialized stage); for Freire, critical consciousness has to develop from below—by being active, it cannot be superimposed from top-down on people.

Paulo Freire was also influenced by radical catholic groups that worked throughout Brazil, especially in impoverished and rural areas, to improve the living conditions and also the social structure of the local populace (De Kadt, 1970). Paulo Freire, together with his first wife Elza, was involved in this movement in the city of Recife, Pernambuco (e.g. Kirylo, 2011).

Overall, it is important to mention that, even though Freire's thoughts were influenced by the philosophers and social scientists of his time and of the past, Freire managed to always propose authentic and revolutionary ideas that led to immediate or future practical application.

Importance of Paulo Freire's concept of *Conscientização* today

Paulo Freire's concept of *conscientização* continues to be important and relevant today. After a prolonged period of not using the term *conscientização*, Freire revisited the concept and used the term in the 1990s within a new socio-historical-political-economical context; Freire (1998) writes

> [. . .] I still insist, without falling into the trap of "idealism," on the absolute necessity of conscientization [*conscientização*]. In truth, conscientization [*conscientização*] is a requirement of our human condition. It is one of the roads we have to follow if we are to deepen our awareness of our world, of facts, of events, of the demands of human consciousness to develop our capacity for epistemological curiosity. (p. 55)

The process of reaching critical awareness and acting upon it—named *conscientização*—is imperative to be once again discussed and carried out in our present time. However, Freire (1998) would emphasize the need for it to be contextualized to the present historical circumstances to address material, social, political, cultural, and ideological conditions that can act as obstacles. *Conscientização* can be the "attempt at critical awareness of those obstacles and their raison d'être" (p. 55). Paulo Freire is very determined in emphasizing "the political and ethical relevance of the effort of conscientization [*conscientização*]" (p. 79). In *Pedagogy of Freedom* (1998), Freire is very clear about the threat of neoliberalism and the importance of *conscientização* as a means to recognize the "obstacles" brought about by neoliberalism and as a means to lay the foundation to overcome these "obstacles."

Neoliberalism, or free-market fundamentalism, today is the all-encompassing politico-economic philosophy and permeates all fabrics of life. Rooted in the work of Hayek (1944) and Friedman (1962), it rose to prominence in the wake of the economic troubles of the 1970s and was implemented as the ruling politico-economic philosophy by Reagan and Thatcher in the United States and Britain in the 1980s; at the present time, neoliberalism in various guises, has a stranglehold on societies worldwide (Harvey, 2005). Neoliberal politico-economic philosophy emphasizes the supremacy of the free market, the absence of government intervention, the importance of deregulation, and widespread privatization (ibid.).

Freire (1998) wrote about the effect of neoliberal fatalism on everyday life, including on the field of education with its degradation to job training (as also observed for teacher education) for the neoliberal economy. He pointed out the unethical attitude whereby ". . . human interests are abandoned whenever they threaten the values of the market" (p. 93). He is adamant in his opposition to neoliberalism and globalization with its ethics of the marketplace that results in "increasing wealth of the few and the rapid increase of poverty and misery for the vast majority of humanity" (p. 114). The exposure of the deleterious effects of neoliberal philosophy on everyday life (and on the field of education) was taken up by other authors (e.g. Aronowitz, 2000; Giroux, 2004; Giroux & Searls Giroux, 2004).

The relevance of Paulo Freire's work and in particular his concept of *conscientização*, however, is clear: gaining a deeper awareness of the social-political-economical reality that dominates one's life and of the ways to change this reality. Following along the path of *conscientização* modern neoliberal philosophy and its global stranglehold can be challenged.

In his body of work, Freire left humanity with a legacy to realize that what makes us human is our capacity to actively insert ourselves into our historical times, not to be passive and/or fatalistic, but to make history. By the way Freire crafted his work, it is also evident that he based his thoughts on those philosophers and thinkers who came before him and those who were his contemporaries—no one creates new ideas and concepts out of a vacuum—but Freire's sense of curiosity, his immersion into the social-political-economical times, his constant effort at contextualizing his work, and his keen analytical abilities allowed him to see beyond and go further. In other words, Freire was not a follower of any particular philosophical idea; he read them, digested them, reinvented them, and recombined ideas into his own philosophy, a philosophy that is centered on the betterment of humankind and rooted in social justice: and it all starts with education.

Notes

1 Translation from the original Brazilian Portuguese by A. Cruz; Freire and Vittoria (2007) and Kirylo (2011) provide a slightly different translation.
2 Translation from the original Brazilian Portuguese by A. Cruz; Freire and Vittoria (2007) and Kirylo (2011) provide a slightly different translation.
3 Translation from the original Brazilian Portuguese by A. Cruz.

References

Anonymous (n.d.). Paulo Freire Kooperation e.V.—Bücher von Paulo Freire. Retrieved from www.freire.de/node/15

Aronowitz, S. (2000). *The knowledge factory: Dismantling the corporate university and creating true higher learning*. Boston, MA: Beacon Press.

Borg, C. and Mayo, P. (2000). "Reflections from a 'third age' marriage: Paulo Freire's pedagogy of reason, hope and passion: An interview with Ana Maria (Nita) Freire." *McGill Journal of Education*, 35 (2), 105–20.

De Kadt, E. J. (1970). *Catholic radicals in Brazil*. London, GB: Oxford University Press.

Elias, J. L. (1976). *Conscientization and deschooling: Freire's and Illich's proposals for reshaping society*. Philadelphia, PA: The Westminster Press.

Freire, P. (1970) "Cultural action and conscientization." *Harvard Educational Review*, 40 (3), 452–77.

— (1971). "A few notions about the word 'conscientization.'" *Hard Cheese*, 1, 23–8.

— (1972). "Conscientizing as a way of liberating." In Anonymous (ed.). *Paulo Freire* (pp. 3–10). The LADOC "Keyhole" Series, 1. Washington, DC: USCC Division for Latin America

— (1984). "Conversation with Paulo Freire," W. B. Kennedy (ed.). *Religious Education*, 79 (4), 511–22.

— (1992/1967). *Educação como práctica da liberdade* (21st edn). Rio De Janeiro, Brazil: Paz E Terra.

— (1994/1970). *Pedagogy of the oppressed*. New York, NY: Continuum.

— (1998). *Pedagogy of freedom: Ethics, democracy, and civic courage*. Lanham, MA: Rowman & Littlefield.

— (2001a/1979). *Conscientização: Teoria e prática da libertação: Uma introdução ao pensamento de Paulo Freire* (3rd edn). Sao Paulo, Brazil: Centauro Editora.

— (2001b). *Educação atualidade Brasileira* (3rd edn). Sao Paulo, Brazil: Cortez Editora.

— (2005/1974). *Education for critical consciousness*. New York, NY: Continuum.

Freire, A. and Vittoria, P. (2007). "Dialogue on Paulo Freire." *Interamerican Journal of Education for Democracy*, 1 (1), 97–117.

Freire, A. M. Araujo (2006). *Paulo Freire—Uma história da vida*. Idaiatuba, Brazil: Villa das Letras Editora.

Friedman, M. (1962). *Capitalism and freedom*. Chicago, IL: University of Chicago Press.

Gerhardt, H.-P. (1993). "Paulo Freire." *Prospects: The Quarterly Review of Comparative Education*, 23 (3/4), 439–58. Retrieved from www.vidyaonline.org/thinkers/freiree.pdf

Giroux, H. A. (2004). *The terror of neoliberalism: Authoritarianism and the eclipse of democracy*. Boulder, CO: Paradigm.

Giroux, H. A. and Giroux, Searls S. (2004). *Take back higher education: Race, youth, and the crisis of democracy in the post-civil rights era*. New York, NY: Palgrave Macmillan.

Harvey, D. (2005). *A brief history of neoliberalism*. Oxford, UK: Oxford University Press.

Hayek, F. (1944). *The road to serfdom*. Chicago, IL: University of Chicago Press.

Kirylo, J. D. (2011). *Paulo Freire—The man from Recife*. New York, NY: Peter Lang.

Macedo, D. (1985). "Translator's preface." In P. Freire. *The politics of education: Culture, power, and liberation* (pp. vii–ix). South Hadley, MA: Bergin & Garvey.

Mackie, R. (1981). "Contributions to the thought of Paulo Freire." In R. Mackie (ed.). *Literacy & revolution: The pedagogy of Paulo Freire* (pp. 93–119). New York, NY: Continuum.

Pinto, A. Vieira (1960). *Consciência e realidade nacional* (2 vols). Rio De Janeiro, Brazil: ISEB.

Ramos, A. Guerreiro (1957). *Introdução crítica a sociologia Brasileira*. Rio De Janeiro, Brazil: Editorial Andes.

Roberts, P. (2010). *Paulo Freire in the 21st century: Education, dialogue, and transformation*. Boulder, CO: Paradigm.

Schipani, D. S. (1984). *Conscientization and creativity: Paulo Freire and Christian education*. Lanham, NY: University of America Press.

Schugurensky, D. (1998). "The legacy of Paulo Freire: A critical review of his contributions." *Convergence*, 31 (1–2), 17–29.

Walker, J. (1981). "The end of dialogue: Paulo Freire on politics and education." In R. Mackie (ed.). *Literacy & revolution: The pedagogy of Paulo Freire* (pp. 120–50). New York, NY: Continuum.

Wilson, T. (2008). "Conscientization." In F. C. Power, R. J Nuzzi, D. Narvaez, D. K. Lapsley, and T. C. Hunt (eds). *Moral education: A handbook* (pp. 100–2). Westport, CT: Praeger.

10
Red-ing the Word, Red-ing the World

Sandy Grande

I was born into a Freirean world. His landmark text, *Pedagogy of the Oppressed*, was translated into English in 1970, right around the time I came into being. Which means, his word defined my world. The implications of this notion compel me to think: while the struggles of colonized peoples remain plethoric, the basic right to be "human," to be a subject in the world, is closer to being realized than it was in the pre Freirean global order. As an effect of his dream to create "a world in which it will be easier to love," (Freire, 1970, p. 24) I recognize my privilege to teach and learn in a world where I can love and be loved.

This chapter examines Paulo Freire's landmark text *Pedagogy of the Oppressed* through the frames of critical Indigenous theory (e.g. Red Pedagogy). While the collective works of Freire are expansive and variegated, from his earliest writings on adult education to his last, he threads a corpus of ideas that are not only evident in *Pedagogy of the Oppressed* but also remain foundational to the field. At issue is how the promise of critical pedagogy and liberation from oppression interfaces with Indigenous visions for schooling and society. While the critique of Freire and the broader field of critical pedagogy as too white, too "Western," and/or patriarchal is well-rehearsed, this analysis is distinctive in that it steps outside the race, class, gender triptych. Specifically, the focus remains on the structural determinations of capital at the heart of *Pedagogy of the Oppressed*. The key distinction is that a Red Pedagogy (Grande, 2004) centers the critique of capitalism within the broader context of settler colonialism (as opposed to Marxism).

Settler colonialism is distinctive from other forms of colonialism in that it is "first and foremost a territorial project" where land (as opposed to natural or human resources) is the precondition (Wolfe, 2006, p. 388). Since the priority is to eradicate, dissolve, and remove Indigenous peoples in order to expropriate their lands, Wolfe (2006) defines "the logic of elimination" as the central organizing principal of settler colonialism; a logic that not only includes genocide but also "officially encouraged miscegenation, the breaking down of native title into alienable individual freeholds, native citizenship, child abduction, religious conversion, resocialization in total institutions such as missions or boarding schools, and a whole range of cognate biocultural assimilations" (p. 388). In other words, he writes, "invasion is a structure not an event" (ibid.).

When invasion is understood as structure rather than event, it is more easily recognized as an ongoing and not "historical" political project. Narrating this history requires "charting the continuities, discontinuities, adjustments, and departures" of the logic that once motivated frontier genocide "transmutes into different modalities, discourses and institutional formations" in relation to the "development and complexification of society" (p. 402). As such, I submit that until we struggle with the question of how and whether the modern settler state can survive this original and seminal abandonment of Indigenous peoples and still claim legitimacy it will continue to live in the shadow of illegitimacy. Thus, one of my central claims is that settler colonialism not only impedes the struggles of Indigenous peoples but also arrests the development of American democracy.

Among critical scholars, the global deployment of neoliberal policies following September 11 ignited a storm of critique, linking the "rise" of the authoritarian state to a new imperialism/era of empire (McLaren, 2005; Darder & Mirón, 2006; Giroux 2006; Macrine, 2009). In a similar vein, Kaplan (2004) writes:

> Across the political spectrum, policy makers, journalists and academics are . . . talking endlessly about empire. It's fashionable, in fact, to debate whether this is a new imperialism or business

as usual, whether the United States should be properly called imperial or hegemonic, whether it is benevolent or self-interested, whether it should rely on hard power or soft power, whether this empire closely resembles the British Empire or the Roman, and whether it is in ascendancy or decline. (p. 2)

Indeed, the shift toward an open imperialism backed by military force lay bare the violence of the late capitalist state, ushering in the predatory practices of what Marxist geographer David Harvey terms capital accumulation by dispossession. (Gordon, 2006, p. 18)

Running parallel to this dominant discourse are the voices of Indigenous scholars for whom the most recent rise of US hegemony does not represent an imperial shift but rather is indicative of a "deepening, hastening and stretching of an already-existing empire" (Alfred & Corntassel, 2005, p. 601). Analyses that employ critical Indigenous theories, begin with the understanding that this nation only came into being through the mass dispossession of Native peoples, meeting all the criteria of an empire: conquest, land grabbing, removal, enclosure, privatization of the commons, and cultural hegemony. Though theorized in critical pedagogy as a new formation of power neoliberalism is, from a critical Indigenous perspective, just the latest display of settler consciousness. The transnational players of first wave colonization (e.g. the Virginia Company of London, Massachusetts Bay Company) have simply been replaced by the likes of British Petroleum and Monsanto, while the old monarchs of empire have morphed into the G8. But the rules of engagement remain the same: disposing, convert, control, profit.

Thus, returning to Freire, this chapter not only aims to examine the "roots" of his work but also to bring into sharper relief the distinction between the political projects of critical Indigenous theory as it stands alongside (and in dialectical relation with) critical pedagogy. Specifically, whereas *Pedagogy of the Oppressed* extends a class analysis that centers critical consciousness and empowerment in defining a pedagogy for liberation, this chapter offers an analysis of settler colonialism that foregrounds the centrality of land as a means of defining a pedagogy for decolonization. The shift from oppression to dispossession not only serves as a reminder of the materiality of invasion but also of the ongoing relationship activated between "logic of elimination" (Wolfe, 2006, p. 1) and continuous consolidation of the settler state. The aim here is not to devalue Freire but rather to deepen his immeasurable contributions.

Indeed, Freire had every expectation that his pedagogical framework would be critically engaged and continuously reinvented. Indeed, perhaps the most compelling attribute of Freire's work is the observable development of his thinking over time, the public confessions of his aporias and unflinching commitment to the dialogue. At every turn, he registered his resistance to the notion of critical pedagogy as a practice or methodology to be imported. So in the name of authentic praxis, I offer the following words, to and with Freire, in dialogue and radical love.

The analysis begins with a brief synopsis of Freire's seminal ideas as expressed in *Pedagogy of the Oppressed*, next it moves to rearticulating the current relevance of his work while also advocating for an (Indigenous) reframing. The final section outlines preliminary steps toward defining a collective struggle between Indigenous and nonIndigenous peoples.

Freire's word

To provide some context, early 1960s Brazil was a ferment of reform efforts that proliferated a menagerie of student, labor, and other "leftist" organizations working to bring critical consciousness to the disenfranchised masses. Seen as a threat to power (i.e. profit) armed forces toppled President João Goulart's democratic administration in a US backed military coup détat in 1964, replacing it with a military regime that lasted for the next 20 years. A backlash of student protest emerged in the late 1960s alongside the global zeitgeist of student movements against imperialist politics. On December 15, 1968, Brazil's armed forces signed (Institutional Act No. 5) the fifth of 17 major decrees that suspended civil rights guarantees through the extension of executive (sovereign) power (Alves de Abreu, 1997). It was under this state of intensified repression that Freire activated his pedagogical project. Within this theater of oppression, Freire's work was considered both revolutionary and dangerous; as an affront to power. Why else would teaching Brazilian peasants to read and rise to critical consciousness be an incarcerable act?

The core idea of *Pedagogy of the Oppressed* is deceptively simple: if education can be used as a tool for dehumanization, it can also be transformed for the purposes of humanization. To be clear, Freire's view of humanity was productivist. That is, beyond the mere state of being, he submits that to be "fully" human is to inhere in the ability to discover and discern one's presence in the existing world (critical consciousness) and also act to change it (transformative agency). Thus, his notion of consciousness is grounded in the material world, a Marxist tenet whereby the processes of social, political, and intellectual life are conditioned by the mode of production. In other words, "it is not the consciousness of men that determines their existence, but their social existence that determines their consciousness" (Marx, 1859, Preface). Freire's views on humanity set the foundation for the other core constructs of critical pedagogy—dialectics, *conscientização*, agency, and dialogue—all of which Freire defines to be in radical contingency with each other.

For example, the dialectical relationship between critical consciousness and agency is what forms, for Freire, the essential difference of humanness; one that not only moves us from object to subject but also distinguishes us from "animals." Marx proposes a similarly productivist view of humanity wherein "man" can only realize (and transcend) "himself" through the processes of "his" own labor. The following excerpt from *Capital* (1990/1976) evidences this view while also brining into sharper relief the anthropocentrism that underlies it. He writes:

Labour is, in the first place, a process in which both man and Nature participate, and in which man of his own accord starts, regulates, and controls the material re-actions between himself and Nature. He opposes himself to Nature as one of her own forces, setting in motion arms and legs, head and hands, the natural forces of his body, in order to appropriate Nature's productions in a form adapted to his own wants. By thus acting on the external world and changing it, he at the same time changes his own nature . . . We are not now dealing with those primitive instinctive forms of labour that remind us of the mere animal. An immeasurable interval of time separates the state of things in which a man brings his labour-power to market for sale as a commodity, from that state in which human labour was still in its first instinctive form. We pre-suppose labour in a form that stamps it as exclusively human. (pp. 283–4)

Thus, to summarize, at the heart of Freire's "pedagogy of the oppressed" are the following suppositions: 1) the state of "oppression" is an effect of the dialectical relationship between material conditions and consciousness; 2) the state of liberation is only possible through a dialogic relationship between oppressor and oppressed (Friere, 1970, p. 43); 3) the dialogic process is understood more broadly as praxis; the process of reflecting and acting upon the world in order to transform it; p. 54); 4) this dialogic relationship is otherwise understood as word=work=praxis (p. 87); and the word and the world, the word=the world (p. 65).

Clearly, the Freirean path toward liberation is highly rational, intentional, and volitional. The pedagogical implications of these suppositions render teaching into a political act. That is, if "knowing" is coming to the critical realization that "reality" is not fixed but mutable then one's conditions, as well as the world's, can be changed. Moreover, if coming to know requires one to be in dialogue it also means that educators cannot simply be "depositing [their] ideas into another" (p. 77) but requires them to treat students as fully human subjects (not objects).

The question remains, however, to what degree Freirean notions of critical consciousness, human agency, transformation, and liberation inhere the potential to undermine Indigenous ways of knowing and being: the power of ancestral knowledge, tradition, and the connection between human beings and the rest of nature. Thus, while we need to reinvigorate his critique of capitalism, I argue that the Marxist roots of this critique must be reconsidered through the frames of critical Indigenous theory. Since I have written elsewhere about how critical pedagogy remains instrumental to this project, (see Grande, 2004), I articulate below how the current crises of the settler state not only underscore its current relevance but also necessitate a reframing of Freire's work.

Relevance of the radical:
Indigenizing Freire

(Ironically?) the circuits of power operating in the United States today resemble those in motion in 1960s Brazil. Within the "new security paradigm" (i.e. the Patriot Act or our own version of Institutional Act No. 5) it is clear that the forces of settler colonialism are not only ongoing but also metastasizing to engulf beyond the "primitive." Indeed under the regime of global, neoliberal capitalism, the poor, working, and middle classes have been subject to the forces of dispossession as well as imperiled by an open imperialism—backed by the military force and violence of the settler state. Thus, while the global deployment of neoliberalism may have intensified both the scope and pace of dispossession, it is critical to recognize that it is nothing new. To do so both erases (eliminates) and elides the experience of Indigenous peoples who have for over 500 years lived in the shadow of the empire and unrelenting power of the settler state.

Thus, where 1964 Brazil may have needed a *Pedagogy of the Oppressed*, the twenty-first century US global order needs a pedagogy of the dispossessed. To begin, there needs to be broad recognition and continued theorizing of how critical pedagogy dissolves colonialism into capitalism by courting a limited and precarious equality predicated on (or more pointedly in exchange for) the "elimination of the Native" (Wolfe, 2006, p. 1). Insofar as the "democratic promise" of critical pedagogy remains implicitly waged upon a series of non-promises to Indigenous peoples it runs the risk of reinscribing settler consciousness. While this is especially true of liberal, postmodern forms of critical pedagogy, more "revolutionary" forms are also complicit if they adhere to early Marxist notions of "primitive accumulation."

Consider, for example, Joel Kovel's articulation of what he terms a prefigurative ecosocialism and situates his pedagogy against liberal forms of "environmentalism." He writes:

> Where environmentalism seeks first of all to protect external nature from assault, a prefigurative ecosocialism combines this goal with anti-capitalist activity—which implies, as we have seen, anti-imperialist and anti-racist activity, and all that devolves from these . . . In the great wealth of interstitial openings the

general rule is that whatever has promise of breaking down the commodity form is to be explored and developed. This can extend from organizing labor (re-configuring the use-value of labor-power), to building cooperatives (ditto, by a relatively free association of labor), to creating alternative local currencies (undercutting the value-basis of money), to making radical media (undoing the fetishism of commodities). In every instance, the challenge is to build small beach-heads—liberated zones that can become the focal points of resistance and combine into larger ensembles. (2002, pp. 251–2)

Though explicitly anti-capitalist, Kovel's critique is additive, seeking only to marry ecosocialism with environmentalism. As such, he leaves intact central dualism; the hierarchical relationship between human beings and an "external nature" (emphasis in original). Even more problematic is Kovel's failure to acknowledge the existence of Indigenous political economies that have always resisted capitalist imperatives, situating human beings within the broader spectrum of "nature" and not as "external." The "eco-socialist" imaginary, thus, limits its own revolutionary possibility. Specifically, by presuming a temporal primitive accumulation (rather than enduring settler colonialism) it is left only to imagine the development of "small beach-heads" and rendered blind to the vision of a broader political solidarity with Indigenous peoples.

As the latest remix of settler colonialism (e.g. neoliberalism) sacrifices more bodies and souls at the altar of capitalism, we must move beyond political and pedagogical paradigms that are centered on abstract, decontextualized notions of liberation/democracy. Indeed, there is probably no other time in the history of our nation that it is more imperative to decolonize our minds, bodies, and spirits and challenge the legitimacy of the settler state. The level of executive privilege normalized in the aftermath of 9/11 has deployed a politics of fear that has emboldened the formation of a virtual police state that obliterates the normative aspect of law with impunity while still claiming to enforce it.

Under such conditions, Agamben's (2005) *State of Exception* insists that the rapid deterioration of civil liberties is misunderstood as the problem rather than a symptom of a more pernicious shift in political geography—wherein the "state of exception" has become the (legal) norm. In reviewing Agamben's book, Bull

(2004) paraphrases Agamben's position when he writes that the West's political model has "moved from Athens to Auschwitz" [where] "the concentration camp rather than the city state" (p. 3) has become the nomos. In other words, under the new security paradigm we are "no longer citizens but detainees" (ibid.). Agamben refers to the noncitizen as the modern homo sacer, which is to say "a creature legally dead while biologically still alive" (Žižek, 2007, n.p.). The homo sacer is always and already Indigenous; the original exempt, banished, disappeared, abandoned, exiled, fragmented, never intended for inclusion (Mitchell, 2006).

Within this context, it is imperative that Indigenous peoples are not conscripted into the Marxist/Freirean paradigm of an oppressed class—we are not just "other" or even "different"—but rather in our totality represent a competing moral vision to capitalism and the settler state. It is this base understanding that will help activate an explicitly decolonial project that refuses displacement and dispossession and advocates instead for a spatial democracy that presupposes Indigenous sovereignty. The task is to define political/pedagogical strategies that go beyond resisting oppression and its attendant methodologies (i.e. banking education) and work instead to interrogate, disrupt, and replace the epistemological underpinnings of the settler world order.

The red road ahead

Freire's *Pedagogy of the Oppressed* helps to reveal how the capitalization of knowledge has contributed to our inability to develop a collective, enduring, and generational consciousness. Specifically, the atomization and commodification of knowledge gave rise to a banking pedagogy that was designed to obfuscate the presence of any grand narrative that would enable us to see our mutual captivity. As critical scholars we must further Freire's project and do the more deliberate work of history, of connecting past with present. We cannot afford to get lost in the myriad refractions of "oppression" and need, instead, to turn our attention to a deep examination of the forms of settler-consciousness that enable them in the first place. That is we need to work beyond and below the surface, searching for patterns of interconnection while keeping an eye toward the process by which relations of mutuality are either abandoned or eroded by relations of capital—to, in effect, decolonize.

In moving toward this end, we must begin with the Freirean gesture of naming the problematic. Secondly, we need to define our differential roles in the struggle for decolonization. And, thirdly, we need to act in solidarity with each other, creating broad-based coalitions for justice and dignity. So, first naming the problem. While the poor and colonized disproportionately suffer the ill effects of the settler state, a Red Pedagogy decenters poverty and situates extreme wealth as the determinative problem of our time. It is not suffering we need cleanse from our moral compass but rather greed. For all the good works accomplished by liberal organizations (e.g. Oxfam, UNICEF), they leave uncontested the hoarding of human and natural resources by the world's elite. Thus, where Jeffrey Sachs, author of *The End of Poverty*, poses the question "will we have the good judgment to use our wealth wisely, to heal a divided planet, to end the suffering of those still trapped by poverty, and to forge a common bond of humanity, security, and shared purpose across cultures and regions?" (2005, p. 3). I ask whether we will have the good judgment to use our critical Indigenous knowledges wisely, to heal a divided planet, to end the moral poverty of those still trapped by wealth, and to forge a common coalition of all beings?

To be clear, Indigenous knowledge is critical to the future sustainability of our planet, not because it holds any magic or ancient "wisdom" but because it represents a competing moral vision to the dominant patterns of thinking and being. And insofar as such patterns have contributed to the existing political, economic, and environmental crises of our time, it is incumbent upon us to protect the complex ecologies that sustain Indigenous communities. The time could not be more urgent to recognize Indigenous sovereignty. Indigenous scholars in particular need to call attention to the ways in which settler democracy continues to fail; inhering the politics of exclusion, inequality, violence as well as the absence of autonomy. Indigenous communities are uniquely poised to represent a true alter-Native to settler colonialism since despite our myriad struggles we have remained autonomous entities with political sovereignty; our very being confounds the infamous Thatcher-ism that there is no alternative.

Serving as allies in this scenario are other nonIndigenous scholar-activists who can engage social transformation from the outside in. That is, to assume the stance of advocate, not just for Indigenous rights but for Whitestream transformation. Perhaps most importantly it means standing on the front lines to help contain the mestatasizing neoliberalism that envelops the globe. Together we need to wage a (Gramscian) "war of position" where counter-hegemonic organizations merge together to form a new historic bloc of solidarity.

Finally, while the pressures of an increasingly globalized world put into sharper relief the grave implications of settler colonialism, the emergence of the global may also hold possibility; the potential for "unraveling of the privileged history of the West" (De Lissovoy, 2008, p. 5). Thus, the prospect of decentering or more accurately decolonizing the dominant social order is arguably more palpable now than ever. As such, I see this is as a moment to recalibrate, reconceptualize, and, most importantly, reterritorialize our understandings of sociopolitical and pedagogical relations. The pedagogical imperative is to redefine schooling and education not only as processes of renegotiating capitalist relations but also of defining alter-Native modes of being. Within these efforts, it is vitally important that all peoples struggling against the ravages of the colonial present work in solidarity with the hope of a deeper, more powerful, and politicized collectivity. I offer the following words as a first salvo in the revolutionary process toward reclamation and renewal.

References

Agamben, G. (2005). *State of exception.* Chicago, IL: University of Chicago Press.

Alfred, T. and Corntassel, J. (2005). "Being indigenous: Resurgences against contemporary colonialism." *Government and Opposition,* 40, 601.

Alves de Abreu, A. (1997). "History and memory: Brazil's guerrilla trap." *History Today.* 47 (12). Retrieved from: www.historytoday.com/alzira-alves-de-abreu/history-and-memory-brazils-guerrilla-trap

Bull, M. (2004). "States don't really mind their citizens dying (provided they don't all do it at once): they just don't like anyone else to kill them." *London Review of Books*, 26 (24), 3–6.

Darder, A. & Mirón, L. (2006). "Critical pedagogy in a time of uncertainty: A call to action." *Cultural Studies, Critical Methodologies*, 6 (1), 5–20.

De Lissovoy, N. (2008). *Power, crisis, and education for liberation: Rethinking critical pedagogy.* New York, NY and London, GB: Palgrave Macmillan.

Freire, P. (1970). *Pedagogy of the Oppressed.* New York, NY: Herder and Herder.

Giroux, H. (2006). "Dirty democracy and state terrorism: The politics of the new authoritarianism in the United States." *Comparative Studies of South Asia, Africa and the Middle East*, 26 (2), 163–77.

Gordon, T. (2006). "Canadian capitalism and dispossession of Indigenous peoples." *The New Socialist*, 58, 18.

Grande, S. (2004) *Red pedagogy.* Baltimore, MD: Rowman and Littlefield.

Kaplan, A. (2004). "Violent belongings and the question of empire today: Presidential Address to the American Studies Association." *American Quarterly*, 56 (1), 2.

Kovel, J. 2002. *The enemy of nature: The end of capitalism or the end of the world?* Nova Scotia, Canada: Fernwood/London, GB and New York, NY: Zed Books.

Macrine, S. (2009). *Critical pedagogy in uncertain times: Hope and possibilities (education, politics, and public life).* New York, NY: Palgrave Macmillan.

McLaren, P. (2005). "Critical pedagogy in the age of neo-liberal globalization." In P. McLaren (ed.). *Capitalists and conquerors: A critical pedagogy against empire* (pp. 19–73). Lanham, MD: Rowman & Littlefield.

Mitchell, K. (2006). "Geographies of identity: the new exceptionalism." *Progress in Human Geography*, 30 (1), 95–106.

Marx, K. (1859). *A Contribution to the Critique of Political Economy.* Moscow: Progress Publishers (1977, with some notes by R. Rojas).

— (1990/1976). *Capital: Volume 1: A critique of political economy*, trans. B. Fowkes. London, England: Penguin Books.

Sachs, J. (2005). *The end of poverty: Economic possibilities for our time.* New York, NY: Penguin Books.

Wolfe, P. (2006). "Settler colonialism and the elimination of the native." *Journal of Genocide Research*, 8 (4) (December), 387–409.

Žižek, S. (2007). "Knight of the living dead." *New York Times*. March 24, 2007.

11

Epilogue: Freire's Roots in his Own Words

Paulo Freire

As the editors of this book, we thought it would be fitting to conclude with chapter one of Pedagogy of Hope: Reliving Pedagogy of the Oppressed, *since it is such a rich source for understanding some of the people and events that shaped Freire's thinking and to leave you with the joyful self-reflective tone of his voice. Paulo created a rich set of notes for this chapter which can be found in the notes section of* Pedagogy of Hope.

In 1947 I was teaching Portuguese at Colégio Oswaldo Cruz, the same school where I had completed my secondary education and, also, as a special favor of the school's director, Dr Aluizio Pessoa de Araújo, my preparatory course for law school. It was at that time that I received the invitation to become part of the recently created Industrial Social Service, SESI, the Regional Department of Pernambuco, set up by the National Industrial Confederation and given legal status by presidential decree.

The invitation was transmitted through a great friend of mine and fellow alumnus of Colégio Oswaldo Cruz, a person to whom I am bound by close ties of friendship, which our political disagreements have never disturbed, to this very day. Our disagreements had to be. They expressed our diverging views of the world, and our understanding of life itself. We have got through some of the most difficult moments of our lives tempering our disagreements, thereby defending our right and our duty to preserve mutual love by ensuring that it will rise above our political opinions and ideological positions. Without our knowing it, at the time, we were already—each in his or her own way—postmodern! In fact, in our mutual respect, we were actually experiencing the rock-bottom foundation of politics.

His name is Paulo Rangel Moreira. Today he is an attorney of renown, and professor of law at the Federal University of Pernambuco. One bright afternoon in Recife, he came to our house in the Casa Forte district, 224 Rita de Souza Street, and told us—Elza, my first wife, and me—of SESI's existence and what it could mean for us. He had already accepted the invitation extended to him by the young president of the organization, engineer and industrialist Cid Sampaio, to coordinate its social service projects. Every indication was that he would soon move to the legal department of the organization—his dream—to work in the field of his own expertise.

I listened, we listened—silent, curious, reticent, challenged—to Paulo Rangel's optimistic discourse. We were a little afraid, too, Elza and I. Afraid of the new, perhaps. But there was also within us willingness and a taste for risk, for adventure.

Night was "falling." Night had "fallen." In Recife, night "arrives" suddenly. The sun is "surprised" to find itself still shining, and makes a run for it, as if there were no time to lose.

Elza flicked on the light. "And what will Paul do in this organization?" she asked. "What will it be able to offer Paul besides the salary he needs? How will he be able to exercise his curiosity, what creative work will he be able to devote himself to so that he won't die of sadness and longing for the teaching job he likes so much?"

We were in our last year of law school, in the middle of the school year. Something had already happened, right about the time of the invitation that was to become very important in my life. I have already referred to it in interviews, and it has been mentioned in biographical notes in books and periodicals. It had made Elza laugh with satisfaction at seeing something happen that she had almost guessed would happen—something she had counted on happening since the beginning of our life together. At the same time, her laugh was a pleasant one, without anything like "I told you so" about it, but just full-to-the-brim of gladness.

I had come home at the end of the day with the tasty sensation of someone correcting a mistake he or she has been making. Opening the door, Elza asked me a question that, on so many people's lips, is not much more than a kind of bureaucratic formality, but which when asked by Elza was always a genuine question, never a rote formula. It expressed lively curiosity, and betokened true investigation. She asked, "Everything all right at the office today?"

And I told her about the experience that had put an end to my brand-new career as a lawyer. I really needed to talk. I needed to recite, word for word, what I had just told the young dentist I had sitting in front of me in my very new office. Shy, frightened, nervous, his hands moving as if suddenly unhooked from his mind, detached from his conscious body, and become autonomous, and yet unable to do anything "on their own," do anything with themselves, or connect with the words that tumbled out of his mouth (God knows how)—the young dentist had said something to me that I needed to speak with Elza about at once. I needed to talk with Elza at that special moment, just as in other, equally special moments in the course of our life. I needed to speak of the spoken, of the said and the not said, of the heard, of the listened to. To speak of the said is not only to resay the said, but to relive the living experience that has generated the saying that now, at the time of the resaying, is said once more. Thus, to resay, to speak of the said, implies hearing once again what has been said by someone else about or because of the saying that we ourselves have done.

"Something very exciting happened to me this afternoon—just a few minutes ago," I said to Elza. "You know what? I'm not going to be a lawyer. It's not that I see nothing special, nothing captivating, about law. Law is a basic need. It's a job that has to be done, and just as much as anything else, it has to be based on ethics, and competence, and seriousness, and respect for people. But law isn't what I want." Then I spoke of what had been, of things experienced, of words, of meaningful silences, of the said, of the heard. Of the young dentist before me whom I had invited to come talk with me as his creditor's attorney. The young man had set up his dental office, at least partially, and had not paid his debts.

"I made a mistake," he said. "I guess I was overoptimistic. I took out a loan I can't pay back. But I'm legally required to have certain instruments in order to practice dentistry. So, well, sir . . . you can take our furniture, in the dining room, the living room . . ." And then, laughing a shy laugh, without the trace of a sneer—with as much humor as irony—he finished up: ". . . Only you can't have my eighteen-month-old baby girl."

I had listened in silence. I was thinking. Then I said to him, "I think you and your wife and your little girls and your dining room and your living room are going to sit in a kind of suspended animation for a while, as far as your debt-troubles are concerned. I'm going to have to wait till next week to see my client and tell him I'm dropping the case. It'll take him another week or so to get another down-and-outer like me to be his attorney. This will give you a little breathing space, even if it is just suspended animation. I'd also like to tell you that, like you, I'm closing down my career before it's even gotten started. Thanks."

The young man, of my own generation, may for all I know have left my office without much of a grasp of what had been said and heard. I squeezed his cold hand warmly with mine. Once he was home again and had thought over what had been said, who knows, he might have begun to understand some of the reasons that had led me to say what I had said.

That evening, relaying to Elza what had been said, I could never have imagined that, one day, so many years later, I would write Pedagogy of the Oppressed, whose discourse, whose proposal, has something to do with the experience of that afternoon, in terms of what it, too, meant, and especially in terms of the decision to accept Cid Sampaio's invitation, conveyed to me by Paulo Rangel. I abandoned the practice of law for good that afternoon, once I had heard Elza say, "I was hoping for that. You're an educator." Not many months after, as the night that had arrived in such haste began, I said yes to SESI's summons to its Division of Education and Culture, whose field of experience, study, reflection, and practice was to become an indispensable moment in the gestation of Pedagogy of the Oppressed.

Never does an event, a fact, a deed, a gesture of rage or love, a poem, a painting, a song, a book have only one reason behind it. In fact, a deed, a gesture, a poem, a painting, a song, a book are always wrapped in thick wrappers. They have been touched by manifold whys. Only some of these are close enough to the event or the creation to be visible whys. And so I have always been more interested in understanding the process in and by which things come about than in the product in itself.

Pedagogy of the Oppressed could not have gestated within me solely by reason of my stint with SESI. But my stint with SESI was fundamental to its development. Even before Pedagogy of the Oppressed, my time with SESI wove a tapestry of which Pedagogy was a kind of inevitable extension. I refer to the dissertation I defended in what was then the University of Recife, and later the Federal University of Pernambuco: "Educação e atualidade brasileira." I later reworked my dissertation and published it as Educação como práctica da liberdade, and that book basically became the forerunner of Pedagogy of the Oppressed.

Again, in interviews, in dialogues with intellectuals, including non-Brazilians, I have made references to more remote tapestries that enveloped me, by bits and pieces, from my childhood and adolescence onward, antedating my time with SESI, which was without any doubt a "founding time," a foundational time.

These bits and pieces of time actually lived in me—for I had lived them—awaiting another time, which might not even have come as it came, but into which, if it did come, earlier bits and pieces of time were destined to extend, in the composition of the larger fabric.

At times, it happens to us not to perceive the "kinship" among the times we have experienced, and thus to let slip the opportunity to "solder together" disconnected cognitions, and in so doing to allow the second to shed light on the doubtful brilliance of the first.

There was my experience of infancy and adolescence with youngsters who were the children of rural and urban workers, my life as a child with children whose opportunities for life were so utterly minimal, the way in which most of their parents treated us—Temístocles, my immediately elder brother, and me—their "fear of freedom," which I never understood, nor called it this at the time, their subservient attitude toward their employers, the boss, the owner, which later, much later, I read in Sartre was one of the expressions of the "connivance" of the oppressed with the oppressors. There were their oppressed bodies, the unconsulted hosts of the oppressors' parasitism.

It is interesting, in a context of childhood and adolescence, in the connivance maintained with the wickedness of the powerful—with the weakness that needed to turn into the strength of the dominated—that the time of SESI's foundation, that time of "solderings" and "splicings" of old, pure "guesses," to which my new knowledge with its critical emergence gave meaning, was the moment at which I read the why, or some of the whys—the tapestries and fabrics that were books yet to be written that would come to enlighten the vivid memory that was forming me: Marx, Lukács, Fromm, Gramsci, Fanon, Memmi, Sartre, Kosik, Agnes Heller, M. Ponty, Simon Weil, Arendt, Marcuse, and so many others.

Years later, the putting into practice of some of the "solderings" and "splicings" of the inaugural years of SESI sent me into exile—a kind of "golden spike" that enabled me to connect recollections, recognize facts, deeds, and gestures, fuse pieces of knowledge, solder moments, re-cognize in order to cognize, to know, better.

In this effort to recall moments of my experience—which necessarily, regardless of when they were, became sources of my theoretical reflections for the writing of Pedagogy of the Oppressed, as they would continue to be today, as I rethink Pedagogy—I feel that it will be appropriate to refer to an excellent example of such a moment, which I experienced in the 1950s. The experience resulted in a learning process of real importance for me—for my theoretical understanding of the practice of political education, which, if it is to be progressive, must, as I have always asserted, take careful account of the reading of the world being made by popular groups and expressed in their discourse, their syntax, their semantics, their dreams and desires.

I was now working in SESI, and specifically on relations between schools and families. I had begun to experiment with various avenues to an improvement of the meeting of minds: to an understanding of the educational practice being carried out in the schools, on the part of the families; to an understanding of the difficulties that families from popular areas would have in confronting problems in the implementation of their own educational activity. At bottom, I was looking for a dialogue between them from which might result the necessary mutual assistance that, at the same time—as it would imply more involvement of the families in the school— might enhance the political connotation of that involvement in the sense of opening channels of democratic participation to fathers and mothers in the actual educational policy being implemented in the schools.

I had carried out, by that time, a research project covering some one thousand families of students, throughout the urban area of

Recife, the Zonda da Mata, the countryside, and what might be called the "doorway" to the desert hinterland of Pernambuco, where SESI had nuclei or social centers in which it offered its members and their families medical and dental assistance, scholastic help, sports and recreation projects, cultural projects, and so on.

My research, which had nothing of the sophisticated about it, asked the parents questions about their relationship with their daughters and sons. I asked about punishments, rewards, the most frequent punishments, the most frequent reasons for it, their children's reaction to the punishment, any change in their behavior, or want thereof, in the direction desired by the person doing the punishing, and so on.

I recall that, when I had sifted through the results, I was astonished, even more than I had expected to be, at the emphasis on corporal punishment, really violent punishment, in the Recife inner city, the Zonda da Mata, in the rural areas, and hinterland, by contrast with the almost complete absence, not only of violent corporal punishment, but of any punishment of children, along the fishing coast. It seemed that, along the coast, under the maritime sky, the legends of individual freedom with which the culture is drenched, the fishers' confrontation, in their precarious jangadas or rafts, with the forces of the sea, the independent jobber's work done by persons free and proud, the imagination that lends such color to the fishers' fantastic stories—it seemed that all of this had some connection with the taste for a liberty diametrically opposed to the use of violent punishment.

I do not know myself to what extent we might consider the fishers' lifestyle too permissive, wanting boundaries, or whether, on the contrary, with their emphasis on freedom, and conditioned by their own cultural context, the fishers are simply relying on nature itself, on the world, on the sea, in an with which their children win an experience of themselves, to be the source of freedom's necessary limits. It was as if, softening or trimming down their duty as their children's educators, fathers and mothers shared them with the sea, with the world itself, to which it would fall, through their children's practice, to delineate their responsibilities. In this fashion, the children would be expected to learn naturally what they might and might not do.

Indeed, the fishers lived a life of enormous contradiction. On one side, they felt free and bold, confronting the sea, in fellowship with its mysteries, doing what they called "scientific fishing," of which they had spoken to me in the sunsets when, relaxing with them in their primitive shelters, their caiçaras, I learned to understand them better by listening to them. On the other hand, they were viciously plundered, exploited, now by the middlemen who bought for nothing the product of their hard labor, now by the moneylenders who financed their work tools.

Sometimes, as I listened to them—in my conversations with them in which I learned something of their syntax and semantics, without which I could not have worked with them, or at any rate not effectively—I wondered whether they didn't perhaps notice how unfree they really were.

I recall that, in the fishing season, we delved into the reason why various students were missing school so frequently. Students and parents, separately, replied. The students, "Because we're free." The parents, "Because they're free. They'll go back some day."

Punishments in the other areas of the state that I researched ranged from tying a child to a tree, locking them in a room for hours on end, giving them "cakes" with thick, heavy switches, forcing them to kneel on stones used to grind corn, thrashing them with leather straps. This last was the principal punishment in a town of the Zona da Mata that was famous for its shoemaking.

Those punishments were applied for trivial reasons, and people watching the fishing were told, "Hard punishment makes hard people, who are up to the cruelty of life." Or, "Getting hit makes a real man out of you."

One of my concerns, at the time, as valid then as it is now, was with the political consequences of that kind of relationship between parents and children, which later becomes that between teachers and pupils, when it came to the learning process of our infant democracy. It was as if family and school were so completely subjected to the greater context of global society that they could do nothing but reproduce the authoritarian ideology.

I acknowledge the risks to which we expose ourselves in confronting such problems. On the one hand, there is the danger of voluntarism, ultimately a kind of "idealism of the strife: that ascribes to the will of the individual with the power to do all things. On the other hand, there is the peril of a mechanistic objectivism that refuses to ascribe any role to subjectivity in the historical process.

Both of these conceptions of history, and of human beings in that history, end by definitively canceling the role of education. The first, because it attributes to education a power that it does not have; the second, because it denies that it has any power at all.

As for the relationship between authority and freedom—the subject of the research project that I have mentioned—we also run the risk either of denying freedom the right to assert itself, thus exacerbating the role of authority; or else of atrophying the latter and thus hypertrophying the former. In other words, we run the risk of succumbing to the seduction or tyranny of liberty, or to the tyranny of authority, thus acting at cross-purposes, in either hypothesis, with our incipient democracy.

This was not my position then and it is not my position now. And today as yesterday, while on perhaps better foundations than yesterday, I am completely persuaded of the importance, the urgency, of the democratization of the public school, and of the ongoing training of its educators, among whom I include security people, cafeteria personnel, and custodians, and so on. Their formation must be ongoing and scientific. Nor should it fail to instill a taste for democratic practices, among which should be an ever more active intervention on the part of educands and their families as to which direction the school is going. This has been one of the tasks to which I have devoted myself recently, so many years after having first observed this need, and spoken of it in my 1959 academic treatise, "Educação e atualidade brasileira," to address it again as secretary of education for the City of São Paulo from January 1989 to May 1991. Here is the challenge of the democratization of the public school, so neglected by the military governments that, in the name of the salvation of the country from the curse of communism and form corruption, all but destroyed that country.

Finally, with the results of my study in hand, I scheduled a kind of systematic visitation of all of the SESI nuclei or social centers in the state of Pernambuco where we maintain primary school, as they were called at the time, to go there and speak to the parents about the findings of the inquiry. And to do something more: to join to communication of the findings of the investigation a discussion about the problem of the relationship between authority and freedom, which would necessarily involve the question of punishment and reward in education.

The tour for discussion with the families was preceded by another, which I made in order to debate, in seminars as rigorous as it was possible to have, the same question with teachers.

I had put together—in collaboration with a colleague, Jorge Monteiro de Melo, recently deceased, whose seriousness, honesty, and devotion I now reverence—an essay on scholastic discipline, which, alongside the results of the study, became the object of our preparatory seminar in our meetings with the families. In this fashion, we prepared ourselves, as a school, to welcome the students' families—the natural educators of those of whom we were the professional educators.

Back then, I was accustomed to give long talks on the subjects that had been selected. I was repeating the traditional route of discourse about something that you would give an audience. Then I would shift the format to a debate, discussion, dialogue about the subject with the participants. And, while I was concerned about the order and development of ideas, I proceeded almost as if I were speaking to university students. I say, "almost," because actually my sensitivity had already made me aware of the differences in language, the syntactical and semantic differences, between the working persons with whom I was working and my own language. Hence my talks were always punctuated with, "In other words," or "That is to say . . ." On the other hand, despite some years of experience as an educator, with urban and rural workers, I still nearly always started out with my world, without further explanation, as if it ought to be the "south" to which their compass ought to point in giving them bearings. It was as if my word, my theme, my reading of the world, in themselves, were to be their compass.

It was a long learning process, which implied a journey, and not always an easy one, nearly always painful, to the point that I persuaded myself that, even when my thesis and proposal were sure, and I had no doubt in their respect, it was nevertheless imperative, first, to know whether this thesis and proposition coincided with the reading of the world of the groups or social class to whom I was speaking; second, it was incumbent upon me to be more or less abreast of, familiar with, their reading of the world, since only on the basis of the knowledge in its content, or implicit in it, would it be possible for me to discuss my reading of the world, which in turn, maintains, and is based on, another type of knowledge.

This learning process, this apprenticeship, whose story is a long one, is rehearsed in my university dissertation, cited above, continues being sketched in Educação como práctica da liberdade, and becomes explicit once and for all in Pedagogy of the Oppressed. One moment—I could even say, a solemn one, among others, of this apprenticeship—occurred during the one-day seminar to which I have referred, which consisted of talks in which I discussed authority, freedom, and punishment and reward in education. It happened precisely in the SESI nucleus or social center named for President Dutra, at Vasco da Gama–Amarela House—in Recife.

Basing my presentation on an excellent study by Piaget on the child's moral code, his and her mental representation of punishment, the proportion between the probable cause of punishment and the punishment itself, I spoke at length. I quoted Piaget himself on the subject, and argued for a dialogical, loving relationship between parents and children in place of violent punishments.

My mistake was not in citing Piaget. In fact, how much richer my presentation could have been if I had talked about him very concretely, using a map, and showing where Recife is, then the Brazilian Northeast, then move out to the whole of Brazil, show where Brazil is in South America, relate that to the rest of the world, and finally, point to Switzerland, in Europe, the land of the author I was quoting. It would have been not only richer, but more challenging and instructive, to do that. But my actual mistake was, first, in my use of my language, my syntax, without more effort to get close to the language and syntax of my audience; and second, in my all but oblivion of the hard reality of the huge audience seated before me.

When I had concluded, a man of about forty, still rather young but already worn out and exhausted, raised his hand and gave me the clearest and most bruising lesson I have ever received in my life as an educator.

I do not know his name. I do not know whether he is still alive. Possibly not. The wickedness of the country's socioeconomic structures, which take on stronger colors in the Brazilian Northeast—suffering, hunger, the indifference of the mighty—all this must have swallowed him up long since.

He raised his hand and gave a talk that I have never been able to forget. It seared my soul for good and all. It has exerted an enormous influence on me. Nearly always, in academic ceremonies in which I have had an honorary doctorate conferred on me by some university, I acknowledge how much I owe, as well, to persons like the one of whom I am now speaking, and not only to scholars— other thinkers who have taught me, too, and who continue to teach me, teachers without whom it would have been impossible for me to learn, like the laborer who spoke that night. Actually, were it not for the scientific rigor that offers me greater opportunities for precision in my findings, I should not be able critically to perceive the importance of common sense and the good sense therein residing. In almost every academic ceremony in which I am honored, I see him standing in one of the aisles of that big auditorium of so long ago, head erect, eyes blazing, speaking in a loud, clear voice, sure of himself, speaking his lucid speech.

"We have just heard," he began, "some nice words from Dr. Paulo Freire. Fine words, in fact. Well spoken. Some of them were even simple enough for people to understand easily. Others were more complicated. But I think I understood the most important things that all the words together say.

"Now I'd like to ask the doctor a couple of things that I find my fellow workers agree with."

He fixed me with a mild, but penetrating gaze, and asked: "Dr. Paulo, sir—do you know where people live? Have you ever been in any of our houses, sir?" And he began to describe their pitiful houses. He told me of the lack of facilities, of the extremely minimal space in which all their bodies were jammed. He spoke of the lack of resources for the most basic necessities. He spoke of physical exhaustion, and of the impossibility of dreams for a better tomorrow. He told me of the prohibition imposed on them from being happy—or even of having hope.

As I followed his discourse, I began to see where he was going to go with it. I was slouching in my chair, slouching because I was trying to sink down into it. And the chair was swiveling, in the need of my imagination and the desire of my body, which were both in flight, to find some hole to hide in. He paused a few seconds, ranging his eyes over the entire audience, fixed on me once more, and said, "Doctor, I have never been over to your house. But I'd like to describe it for you, sir. How many children do you have? Boys or girls?"

"Five," I said—scrunching further down into my chair. "Three girls and two boys."

"Well, Doctor, your house must be the only house on the lot, what they call an oitão livre house," a house with a yard. "There must be a room just for you and your wife, sir. Another big room, that's for the three girls. There's another kind of doctor, who has a room for every son or daughter. But you're not that kind—no, sir. You have another room for the two boys. A bathroom with running water. A kitchen with Arno appliances. A maid's room— much smaller than your kids' rooms—on the outside of the house. A little garden, with an 'ingress' (the English word) lawn," a front lawn. "You must also have a room where you toss your books, sir—a 'study,' a library. I can tell by the way you talk that you've done a lot of reading, sir, and you've got a good memory."

There was nothing to add or subtract. That was my house. Another world, spacious and comfortable.

"Now Doctor, look at the difference. You come home tired, sir, I know that. You may even have a headache from the work you do. Thinking, writing, reading, giving these kind of talks that you're giving now. That tires a person out too. But, sir," he continued, "it's one thing to come home, even tired, and find the kids all bathed, dressed up, clean, well fed, not hungry—and another thing to come home and find your kids dirty, hungry, crying, and making noise. And people have to get up at four in the morning the next day and start all over again—hurting, sad, hopeless. If people hit their kids, and even 'go beyond bounds,' as you say, it's not because people don't love their kids. No, it's because life is so hard they don't have much choice."

This is class knowledge, I say now.

This talk was given about thirty-two years ago. I have never forgotten it. It said to me, despite the fact that I didn't understand this at the time, much more than immediately communicated.

In his intonations, his laborer's syntax and rhythm, the movements of his body, his hands of an orator, in the metaphors so common to popular discourse, he called the attention of the educator there in front of him, seated, silent, sinking down into his chair, to the need, when speaking to the people, for the educator to be up to an understanding of the world the people have. An understanding of the world which, conditioned by the concrete reality that in part explains that understanding, can begin to change through a change in that concrete reality. In fact, that understanding of the world can begin to change the moment the unmasking of concrete reality begins to lay bare the "whys" of what the actual understanding had been up until then.

A change in understanding, which is of basic importance, does not itself, however, mean a change in the concrete.

The fact that I have never forgotten the fabric in which that discourse was delivered is significant. The discourse of that faraway night is still before me, as if it had been written text, an essay that I constantly had to review. Indeed, it was the culmination of the learning process I had undertaken so long ago—that of the progressive educator: even when one must speak to the people, one must convert the "to" to a "with" the people. And this implies respect for the "knowledge of living experience: of which I always speak, on the basis of which it is possible to go beyond it.

That night, in the car on the way back home, I complained to Elza rather bitterly. Though she rarely accompanied me to meetings, when she did she made excellent observations that always helped me.

"I thought I'd been so clear," I said. "I don't think they understood me."

"Could it have been you, Paulo, who didn't understand them?" Elza asked, and she went on: "I think they got the main point of your talk. The worker made that clear in what he said. They understood you, but they needed to have you understand them. That's the question."

Years later, *Pedagogy of the Oppressed* spoke of the theory that became steeped in practice that night, a night whose memory went with me into exile along with the remembrance of so many other fabrics lived.

The moments we live either are instants in a process previously inaugurated, or else they inaugurate a new process referring in some way to something in the past. This is why I have spoken of the "kinship" among times lived—something we do not always perceive, thereby failing to unveil the fundamental why of the way in which we experience ourselves at each moment.

I should like to refer, now, to another of these times, another fabric that powerfully scored my existential experience and had a noticeable influence on the development of my pedagogical thought and educational practice.

Stepping back, now, from the moment to which I am about to refer, which I experienced between the ages of twenty-two and twenty-nine—part of it, then, while I was working in SESI—I see it as not just a moment but a process, whose point of departure occurred toward the end of my childhood and the beginning of my teen years, in Jaboatão.

During the period I am talking about, from the ages of twenty-two to twenty-nine, I used to be overcome by a sense of despair and sadness from time to time. I was a terrible sad sack at these moments, and I suffered terribly from it. Nearly always, I would spend two or three days, or even longer, like this. Sometimes this state of mind would attack me without warning—in the street, in my office, at home. Sometimes it would come gradually, and get the best of me piecemeal. Regardless of which way it came, I felt wounded, and bored with the world, as if I were submerged in myself, in the pain whose reason I did not know, and everything around me seemed strange and foreign. Who wouldn't despair?

One time, a schoolmate from high school managed to hurt and offend me by telling me about something in my behavior of the previous two or three days that he couldn't understand. "You wouldn't talk to me! On Empress Street! I was heading for Hospice Street, and you were walking on the other side of the street going the other way. I crossed over, and waved a big hello. I thought you'd stop and say hi! And you just kept on walking! Why did you pretend you didn't see me?"

There were other, less striking, cases than this one. My explanation was always the same. "I didn't see you. Look, I'm your friend! I wouldn't do something like that!"

Elza always had deep understanding for me when this happened, and she helped me in every way she could. And the finest help she could give me, and she gave it, was not to so much as suggest to me that my attitude toward her was changing.

After I had had these experiences for some time, especially as they were beginning to happen more and more often, I began to try to see it in the framework, in which it occurred, see it as a part of the bigger picture. What were the elements, or surrounding elements, of the actual moment at which I felt that way?

When I could see the depression coming, I tried to see what it was that was there around me. I tried to see again, tried to remember, what had happened the day before, tried to hear once more what had been said and to whom it had been said, what I had heard and from whom I had heard it. When you come right down to it,

I began to take my depression as an object of curiosity and investigation. I "stepped back" from it, to learn its "why." Basically, I needed to shed some light on the framework in which it was being generated.

I began to perceive that it was repeated, almost identically—my depression, this lack of interest in the world, this pessimism: that is occurred more often in the rainy season, and mostly at or around the time of the trips I would make to the Zona da Mata to speak in SESI schools to teachers and pupils' families on educational problems. This observation called my attention to the trips I made with the same objective to the farming zone of the state. But it didn't happen in connection with these trips. So it wasn't trips that were the cause of my depression.

I find it interesting that I can condense into just a few pages the three or four years of search out of the seven during which that moment was repeated.

My first visit to the city of São Paulo occurred when my search happened to be in full swing.

The day after I arrived, I was in my hotel, that afternoon, and the rain began to pour. I went over to the window to peer out at the world outside. The sky was black, and it was really coming down. But one thing was lacking, in the world that I was observing, by comparison with the pouring rain that would be accompanied with such deep depression. What was missing was green, and mud—the black earth soaking up the water, or the yellow clay turning into the slippery, or else slurpy-sticky, mass that "grabs you like a great, big constrictor," as Gilberto Freyre said of massapê, the black clay of the Northeast.

The dark sky of São Paulo that day, and the falling rain, had no effect on me whatsoever. On my return to Recife, I brought with me a mental portrait that the visit to São Paulo had helped me put together. My depressions were doubtless connected to rain, and mud—massapê clay—and the green of the cane brakes and the dark sky. Not connected to any of these elements in isolation, but to the relationship among them. What I needed now, in order to gain a clear understanding of the experience of my suffering, was to discover the remote framework in which these elements had won or had been winning the power to spark my depression. At bottom, in seeking for the deepest "why" of my pain, I was educating my hope. I never expected things just to "be that way." I worked on things, on facts, on my will. I invented the concrete hope in which, one day, I would see myself delivered from my depression.

And so it was that, one rainy afternoon in Recife, under a leaden sky, I went to Jaboatão in quest of my childhood. If it was raining in Recife, in Jaboatão, which was known as the "spout of heaven," there was no describing it. And it was under a heavy rain that I paid my visit to Morro da Saúde, where I had lived as a child. I stopped in front of the house in which I had lived—the house in which my father died in the late afternoon of October 21, 1934. I saw again the long lawn that stretched before the house at the time, the lawn we played soccer on. I saw again the mango trees, their green fronds. I saw my feet again, my muddy feet going up the hill, and me soaked to the skin. I had before me, as on a canvas, my father dying, my mother in stupefaction, my family lost in sorrow.

Then I walked down the hill and went to see once more certain areas where, more out of need than for sport, I had hunted innocent little birds, with the slingshot I had made myself and with which I became an excellent shot.

That rainy afternoon, with the sky dark as lead over the bright green land, the ground soaked, I discovered the fabric of my depression. I became conscious of various relationships between the signs and the central core, the deeper core, hidden within me. I unveiled the problem by clearly and lucidly grasping its "why." I dug up the archeology of my pain.

Since then, never again has the relationship between rain, green, and mud or sticky clay sparked in me the depression that had afflicted me for years. I buried it, that rainy afternoon I revisited Jaboatão. At the same time as I was struggling with my personal problem, I devoted myself to SESI groups of rural and urban workers, worked on the problem of moving from my discourse about my reading of the world to them, and moving them, challenging them, to speak of their own reading.

Many of them had possibly experienced the same process I had lived through—that unraveling the fabric in which the facts are given, discovering their "why." Many, perhaps, had suffered, and not just a little, in redoing their reading of the world under the impulse of a new perception—in which it was not actually destiny or fate or an inescapable lot that explained their helplessness as workers, their impotence in the face of the defeated, squalid body of their companion, and their death for want of resources.

Let me make it clear, then, that, in the domain of socioeconomic structures, the most critical knowledge of reality, which we acquire through the unveiling of that reality, does not of itself alone effect a change in reality.

In my case, as I have just recounted, the unmasking of the "why" of my experience of suffering was all that was needed to overcome it. True, I was freed from a limitation that actually threatened both my professional activity and my life in the community of my fellow human beings. It had come to the point that I was politically limited, as well.

A more critical understanding of the situation of oppression does not yet liberate the oppressed. But the revelation is a step in the right direction. Now the person who has this new understanding can engage in a political struggle for the transformation of the concrete conditions in which the oppression prevails. Here is what I mean. In my case, it was enough to know the fabric in which my suffering had been born in order to bury it. In the area of socioeconomic structures, a critical perception of the fabric, while indispensable, is not sufficient to change the data of the problem, any more than it is enough for the worker to have in mind the idea of the object to be produced: that object has to be made.

But the hope of producing the object is as basic to the worker as the hope of remaking the world is indispensable in the struggle of oppressed men and women. The revelatory, gnosiological practice of education does not of itself effect the transformation of the world: but it implies it.

No one goes anywhere alone, least of all into exile—not even those who arrive physically alone, unaccompanied by family, spouse, children, parents, or siblings. No one leaves his or her world without having been transfixed by its roots, or with a vacuum for a soul. We carry with us the memory of many fabrics, a self soaked in our history, our culture; a memory, sometimes scattered, sometimes sharp and clear, of our childhood, of our adolescence; the reminiscence of something distant that suddenly stands out before us, in us, a shy gesture, an open hand, a smile lost in a time of misunderstanding, a sentence, a simple sentence possibly now forgotten by the one who said it. A word for so long a time attempted and never spoken, always stifled in inhibition, in the fear of being rejected—which, as it implies a lack of confidence in ourselves, also means a refusal of risk.

We experience, of course, in the voyage we make, a tumult in our soul, a synthesis of contrasting feelings—the hope of immediate deliverance from the perils that surround us, relief at the absence of the inquisitor (either the brutal, offensive interrogator, or the tactically polite prosecutor to whose lips this "evil, dangerous subversive" will yield, it is thought, more easily), along with, for the extension of the tumult of and in the soul, a guilt-feeling at leaving one's world, one's soil, the scent of one's soil, one's folks. To the tumult in the soul belongs also the pain of the broken dream, utopia lost. The danger of losing hope. I have known exiles who began to buy a piece of furniture or two for their homes only after four or five years in exile. Their half-empty homes seemed to speak, eloquently, of their loyalty to a distant land. In fact, their half-empty rooms not only seemed to wish to speak to them of their longing to return, but looked as if the movers had just paid a visit and they were actually moving back. The half-empty house lessened the sentiment of blame at having left the "old sod." In this, perhaps, lies a certain need that I have so often perceived in persons exiled: the need to feel persecuted, to be constantly trailed by some secret agent who dogged their step and whom they alone ever saw. To know they were so dangerous gave them, on the one hand, the sensation of still being politically alive; and on the other, the sensation of a right to survive, through cautious measures. It diminished their guilt feelings.

Indeed, one of the serious problems of the man or woman in exile is how to wrestle, tooth and nail, with feelings, desire, reason, recall, accumulated knowledge, worldviews, with the tension between a today being lived in a reality on loan and a yesterday, in their context of origin, whose fundamental marks they come here charged with. At bottom, the problem is how to preserve one's identity in the relationship between an indispensable occupation in the new context, and a preoccupation in which the original context has to be reconstituted. How to wrestle with the yearning without allowing it to turn into nostalgia. How to invent new ways of living, and living with others, thereby overcoming or redirecting an understandable tendency on the part of the exiled woman or man always to regard the context of origin (as it cannot be got rid of as a reference, at least not over the long haul) as better than the one on loan. Sometimes it is actually better; not always, however.

Basically, it is very difficult to experience exile, to live with all the different longings—for one's town or city, one's country, family, relatives, a certain corner, certain meals—to live with longing, and educate it too. The education of longing has to do with transcendence of a naively excessive optimism, of the kind, for example, with which certain companions received me in October 1964 in La Paz: "You're just in time to turn around. We'll be home for Christmas."

I had arrived there after a month or a little more than a month in the Bolivian embassy in Brazil, waiting for the Brazilian government to deign to send me the safe-conduct pass without which I should not be allowed to leave. Shortly before, I had been arrested, and subjected to long interrogations by military personnel who seemed to think that, in asking these questions of theirs, they were saving not only Brazil but the whole world.

"We'll be home for Christmas."

"Which Christmas?" I asked, with curiosity, and even more surprise.

"This Christmas!" they answered, with unshakable certitude.

My first night in La Paz, not yet under the onslaughts of the altitude sickness that were to fall upon me the next day, I reflected a bit on the education of longing, which figures in Pedagogy of Hope. It would be terrible, I thought, to let the desire to return kill in us the critical view, and make us look at everything that happens back home in a favorable way—create in our head a reality that isn't real.

Exile is a difficult experience. Waiting for the letter that never comes because it has been lost, waiting for notice of a final decision that never arrives. Expecting sometimes that certain people will come, even going to the airport simply to "expect," as if the verb were intransitive.

It is far more difficult to experience exile when we make no effort to adopt its space-time critically—accept it as an opportunity with which we have been presented. It is this critical ability to plunge into a new daily reality, without preconceptions, that brings the man or woman in exile to a more historical understanding of his or her own situation. It is one thing, then, to experience the everyday in the context of one's origin, immersed in the habitual fabrics from which we can easily emerge to make our investigations, and something else again to experience the everyday in the loan context that calls on us not only to become able to grow attached to this new context, but also to take it as an object of our critical reflection, much more than we do our own from a point of departure in our own.

I arrived in La Paz, Bolivia, in October 1964, and another coup d'état took me by surprise. In November of the same year I landed in Arica, in Chile, where I startled my fellow passengers, as we were making our descent toward the airport, by calling out, loud and strong, "Long live oxygen!" I had left an altitude of four thousand meters and was returning to sea level. My body once more rapidly became as viable as it had been before. I moved with facility, rapidly, without exhaustion. In La Paz, carrying a package, even a little one, meant an extraordinary effort for me. At forty-three I felt old and decrepit. In Arica, and on the next day in Santiago, I got my strength back, and everything happened almost instantly, as if by sleight of hand. Long live oxygen!

I arrived in Chile with my whole self: passion, longing, sadness, hope, desire, dreams in smithereens but not abandoned, offenses, knowledge stored in the countless fabrics of living experience, availability for life, fears and terrors, doubts, a will to live and love. Hope, especially.

I arrived in Chile, and a few days later started to work as a consultant for renowned economist Jacques Chonchol, president of the Instituto de Desarrollo Agropecuario (Institute for the Development of Animal Husbandry)—the INDAP—subsequently to be minister of agriculture in the Allende government.

Only in mid-January of 1965 were we all back together. Elza, the three girls, and the two boys, with all their terrors, their doubts, their hopes, their fears, their knowledge gotten and being gotten, started a new life with me again in a strange land—a foreign land to which we were giving ourselves in such wise that it was receiving us in a way that the foreignness was turning into comradeship, friendship, siblingship. Homesick as we were for Brazil, we had a sudden special place in our hearts for Chile, which taught us Latin America in a way we had never imagined it.

I reached Chile a few days after the inauguration of Eduardo Frey's Christian Democratic government. There was a climate of euphoria in the streets of Santiago. It was as if a profound, radical, substantial transformation of society had occurred. Only the forces of the Right, at one extreme, and those of the Marxist-Leninist

Left at the other, for different reasons, obviously, did not share the euphoria. How vast it was! What a certitude there was, rooted in the minds of Christian Democracy activists, that their revolution was fixed on solid ground, that no threat could ever get near it! One of their favorite arguments, more metaphysical than historical, was what they called the "democratic and constitutionalist tradition of the Chilean armed forces."

"Never will there be an uprising against the established order," they said, sure as sure can be, in conversations with us.

I remember a meeting that did not go very well at the home of one of these militants, with some thirty of them, in which Plínio Sampaio, Paulo de Tarso Santos, Almino Affonso, and I, participated.

We argued that the so-called tradition of loyalty on the part of the armed forces to the established, democratic order was not an immutable quality, an intrinsic property of the military, but a mere "historical given," and therefore that this "tradition" might become historically shattered and a new process take its place. They answered that Brazilians in exile gave them "the impression of being crybabies who've had their toys taken away," or "frustrated, helpless children." There was no conversing with them.

A few years later the Chilean armed forces decided to change positions. I hope it was without the contribution of any of those with whom we were conversing that night, as I hope as well that none of them had to pay as dearly as thousands of other Chileans did— along with other Latin Americans—under the weight of the perversity and cruelty that came crashing down on Chile in September 1973. It was not by chance, then, that the most backward of the elite, in whom even timid liberal positions stirred threat and fear, frightened at the reformist policy of Christian Democracy, which was then regarded as a kind of middle road, dreamed of the need to put an end to all this bold, too-risky business. Just imagine what Allende's victory meant, then, not only for the Chilean elite, but for the outsiders of the North!

I visited Chile twice during the time of the Popular Unity government, and used to say, in Europe and in the United States, that anyone who wanted to get a concrete idea of the class struggle, as expressed in the most divergent ways, really ought to pay a visit to Chile. Especially, if you wanted to see—practically touch with your hands—the tactics of the dominant classes employed in the struggle, and the richness of their imagination when it came to waging a more effective struggle for the resolution of the contradiction between power and government, I would tell my audiences, you really must go to Chile. What had happened is that power, as a fabric of relations, decisions, and force, continued to be the main thing with them, while the government, which was in charge of policy, found itself being propelled by progressive forces, forces in discord with the others. This opposition, this contradiction, had to be overcome, so that both power and government would be in their hands again. The coup was the solution. And so, even within the Christian Democratic party, the Right tended to place obstacles in the way of the democratic policy of the more advanced echelons, especially of the youth. As the process developed, a clearer and clearer tendency to radicalization, and breach between the discordant options, appeared, precluding a peaceful coexistence between them, either in the party or in society itself.

On the outside, the Marxist-Leninist Left, the Communist party and the Socialist party, had their ideological, political, historical, and cultural reasons for not joining in the euphoria. They regarded it as naïve at best.

In step with the waxing and deepening of the class struggle or conflicts, the rift between the forces of right and Left, among Christian Democrats as in civil society, likewise deepened. Thus arose various tendencies on the Left calculated to regiment militants who, in direct contact with the popular bases, or seeking to understand these grassroots elements through a reading of the classic Marxists, began to call on the carpet the reformism that had finally gained the upper hand in the strategic plans of Christian Democratic policy.

The Movimiento Independente Revolucionário, the MIR, was born in Concepción, and was constituted of revolutionary youth who disagreed with what seemed to them to be a deviation on the part of the Communist party—that of a "coexistence" with elements of "bourgeois democracy."

It is interesting, however, that the MIR, which was constantly to the Left of the Communist party, and afterwards, of the Popular Unity government itself, always manifested a sympathy for popular education, something the parties of the traditional Left generally lacked.

When the Communist party and the Socialist party refused, dogmatically, to work with certain poblaciónes who, they said, were without a "class consciousness," so that they mobilized only for ad hoc protests and automatically demobilized whenever their demands were met, the MIR thought it necessary, first to prove the correctness of this attitude toward the Lumpenproletariat, the "great unwashed," and second, to observe whether, admitting the hypothesis that their proposition had been verified in certain situations, it would be verified again in a different historical moment. In other words, while there was some truth in the proposition, it could not be taken as a metaphysical postulate.

And so it came about that, now under the Popular Unity government, the MIR launched an intensive campaign of mobilization and organization—itself a piece of political pedagogy—in which it included a series of educational projects in the popular areas. In 1973, I had the opportunity to spend an evening with the leaders of the población—settlement or "new city"—of Nueba Hablana, which, contrary to the dour forecast, after obtaining what it had been demanding, its own villa, continued active and creative, maintaining countless projects in the area of education, health, justice, social security, and sports. I paid a visit to a lineup of old buses, donated by the government, whose bodies, converted and adapted, had become neat, nicely set up little schoolrooms, which the children of the población attended. In the evenings, the bus-schoolrooms would fill with literacy-program clients, who were learning to read the word through a reading of the world. Nueba Habana had a future, then, if an uncertain one, and the climate surrounding it and the experimental pedagogy being plied within it was one of hope.

Alongside the MIR arose the Movimiento de Acción Popular Unitaria, and the Christian Left, further splintering the Christian Democrats. A sizable contingent of more advanced youth among the Christian Democrats joined the MAPU, or else the Christian Left, and even migrated to the MIR as well, or the Communist and Socialist parties.

Today, nearly thirty years later, one readily perceives what, at the time, only a few grasped, and already urged. They were sometimes regarded as dreamers, utopians, idealists, or even as "selling out to the gringos." At this distance, it is easy to see that only a radical politics—not a sectarian one, however, but one that seeks a unity in diversity among progressive forces—could ever have won the battle for a democracy that could stand up to the power and virulence of the Right. Instead, there was only sectarianism and intolerance—the rejection of differences. Tolerance was not what it ought to be: the revolutionary virtue that consists in a peaceful coexistence with those who are different, in order to wage a better fight against the adversaries.

The correct road for the progressive forces standing to the Left of the Christian Democrats would have been to move—within ethical limits of the concession on policy—closer and closer to them, not in order to take over the party, nor again in such a manner as to drive it to the Right, nor, indeed, so as to be absorbed into it. And for its own part, Christian Democracy, in all intolerance, rejected dialogue. There was no credibility on either side.

It was precisely by virtue of the inability of all forces to tolerate one another that Popular Unity came to power . . . without power.

From November 1964 to April 1969, I followed the ideological struggle closely. I witnessed, sometimes with surprise, retreats in the area of political ideology by persons who had proclaimed their opinion for the transformation of society, then became frightened and repentant, and made a fearful about-face in midcourse and turned into hidebound reactionaries. But I also saw the advances made by those who confirmed their progressive discourse by walking consistently, refusing to run from history. I likewise witnessed the progress of persons whose initial position had been timid, to say the least, but who became stronger, ultimately to assert themselves in a radicalness that never extended to sectarianism.

It would really have been impossible to experience a process this rich, this problem-fraught, to have been touched so profoundly by the climate of accelerated change, to have shared in such animated, lively discussion in the "culture circles" in which educators often had to beg the peasants to stop, since they had already gone on practically the whole night, without all of this later winning explication in this or that theoretical position of mine in the book that, at the time, was not even a project.

I was impressed, when I heard about it in evaluation meetings, or when I was actually present, by the intensity of the peasants' involvement when they were analyzing their local and national reality. It took them what seemed like forever to spill everything that was on their minds. It was as if the "culture of silence" was suddenly shattered, and they had discovered not only that they could speak, but that their critical discourse upon the world, their world, was a way of remaking that world. It was if they had begun to perceive that the development of their language, which occurred in the course of their analysis of their reality, finally showed them that the lovelier world to which they aspired was being announced, somehow anticipated, in their imagination. It was not a matter of idealism. Imagination and conjecture about a different world than the one of oppression, are as necessary to the praxis of historical "subjects" (agents) in the process of transforming reality as it necessarily belongs to human toil that the worker or artisan first have in his or her head a design, a "conjecture," of what he or she is about to make. Here is one of the tasks of democratic popular education, of a pedagogy of hope: that of enabling the popular classes to develop their language: not the authoritarian, sectarian gobble-dygook of "educators," but their own language—which, emerging from and returning upon their reality, sketches out the conjectures, the designs, the anticipations of their new world. Here is one of the central questions of popular education—that of language as a route to the invention of citizenship.

As Jacques Chonchol's consultant in the Institute for the Development of Animal Husbandry, in the area of what was then called in Chile human promotion, I was able to extend my collaboration to the Ministry of Education, in cooperation with people working in adult literacy, as well as to the Corporation for Agrarian Reform.

Quite a bit later, almost two years before we left Chile, I began to work as a consultant for these same organizations on the basis of my position in another, the Instituto de Capacitación e Investigación en Reforma Agraria (Institute for Ways and Means and Research in Agrarian Reform or ICIRA), a joint organization of the United Nations and the Chilean government. I worked there for UNESCO, against the will and under the consistent niggardly protest of the Brazilian military government of the period.

And it was as consultant for the Institute for the Development of Animal Husbandry, for the Ministry of Education, and for the Corporation for Agrarian Reform, that, as I traveled practically all over the country, always in the company of young Chileans, who were mostly progressives, I listened to peasants and discussed with them various aspects of their concrete reality. I urged upon agronomists and agricultural technologists a political, pedagogical, democratic understanding of their practice. I debated general problems of educational policy with the educators of the cities and towns I visited.

I still have in my memory today, as fresh as ever, snatches of discourses by peasants and expressions of their legitimate desires for the betterment of their world, for a finer, less-ugly world, a world whose "edges" would be less "rough," in which it would be possible to love—Guevara's dream, too.

I shall never forget what a UN sociologist, an excellent intellectual and no less excellent a person, a Dutchman who wore a red beard, told me after we had assisted, all enthusiastic and full of confidence in the working class, at a two hour discussion on their eagerness for the establishment of agrarian reform by the government (still the Christian Democrats) in a remote corner of Chile. The peasants had been discussing their right to the land, their right to the freedom to produce, to raise crops and livestock, to live decently, to be. They had defended their right to be respected as persons and as workers who were creators of wealth, and they had demanded their right of access to culture and knowledge. It is in this direction that those historico-social conditions intersected in which the *Pedagogy of the Oppressed* could take root—and this time I am not referring to the book I wrote—which, in turn, is here being matched by, or prolonged into, a needed pedagogy of hope.

With the meeting over, as we were leaving the wagon shed where it had been held, my Dutch friend with the red beard put his hand on my shoulder and said—choosing his phrases carefully, and speaking with conviction: "It's been worth four days of wandering through these corners of Chile, to hear what we heard tonight." And he added, good-humoredly, "These peasants know more than we do."

I think it is important, at this point, to call attention to something I have emphasized in Pedagogy of the Oppressed: the relationship prevailing between political lucidity in a reading of the world, and the various levels of engagement in the process of mobilization and organization for the struggle—for the defense of rights, for laying claim to justice.

Progressive educators have to be on the alert where this datum is concerned, in their work of popular education, since not only the content, but the various manners in which one approaches the content, stand in direct relation with the levels of struggle referred to above.

It is one thing to work with popular groups, and experience the way in which those peasants operated that night, and something else again to work with popular groups who have not yet managed to "see" the oppressor "outside."

This datum continues valid today. The neoliberal discourses, chock-full of "modernity," do not have sufficient force to do away with social classes and decree the nonexistence of differing interests among them, any more than they have the strength to make away with the conflicts and struggle between them.

It happens that struggle is a historical and social category. Therefore it has historicity. It changes from one space-time to another space-time. The fact of the struggle does not militate against the possibility of pacts, agreements between the antagonistic parties. In other words, agreements and accords are part of the struggle, as a historical, and not metaphysical, category.

There are historical moments in which the survival of the social whole, which is in the interest of all the social classes, imposes upon those classes the necessity of understanding one another— which does not mean that we are experiencing a new age devoid of social classes and of conflicts.

The four-and-one-half years that I lived in Chile, then, were years of a profound learning process. It was the first time, with the exception of a brief visit to Bolivia, that I had had the experience of distancing myself geographically, with its epistemological consequences, from Brazil. Hence the importance of those four-and-one-half years.

Sometimes, on long automobile trips, with stops in cities along the way—Santiago to Puerto Mont, Santiago to Arica—I gave myself over to the quest for myself, refreshing my memory when it came to Brazil, about what I had done here, with other persons, mistakes made, the verbal incontinence that few intellectuals of the Left had escaped and to which any today still devote themselves, and through which reveal a terrible ignorance of the role of language in history.

"Agrarian reform, like it or lump it!" "Either this congress votes laws in the people's interests or we'll close it."

Actually, all of this verbal incontinence, this explosion of verbiage has no connection, none whatsoever, with a correct, authentic progressive position. It has no connection with a correct understanding of struggle as political, historical practice. It is quite true, as well, that all of this volubility, precisely because it is not done in a vacuum, ends by generating consequences that retard needed changes even more. At times, however, the irresponsible chatter also generates a discovery of the fact that verbal restraint is an indispensable virtue for those who devote themselves to the dream of a better world—a world in which women and men meet in a process of ongoing liberation.

Basically, I sought to reunderstand the fabrics, the facts, the deeds in which I had been wrapped and enveloped. Chilean reality, in its difference from our own, helped me to a better understanding of my experiences, and the latter, reseen, helped me to understand what was happening and could be happening in Chile.

I traversed a great part of that country on trips on which I really learned a great deal. Side by side with Chilean educators, I learned by helping administer training courses for persons proposing to work at the grass roots in agrarian reform projects, those who would work with the peasants on the fundamental problem of the reading of the word, always preceded by a reading of the world. The reading and writing of the word would always imply a more critical rereading of the world. Hence the hope that necessarily steeps Pedagogy of the Oppressed. Hence also the need, in literacy projects conducted in a progressive perspective, for a comprehension of language, and of its role, to which we have referred, in the achievement of citizenship.

It was by attempting to include a maximal respect for the cultural differences with which I had to struggle, one of them being language—in which I made an effort to express myself, as best I could, with clarity—that I learned so much of reality, and learned it with Chileans.

Respect for cultural differences, respect for the context to which one has come, a criticism of "cultural invasion," of sectarianism, and a defense of radicalness, of which I speak in Pedagogy of the Oppressed—all of this was something that, having begun to be part of my experience years before in Brazil, whose knowledge I had brought with me into exile, in the memory contained within my own self, was intensely, rigorously experienced by me in my years in Chile.

These elements of knowledge, which had been critically constituted in me since the inauguration of SESI, were consolidated in Chilean practice, and in the theoretical reflection I made upon that practice—in enlightening readings that made me laugh for joy, almost like a teenager, at finding in them a theoretical explanation of my practice, or the confirmation of the theoretical understanding that I had had of my practice. Santiago, to mention just the team of Brazilians living there, sometimes de jure—in exile— sometimes just de facto, unquestionably provided us with a rich opportunity. Christian Democracy, which spoke of itself as a "revolution in freedom," attracted countless intellectuals, student and union leaders, and groups of leftist political leaders from all over Latin America. Santiago, especially, had become a place, or grand context of theory-of-practice, in which those who arrived from other corners of Latin America would discuss, with Chileans and foreigners living there, both what was going on in Chile and what was going on in their own countries.

Latin America was effervescent in Santiago. Cubans were there, threatened as much as ever by the reactionary forces that, all filled with themselves, spoke of the death of socialism. The Cubans showed that changes could be made. There were the guerrilla theories, the "focus theory," the extraordinary charismatic personality of Camilo Torres—in whom no dichotomy existed between transcendentality and worldliness, history and metahistory—liberation theology was there (so soon to provoke fear, trembling, and rage), Guevara's capacity for love was there, as in the line he wrote to Carlos Guijano, as sincere as it was arresting: "Let me tell you, at the risk of appearing ridiculous, that the genuine revolutionary is animated by feelings of love. It is impossible to imagine an authentic revolutionary without this quality."

In May 1968 came the student movements in the outside world, rebellious, libertarian. There was Marcuse, with his influence on youth. In China, Mao Tse-tung and the cultural revolution.

Santiago had become almost a kind of "bedroom community" for intellectuals, for politicians of the most varied persuasions. In this sense, perhaps Santiago was, in itself, at that time, the best center of "learning" and knowledge in Latin America. We learned of analyses, reactions, and criticisms by Colombians, Venezuelans,

Cubans, Mexicans, Bolivians, Argentinians, Paraguayans, Brazilians, Chileans, and Europeans—analyses ranging from an almost unrestricted acceptance of Christian Democracy to its total rejection. There were sectarian, intolerant criticisms, but also open, radical criticisms in the sense that I advocate.

Some of my companions in exile and I learned not only from encounters with many of the Latin Americans I have mentioned who passed through Santiago, but from the excitement of a "knowledge of living experience," from the dreams, from the clarity, from the doubts, from the ingenuousness, from the "cunning" of the Chilean workers—more rural than urban, in my case.

I remember now a visit I made, with a Chilean companion, to an agrarian reform project some hours' distance from Santiago. A number of evening "culture circles" were in operation there, and we had come to follow the process of the reading of the word and rereading of the world. In the second or third circle we visited, I felt a strong desire to try a dialogue with a group of peasants. Generally I avoided this because of the language difficulty. I was afraid my language gaffes might prejudice the smooth functioning of the work. That evening I decided to lay this concern aside, and, asking permission from the educator coordinating the discussion, I asked the group whether they were willing to have a conversation with me.

They accepted, and we began a lively dialogue, with questions and replies on both sides—promptly followed, however, by a disconcerting silence.

I too remained silent. In the silence, I remembered earlier experiences, in the Brazilian Northeast, and I guessed what was going to happen. I knew and expected that, suddenly, one of them, breaking the silence, would speak in his or her name and that of his or her companions. I even knew the tenor of that discourse. And so my own waiting, in the silence, must have been less painful than it was for them to listen to the silence.

"Excuse us, sir," said one of them, ". . . excuse us for talking. You're the one who should have been talking, sir. You know things, sir. We don't."

How many times I have heard this statement in Pernambuco, and not only in the rural zones, but even in Recife. And it was at the price of having to hear statements like that that I learned that, for the progressive educator, there is no other route than to seize the educands' "moment" and begin with their "here" and "now"—but as a stepping-stone to getting beyond, critically, their naïveté. It will do no harm to repeat that a respect for the peasants; ingenuousness, without ironical smiles or malicious questions, does not mean that the educator must accommodate to their level of reading of the world.

What would have been meaningless would have been for me to "fill" the silence of the group of peasants with my words, thus reinforcing the ideology that they had just enunciated. What I had to do was to begin with the acceptance of something said in the discourse of the peasant and make a problem of it for them, and thereby bring them once more to dialogue.

On the other hand, it would have been likewise meaningless—after having heard what the peasant said, begging pardon on behalf of the group for having spoken, when I was the one who knew how to do that, because I "knew"—if I had given them a lecture, with doctoral airs, on the "ideology of power and the power of ideology."

Purely parenthetically, I cannot resist—at a moment like this, as I relive Pedagogy of the Oppressed, and speak of cases like this one that I have experienced, the experience of which has given me theoretical foundations for not only advocating, but experiencing respect for the popular groups in my work as an educator—I cannot resist expressing my regret over a certain type of criticism in which I am pointed to as an "elitist." Or, at the opposite pole, where I am sketched as a "populist."

The far-off years of my experiences in SESI, the years of my intense learning process with fishers, with peasants and urban laborers, among the hillocks and ravines of Recife, had vaccinated me, as it were, against an elitist arrogance. My experience has taught me that educands need to be addressed as such; but to address them as educands implies a recognition of oneself, the educator, as one of two agents here, each capable of knowing and each wishing to know, and each working with the other for an understanding of the object of cognition. Thus, teaching and learning are moments in a larger process—that of knowing, of cognizing, which implies recognizing. At bottom, what I mean is that the educand really becomes an educand when and to the extent that he or she knows, or comes to know, consent, cognoscible objects, and not in the measure that the educator is depositing in the educand a description of the objects or content.

Educands recognize themselves as such by cognizing objects—discovering that they are capable of knowing, as the assist at the immersion of significates, in which process they also become critical "significators." Rather than being educands because of some reason or other, educands need to become educands by assuming themselves, taking themselves as cognizing subjects, and not as an object upon which the discourse of the educator impinges. Herein lies, in the last analysis, the great political importance of the teaching act. It is this, among other elements, that distinguishes a progressive educator from his or her reactionary colleague.

"All right," I said, in response to the peasant's intervention. "Let's say I know and you don't. Still, I'd like to try a game with you that, to work right, will require our full effort and attention. I'm going to draw a line down the middle of this chalkboard, and I'm going to write down on this side the goals I score against you, and on this other side the ones you score against me. The game will consist in asking each other questions. If the person asked doesn't know the answer, the person who asked the question scores a goal. I'll start the game by asking you a question."

At this point, precisely because I had seized the group's "moment," the climate was more lively than when we had begun, before the silence.

First question:
"What is the Socratic maieutic?"
General guffawing. Score one for me.
"Now it's your turn to ask me a question," I said.
There was some whispering, and one of them tossed out the question:
"What's a contour curve?"
I couldn't answer. I marked down one to one.
"What importance does Hegel have in Marx's thought?"
Two to one.
"What's soil liming?"
Two to two.
"What's an intransitive verb?"
Three to two.
"What's a contour curve got to do with erosion?"
Three to three.
"What's epistemology?"

Four to three.
"What's green fertilizer?"
Four to four.
And so on, until we got to ten to ten.
As I said good-bye, I made a suggestion. "Let's think about this evening. You had begun to have a fine discussion with me. Then you were silent, and said that only I could talk because I was the only one who knew anything. Then we played a knowledge game and we tied ten to ten. I knew ten things you didn't, and you knew ten things I didn't. Let's think about this."
On the way back home I recalled the first experience I had had, long before, in the Zona da Mata of Pernambuco, like the one I had just had here.
After a few moments of good discussion with a group of peasants, silence fell on us and enveloped us all. What one of them had said then, in Portuguese, was the same thing as I had heard tonight in Spanish—a literal translation of what the Chilean peasant had said this evening.
"Fine," I had told them. "I know. You don't. But why do I know and you don't?"
Accepting his statement, I prepared the ground for my intervention. A vivacious sparkle in them all. Suddenly curiosity was kindled. The answer was not long in coming.
"You know because you're a doctor, sir, and we're not."
"Right, I'm a doctor and you're not. But why am I a doctor and you're not?"
"Because you've gone to school, you've read things, studied things, and we haven't."

"And why have I been to school?"
"Because your dad could send you to school. Ours couldn't."
"And why couldn't your parents send you to school?"
"Because they were peasants like us."
"And what is 'being a peasant'?"
"It's not having an education . . . not owning anything . . . working from sun to sun . . . having no rights . . . having no hope."
"And why doesn't a peasant have any of this?"
"The will of God."
"And who is God?"
"The Father of us all."

"And who is a father here this evening?"

Almost all raised their hands, and said they were.

I looked around the group without saying anything. Then I picked out one of them and asked him, "How many children do you have?"

"Three."

"Would you be willing to sacrifice two of them, and make them suffer so that the other one could go to school, and have a good life, in Recife? Could you love your children that way?"

"No!"

"Well, if you," I said, "a person of flesh and bones, could not commit an injustice like that—how could God commit it? Could God really be the cause of these things?"

A different kind of silence. Completely different from the first. A silence in which something began to be shared. Then:

"No. God isn't the cause of all this. It's the boss!"

Perhaps for the first time, those peasants were making an effort to get beyond the relationship that I called, in Pedagogy of the Oppressed, that of the "adherence" of the oppressed to the oppressor, in order to "step back" from the oppressor, and localize the oppressor "outside" themselves, as Fanon would say.

From that point of departure, we could have gotten to an understanding of the role of the "boss," in the context of a certain socioeconomic, political system—gotten to an understanding of the social relations of production, gotten to an understanding of class interests, and so on and so on.

What would have been completely senseless would have been if, after the silence that had so brusquely interrupted our dialogue, I had given a traditional speech, crammed with empty, intolerant slogans.

Afterword
Paulo Freire's Intellectual Roots

Peter McLaren

Years ago I was told in a blind review by a distinguished education journal that my paper on Paulo Freire needed drastic revision. The reviewer had kindly offered copious notes criticizing my approach to Freire's work, ending his review with some stern advice that went something like this: "I would advise this author to read the work of Peter McLaren so he or she can get a better grasp of Freire's work." The recommendation that I must read the work of Peter McLaren was interesting in many ways, but I am afraid I did not take this reviewer's comments to heart. I simply continued to read Freire in and against the contexts provided by other writers and thinkers who at that time were making a significant impact on my own pedagogical work and to expand on these insights for its implications for a deeper approach to critical pedagogy. That, it seems to me, is one of the signal purposes of *Paulo Freire's Intellectual Roots: Toward Historicity in Praxis.*

This book would have only scholarly value if Freire's work was necessarily finished. But it offers the reader much more. It provides the necessary theoretical import for translating Freire's work into the contextual specificity of the reader's own pedagogical projects, and thus provides paths for making Freire's work much more meaningful as a form of praxis.

Fortunately for those interested in social and economic justice and the role played by education, there is always something new to be said about Freire's writings because there is always something new to be said about the world and our relationship to it. It is fundamentally and necessarily unfinished because the project that animated his work was the struggle for human liberation. He has left all of us yearning for human freedom, an invaluable if not magisterial corpus that will forever remain unfinished. Each reader who reads Freire enters a privileged zone of pedagogical dynamism in which her actions in and on the world become unraveled like an unspooled film, each image to be scrutinized in the context of the larger mise-en-scène, which amounts to the articulation of pedagogical space, the production of historical time; the creation of characters whose actions are bordered by various ideological frames and determined by what society permits us to record and with what epistemological instruments. Against this knowledge we can reedit our past and live differently in the present and imagine futures of concrete possibility.

Freire's intellectual roots cannot be understood without understanding the intrinsic spirituality that animates his politico-ethical project. Of course, Freire believed that we can grasp the object of our knowledge, that there was a world independent of our existence, and that this world can be directly grasped (although not fully grasped) in itself. But he also argued that the objective world could only be understood in relation to others, to the social character of both our being human and our becoming more fully human. There is in Freire's work what I would call a transformative volition, or protagonistic intent, that is, a movement of the human spirit (that resides in the flesh of our bodies and of our dreams) in and on the world designed to transform the material and social conditions that shape us and are shaped by us so that our capacities are enhanced and our humanity enlarged. This is not meant to be some pulpy or sensationalistic observation to excite the reader's imagination but deals directly with what I consider to represent the enfleshment of Freire's concept of praxis in which he weaves the human body into his materialist dialectics of consciousness and praxis. For Freire, reality was a concrete totality, a reality that is already a structured, self-forming, dialectical whole in the process of coming into existence. As subjects, Freire believes we can break out of the prison house of discourse and its attendant subjectivism by changing the material conditions that shape us in our practical activity. Here Freire seeks to avoid solipsism and idealism through a method of analysis and a conception of the world that involves a dialectical analysis of reality and a dialectical unity with the oppressed. In other words, Freire was concerned with interrogating the causal relationships that inform our material consciousness and subjective volition and intentionality. In the process of understanding the world, we deepen our consciousness precisely through our actions in and on the world that enable us not only to grasp our positionality in the world but to transform the totality of social relations that constitute the contradictory character of our existence. Freire was committed to freeing ourselves and others from the relations bound up in the dialectical contradictions of everyday life. His work was thusly connected to Marx's negative conception of ideology—to actions and symbols that are really only partial and fragmented and therefore distorted. Here Freire admonishes us not to free people from their chains but to prepare them to free themselves through a dialogical praxis linked to a materialist dialectics of consciousness (see Au, 2007). Freire believes that the forms of action people take is a function of how they perceive themselves in the world. What is urgently necessary for Freire is critical action and this stems fundamentally from our dialogical relations with other human beings that leads to a critical consciousness embedded relationally in the word and the world as a form of praxis, an act of knowing through problem-posing/coding/decoding and reconstruction. Dialogue in this fashion not only enables teachers to teach but teachers can also learn from their students.

Attending an *encuentro* in Cherán, Michoacán, where *el pueblo Purépecha en rebeldía* are creating militias to protect themselves from the illegal loggers backed by the narco cartels, I could see the spirit of Freire at work in the attempts of the people to become a self-governing community. Here, Freire's entire pedagogical crasis stands for the God of the Poor against both the exgregiousness and good intentions of the God of the Rich (the God of Violence or the God of Unlimited Progress). The fragrance wafting from Freire's axiological thurible is not cassia or sandlewood, or frankincense and myrrh; rather, it is the sacred sage of the indigenous peoples of Las Americas, signifying unwithholding love and salvific grace. Here Freire's face is hidden behind a signature Zapatista handerchief, his pedagogy of liberation bent on creating the necessary albeit insufficient conditions for a world where the boulevards of the lonely and the despised will no longer be drenched with tears from poor mothers carrying pictures of their daughters, sons, and husbands. There is therefore an eschatological dimension to Freire's work that is designed to remove barriers to a developing, emergentist world transformation in which vertical relations of power (think of the "andar predicando" associated with the vanguard party) are replaced by more symmetrical or horizontal relations of power and privilege (think of the "andar preguntando" view of power relations of the Zapatistas).

The theogony of Freire's works is not derived from Biblical scholarship and the hamartia of Adam nor does he reject this root and branch; rather, it can be linked at least implicitly to the pantheon of indigenous saints that stretch thousands of years into the past and that refuse to be whitened. This could be seen as anathema to those ensepulchured within the dogma of capitalist modernity for whom politics and spirituality are two fundamentally separable spheres, each of which somehow loses its integrity insofar as it loses autonomy to the other. However, Freire sees no contradiction in a pedagogy informed by both practical consciousness and spiritual conviction (see Rivage-Seul, 2006).

Like the Cross in the Box by sculptor Mathias Goeritz, a spiked cross that folds itself neatly into a box with four smooth and glistening surfaces, Freire's work can be folded together into a relatively domesticated corpus that calls for student-centered programs with a stress on functional and cultural literacy, or it can be opened to reveal the razor-edged teeth of more forbidding challenges to the totality of capitalist social relations that imprison us, relations of exploitation and alienation that cause such needless suffering for so much of the world's population (what we have come to know through the Occupy Movements as the 99 percent). For those who embrace the former role for Freire, critical pedagogy is often seen as excessively ideological and oppressively obvious, bludgeoning the student with blatant leftist propaganda. For those who choose to unfold the box into a cross of steel thorns, Freire's work is necessarily directed first and foremost against the structural violence of the state and its brutal insinuation into the totality of transnational capitalist social relations. This structural violence is often naturalized as a commonplace feature that we cannot challenge.

This sentiment was brought to my attention by a perceptive reader of Freire during a recent visit to the Northeast Normal University in China:

> In China, when I finished primary school, I was told by my teachers to adjust to this world, to learn the rules of Chinese society, to leave behind my restiveness and childish behavior. I was told that in doing so, I had arrived at maturity, or sociability. I never doubted this advice until reading Freire's *Pedagogy of the Oppressed*. Slowly, I began to realize something: Why should I adjust to this society? Who created this society? Who made those rules for us to follow? Why should I change myself, drop my curiosity for a more sophisticated attitude, drop my initial dreams for the position that this society "reserved" for me? Paulo Freire's works proved inspirational, his work taught me to realize my power and my right as a human being; he taught me that there is a word called "alternative"; he taught me that not everything is meant to be; he provided me with the opportunity to understand more deeply Plato's parable—we cannot remain staring at our shadows in the cave without turning our bodies around to find the source of the light. Life is a one-way journey, but the way we live our lives is never one-dimensional. (Yan Wang, personal communication)

It was my privilege to have witnessed Freire walking among us, laughing and lightfooted, his tiny shoulders heaving like twin turbines beneath his crisp, freshly starched shirt, his slender legs gliding with a carefree, insouciant lilt, as if he were being helped along by a puckish breeze that served as a counterpoint to his steady, almost relentless gaze. To me it seemed as though he was always peering into the present somewhere from the future, in some future anterior where dreams are on a collision course with what is occurring in the laboratories of everyday life we call reality, where light breaks through dark chambers that cannot be illuminated without love. To understand that collision is to understand the essence of Freire's work. Without a careful reading of Freire's intellectual roots, one can only witness the collision without understanding the systems of intelligibility that make such a collision inevitable and without understanding the possibilities of sublating such a collision in order to bring about alternative futures linked to the sustainability of the planet and humanity as a whole. This is the *grand mysterium* of Freire's work.

Paulo Freire's Intellectual Roots: Toward Historicity in Praxis, edited by Robert Lake and Tricia Kress is a powerful text that demands a careful reading by all of those interested in taking up the Freirean challenge—which is, after all, the fundamental human challenge—of creating those structural and endogenous conditions of possibility that will lead to a concrete future of human creativity, autonomy, and social justice.

References

Au, W. (2007). "Epistemology of the Oppressed: The Dialectics of Paulo Freire's Theory of Knowledge." *Journal for Critical Education Policy Studies*, 5 (2). Retrieved from: www.jceps.com/index.php?pageID=article&articleID=100

Rivage-Seul, D. (2006). *The Emperor's God: Misunderstandings of Christianity*. Berea, KY: Berea College Printing Services.

BIBLIOGRAPHY

Adorno, T. (1998). *Education after Auschwitz: Critical models interventions and catchwords.* New York, NY: Columbia University Press.

Alexander, M. J. and Mohanty, C. T. (1997). "Introduction: genealogies, legacies, movements." In M. J. Alexander and C. Mohanty (eds). *Feminist genealogies, colonial legacies, democratic futures* (pp. xiii–xlii). New York, NY: Routledge.

Allman, P. (1999). *Revolutionary social transformation. Democratic hopes, political possibilities and critical education.* Westport, CT and London, GB: Bergin & Garvey.

Allman, P., Mayo, P., Cavanagh, C., Lean Heng, C., and Haddad, S. (1998). "Introduction. '. . . the creation of a world in which it will be easier to love,'" *Convergence,* XXI (1 and 2), 9–16.

Aricó, J. (1988). *La Cola del Diablo. Itinerario de Gramsci en America Latina.* Caracas, Venezuela: Editorial Nueva Sociedad.

Aronowitz, S. (1993). "Paulo Freire's radical democratic humanism." In P. McLaren and P. Leonard (eds). *Paulo Freire: A critical encounter* (pp. 8–24). London, GB and New York, NY: Routledge.

— (2008). *Against schooling: For an education that matters.* Boulder: CO: Paradigm Publishers.

— (2009). "Forward." In S. L. Macrine (ed.). *Critical pedagogy in uncertain times: Hope and possibilities* (pp. ix–xii). New York, NY: Palgrave MacMillan.

— (2009). "Gramsci's concept of political organization." In J. Francese. *Perspectives on Gramsci: Politics, culture and social theory* (pp. 8–19). Abingdon, UK and New York, NY: Routledge.

Avrich. P. (1980). *The modern school movement: Anarchism and education in the United States.* Princeton, NJ: Princeton University Press.

Bauman, Z. and Tester, K. (2001). *Conversations with Sigmund Bauman.* Malden, MA: Polity Press, p. 4.

Beverly, J. (2000). "The dilemma of subaltern studies at Duke." *Nepantla: Views from the South,* 1, 33–44.

Bhabha, H. (1994). "The enchantment of art: The artist in society." C. Becker and A. Wiens (eds). Chicago: *New Art Examiner,* pp. 24–34.

Borge, C. and Mayo, P. (2007). *Public intellectuals, radical democracy and social movements. A book of interviews.* New York, NY: Peter Lang.

Coben, D. (1998). *Radical heroes: Gramsci, Freire and the politics of adult education*. New York, NY: Garland.

Connell, R. (2007). *Southern theory*. Cambridge, UK: Polity Press.

Corrigan, P. R. D. (1990). *Social forms/human capacities: Essays in authority and difference*. New York, NY and London, GB: Routledge.

Cortesão, L. (2012). "Paulo Freire ve Amilcar Cabral (Paulo Freire and Amilcar Cabral)." *Eleştirel pedagoji—critical pedagogy*, 4 (19), 23–6.

Coutinho, C. N. (1995). *In Brasilé in Gramsci in Europa e in America*. A. A. Santucci (ed.). Rome, Italy and Bari, Italy: Sagittari Laterza, pp. 133–40.

Dale, J. (2003). "Freire, Aristotle, Marx, and Sartre: A critique of the human condition." Paper presented at The Midwest Research to Practice Conference in Adult, Continuing, and Community Education. Columbus, OH: The Ohio State University.

Dale, J. and Hyslop-Margison, E. (2010). *Paulo Freire: Teaching for freedom and transformation: The philosophical influences on the work of Paulo Freire*. Dordrecht, The Netherlands: Springer.

Douglas, F. (1999/1857). *Frederick Douglass: Selected speeches and writing*. Chicago, IL: Lawrence Hill Books.

Dryzek, J. S. (2005). "Deliberative democracy in divided societies: Alternatives to agonism and analgesia." *Political Theory*, 33, 218–42.

Elias, J. L. (1994). *Paulo Freire: Pedagogy of liberation*. Malabar, FL: Krieger.

Engels, F. (1997). "Feuerbach and the end of classical German philosophy." In L. Feuerbach, K. Marx, and F. Engels. *German socialist philosophy* (pp. 183–225). New York, NY: Continuum.

Fernández Díaz, O. (1995). *In America Latina in Gramsci in Europa e in America*. A. A. Santucci, (ed.). Rome, Italy and Bari, Italy: Sagittari Laterza, pp. 141–57.

Fichte, J. (1796/2000). "Foundations of natural right." In F. Neuhouser (ed.). *Foundations of natural right according to the principles of the Wissenschaftslehre* (pp. 260–1). Cambridge, UK: Cambridge University Press.

Freire, P. (1970/2000/2005/2011). *Pedagogy of the oppressed*. New York, NY: Continuum.

— (1972). *Cultural action for freedom*. Harmondsworth, GB. .Penguin.

— (1973). *Education for critical consciousness*. New York, NY: Seabury Press.

— (1976). *Education, the practice of freedom*. London, GB. Writers and Readers Publishing Cooperative.

— (1980). *A day with Paulo Freire*. Delhi, India: ISPCK.

— (1983/1978). *Pedagogy in process: The Letters to Guinea Bissau*. New York, NY: Continuum.

— (1985). *The politics of education: Culture, power, and liberation*. South Hadley, MA: Bergin & Garvey.

— (1993a). "Foreword." In P. McLaren and P. Leonard (eds). *Paulo Freire: A critical encounter* (pp. ix–xii). London, GB and New York, NY: Routledge.

— (1993b). *Pedagogy of the city*. New York, NY: Continuum.

— (1993c). *Pedagogy of hope: Reliving pedagogy of the oppressed*. New York, NY: Continuum Press.

— (1995). *Reply to discussants in Paulo Freire at the institute*. M. de Fugueiredo-Cowen and D. Gastaldo (eds). London, GB: Institute of Education, University of London, pp. 61–7.

— (1996). *Letters to Cristina: Reflections on my life and work*. New York, NY and London, GB: Routledge.

— (1997a). *Mentoring the mentor: A critical dialogue with Paulo Freire* Counterpoints, vol. 60. New York, NY: Peter. Lang.

— (1997b). *Pedagogy of the heart*. New York, NY: Continuum.

— (1998a). *Pedagogy of freedom: Ethics, democracy, and civic courage*. Lanham, MD: Rowman & Littlefield.

— (1998b). *Politics and education: UCLA Latin American studies*; vol. 83. Los Angeles, CA: UCLA Latin American Center.

— (1998c). *Teachers as cultural workers: Letters to those who dare teach*. Boulder, CO: Westview.

— (2000). *Cultural action for freedom* (revised edition). Cambridge, MA: Harvard Educational Review.

— (2003). *El Grito manso*. México, DF: Sigle Veintiuno.

Freire, P. and Faundez, A. (1989). *Learning to question: A pedagogy of liberation*. Geneva, Switzerland: World Council of Churches/New York, NY: Continuum.

Freire, P., Freire, A. M., and Macedo, D. (1998). *The Paulo Freire reader*. New York, NY: Continuum.

Freire, P. and Macedo, D. (1987). *Literacy: Reading the word & the world*. Critical studies in education series. South Hadley, MA: Bergin & Garvey.

— (1996). *Letters to Cristina: Reflections on my life and work*. New York, NY: Routledge.

— (1998). "Introduction." In A. Freire and D. Macedo (eds). *The Paulo Freire reader* (pp. 1–44). New York, NY: Continuum.

Fromm, E. (1942). *The fear of freedom*. London, GB: Routledge & Kegan Paul.

— (1964). *Marx's concept of man*. New York, NY: Frederick Ungar.

Fuentes, L. (2010). "Remembering Paulo: Stories." In T. Wilson, P. Park, and A. Colon-Muniz. *Memories of Paulo* (pp. 133–8). Rotterdam, The Netherlands: Sense.

Fung, A. (2005). "Deliberation before the revolution: Toward an ethics of deliberative democracy." *Political Theory*, 33, 397–419.

Gabriel, M. (2011). *Love and capital: Karl and Jenny Marx and the birth of a revolution.* New York, NY: Little, Brown and Company.

Giroux, H. (1993). "Paulo Freire and the politics of postcolonialism." In P. McLaren and P. Leonard (eds). *Paulo Freire: A critical encounter* (pp. 177–88). London, GB and New York, NY: Routledge.

Gramsci, A. (1957). *The modern prince and other writings*, L. Marks (ed. and trans.). New York, NY: International Publishers.

— (1971). *Selections from the prison notebooks*, Q. Hoare and G. Bowell Smith (eds). New York, NY: International.

— (1975). *Quanderni del carcere, edizione critica* (4 vols). V. Gerratana (ed.). Turin, Italy, Einaudi.

— (1977). *Antonio Gramsci: Selections from political writings (1910–1920)*, Q. Hoare and J. Matthew (eds). New York, NY: International.

Habermas, J. (1973). *Theory and Practice.* Boston, MA: Beacon.

Hegel, G. W. F. (1805). *The philosophy of spirit (Jena Lectures 1805–6)* PART II. Actual Spirit. Retrieved from: www.marxists.org/reference/archive/hegel/works/jl/ch02a.htm.

— (1910 [1807]). *The phenomenology of mind.* Translated with an Introduction and notes J. B. Baillie. London, GB: George Allen & Unwin.

— (1952/1821). *Hegel's philosophy of right.* Translated with Notes by T. M. Knox. Oxford, UK: Oxford University Press.

— (1955). *Hegel's lectures on the history of philosophy*, trans. John Sibree. New York, NY: Dover.

— (1969/1816). *The science of logic*, trans. A. V. Miller. London, GB: George Allen & Unwin.

— (1971) *Hegel's philosophy on mind. Part three of the encyclopedia of the philosophical sciences (1830).* Translated by William Wallace together with the zus~tze in Boumann's text (1845). Translated by A. V. Miller, with a Foreword by J. N. Findlay. Oxford, UK: Oxford University Press.

— (1977/1807). *Phenomenology of spirit.* Oxford, UK: Oxford University Press.

— (1979). *System of ethical life* [1802/3] and *First philosophy of spirit* [1803–4], trans. T. M. Knox. New York, NY: State University of New York Press.

— (1984). *The letters*, trans. C. Butler and C. Seiler. Bloomington, IN: Indiana University Press.

— (2009/1830). *Hegel's logic.* Translated by William Wallace with a Foreword by Andy Blunden. Pacifica, CA: Marxists Internet Archive Publications.

— (2011/1807). *The phenomenology of spirit*, trans. Terry Pinkard. Retrieved from http://web.mac.com/titpaul/Site/Phenomenology_of_ Spirit_page.html

Hess, M. (1964/1843). "The philosophy of the act." In A. Fried and R. Sanders (eds). *Socialist thought, a documentary history* (pp. 260–1). Chicago, IL: Aldine.

Horton, M. and Freire, P. (1990). *We make the road by walking: Conversations on education and social change.* Philadelphia, PA: Temple University Press.

Ireland, T. (1987). *Antonio Gramsci and adult education: Reflections on the Brazilian experience.* Manchester, UK: Manchester University Press.

Ives, P. (2004). *Language and hegemony in Gramsci.* London, GB: Pluto Press/Halifax Nova Scotia, Canada: Fernwood Publishing.

Kane, L. (2001). *Popular education and social change in Latin America.* London, GB: Latin American Bureau.

Kliebard, H. (1986). *The struggle for the American curriculum: 1893– 1958.* Boston, MA: Routledge and Kegan Paul.

Kojéve, A. (1969/1933–9). *Introduction to the reading of Hegel. Lectures on the phenomenology of spirit.* Ithaca: NY: Cornell University Press.

La Belle, T. J. (1986). *Nonformal education in Latin American and the Caribbean: Stability, reform, or revolution?* New York, NY: Praeger.

Langford, P. E. (2005). *Vygotsky's developmental and education psychology.* New York, NY: Psychology Press.

Ledwith, M. (2005). *Community development: A critical approach.* Bristol, UK: Policy Press.

Lenin, V. I. (1972/1916). *Collected works*, vol. 38. London, GB: Lawrence & Wishart.

Lewis, T. E. (2007). "Revolutionary leadership, revolutionary pedagogy: Reevaluating the links and disjunctions between Lukacs and Freire." *Philosophy of Education*, 285–93.

Lukács, G. (1971/1923). *History and class consciousness.* London, GB: Merlin.

— (1975/1938). *The young Hegel.* London, GB: Merlin.

Marx, K. (1932/1845). *The German ideology.* Ch. 3. Retrieved from: www. marxists.org/archive/marx/works/1845/german-ideology/ch03p.htm

— (1956/1844). *The holy family or critique of critical criticism against Bruno and company.* Ch. 6. Retrieved from: www.marxists.org/ archive/marx/works/1845/holy-family/cho06_2.html

— (1975/1845). "Theses on Feuerbach." In L. Churbanov and L. Golman (eds). *Marx Engels collected works* (vol. 5, p. 3). New York, NY: International.

— (1976/1848). "Manifesto of the communist party." In L. Churbanov and L. Golman (eds). *Marx Engels collected works* (vol. w6, p. 3). New York, NY: International.

— (1977). *Capital: Volume one.* New York, NY: Vintage Books.
— (1978). "Thesis on Feuerbach." In R. Tucker (ed.). *The Marx-Engels reader* (pp. 143–5). New York: W.W. Norton.
— (1986/1857). "The method of political economy." In L. Churbanov and L. Golman (eds). *Marx Engels collected works* (vol. 28, p. 37). New York, NY: International.
— (1987). *Economic and philosophic manuscripts of 1844.* Buffalo, NY: Prometheus Books.
— (1996/1867). "Preface to the first German edition of *capital*." In L. Churbanov and L. Golman (eds). *Marx Engels collected works* (vol. 35, p. 7). New York, NY: International.
— (2002). *Marx on religion.* J. C. Raines (ed.). Philadelphia, PA: Temple University Press.
Marx, K. and Engels, F. (1987). "Manifesto of the communist party." In K. Marx. *Economic and philosophic manuscripts of 1844* (pp. 203–43). Buffalo, NY: Prometheus Books.
Mayo, P. (1997). *Imagining tomorrow: Adult education for transformation.* Leicester, UK: NIACE.
— (1999). *Gramsci, Freire and adult education: Possibilities for transformative education.* London, GB and New York, NY: Zed Books.
— (2004). *Liberating praxis Paulo Freire's legacy for radical education and politics.* Rotterdam, The Netherlands: Sense.
— (2005). "Antonio Gramsci and Paulo Freire some connections and contrasts." In *Encyclopedia* No. 17, pp. 77–102; republished 2008 in C. A. Torres and P. Noguera (eds). *Social justice education for teachers: Paulo Freire and the possible dream* (pp. 51–68). Rotterdam, The Netherlands and Taipei, Taiwan: Sense.
— (2007). "Gramsci, the Southern question and the Mediterranean." *Mediterranean Journal of Educational Studies,* 12 (2), 1–17.
— (2009). "Editorial: Antonio Gramsci and educational thought." *Educational Philosophy and Theory,* 41 (6), 601–44.
— (2010). *Intelectual/intelectuais in dicionário Paulo Freire.* D. R. Streck, E. Redin, and J. J. Zitkoski (eds). Belo Horizonte, Brazil: Autentica, pp. 227–9.
Melis, A. (1995). "Gramsci e l'America Latina." In G. Baratta and A. Catone (eds). *Antonio Gramsci e il progresso intellectual di massa* (pp. 227–34). Milano, Italy: Edizioni Unicopli.
Morrow, R. A. and Torres, C. A. (1995). *Social Theory and education. A critique of theories of social and cultural reproduction.* Albany, NY: State University of New York Press.
Newman, F. and Holzman, L. (1993). *Lev Vygotsky: Revolutionary scientist.* New York: NY: Routledge.

Oakeshott, M. (1962). *The voice of poetry in the conversation of mankind. Rationalism in politics and other essays.* London, GB: Metheun, pp. 197–247.

O'Brien, J. (2002). "Be realistic, demand the impossible: Staughton Lynd, Jesse Lemisch, and a committed history." *Radical History Review*, 82, 65–90.

Pinkard, T. (1996). *Hegel's Phenomenology. The Sociality of Reason.* Cambridge, UK: Cambridge University Press.

— (2000). *Hegel: A biography.* Cambridge, UK: Cambridge University Press.

Pollock, S. (1992). "Robert Hass." *Mother Jones*, March/April, 22.

Ransome, O. (1992). *Antonio Gramsci. A new introduction.* Hemel Hempstead, Hertfordshire, UK: Harvester-Wheatsheaf.

Said, E. (2001). *Reflections on exile and other essays.* Cambridge, MA: Harvard University Press.

Sartre, J. P. (1956). *Being and nothingness: a phenomenological essay on ontology.* New York, NY: Pocket Books.

Shor, I. (1987/1980). *Critical Teaching and everyday life.* Chicago, IL and London, GB: University of Chicago Press.

Shor, I. and Freire, P. (1987). *A pedagogy for liberation: Dialogues on transforming education.* Westport, CT: Bergin & Garvey.

Thomas, P. D. (2009). *The Gramsci moment: Philosophy, hegemony and Marxism.* Amsterdam, The Netherlands: Brill.

Torres, C. A. (1990). *The politics of nonformal education in Latin America.* New York, NY: Praeger.

— (1992). *The church, society, and hegemony: A critical sociology of religion in Latin America.* Westport, CT: Greenwood.

Williams, R. R. (1997). *Hegel's ethics of recognition.* Los Angeles, CA: University of California Press.

Wilson, T., Park, P., and Colon-Muniz, A. (2010). *Memories of Paulo.* Rotterdam, The Netherlands: Sense.

Zinn, H. (1999). *Marx in Soho: A play on history.* Cambridge, MA: South End Press.

NOTES ON CONTRIBUTORS

Stanley Aronowitz has taught at the Graduate Center of the City University of New York since 1983, where he is a Distinguished Professor of Sociology. He received his BA at the New School in 1968 and his PhD from the Union Graduate School in 1975. He studies labor, social movements, science and technology, education, social theory, and cultural studies and is director of the Center for the Study of Culture, Technology and Work at the Graduate Center.

He is author or editor of 23 books including Just Around Corner The Paradox of the Jobless Recovery (2005), How Class Works (2003), The Last Good Job in America (2001), The Knowledge Factory (2000), The Jobless Future: Sci-tech and the Dogma of Work (1994, with William DiFazio), and False Promises: The Shaping of American Working Class Consciousness (1992/1973).

He is founding editor of the journal *Social Text* and is currently a member of its advisory board, and he sits on the editorial boards of Cultural Critique and Ethnography. He has published more than 200 articles and reviews in publications such as *Harvard Educational Review, Social Policy, The Nation,* and *The American Journal of Sociology.* Prior to coming to the Graduate School he taught at the University of California-Irvine and Staten Island Community College. He has been visiting professor or scholar at University of Wisconsin, Madison, the University of Paris, Lund University, and Columbia University.

Andy Blunden is a Melbourne writer, who works with the Independent Social Research Network. Andy developed an interest in Hegel in 1980, has held a Hegel Summer School since 1998, and runs the Hegel-by-HyperText website. He is a joint Editor *of Mind, Culture & Activity*, a journal of cultural psychology.

Ana Cruz, a native of Brazil, received her PhD in Education from the University of Tennessee. She is Full Professor of Education at St. Louis Community College—Meramec, St. Louis, Missouri. Ana's research interests include critical pedagogy, social justice education, multicultural/international education, and Music and Deafness. Ana was the Founding Chair of the AERA Paulo Freire SIG and serves on the *Founding Scholars' Advisory Board* of the Paulo and Nita Freire Project for Critical Pedagogy. She is involved with the *International Journal of Critical Pedagogy* (IJCP) as *International Affiliate*, as *Brazilian Portuguese Articles Editor*, and was managing editor.

Vicki Dagostino is currently a Lecturer in the Judith Herb College of Education, Department of Educational Foundations and Leadership. She received her PhD from the University of Toledo in 2008 in Foundations of Education in Educational Sociology with a minor in Educational Psychology. The title of her dissertation is *Towards a Being Based Liberatory Educational Paradigm: A Critical Encounter between Paulo Freire and Erich Fromm*. She is interested in transformative educational practices and the role of the individual in praxis, that is, reflection and action in order to transform the world. Her dissertation explored Freirean "Critical Consciousness" and posited that while critical awareness of social injustice is a necessary component of praxis, it is an insufficient condition for acting transformatively in the world. The psychology of the individual is alluded to, but not fully addressed by Freire, and her dissertation explores the connection of Freire's idea of the purpose of education as they relate to the psychology of the individual in society. In an attempt to do this, she invokes Erich Fromm's social-psychological theory to fill in this missing element and enhance Freire's theory by adding a much-needed understanding of the complexity of freedom and authentic existence. She currently teach courses in Educational Sociology, that is, "Schooling and Democratic Society," and Educational Psychology, that is, "Applied Psychology for Teachers." In both she teaches preservice teachers, and attempts to incorporate Freirean critical consciousness through problem-posing pedagogy.

Pablo Fontdevila—choreographer, dancer, and designer—was born in Tucumán, Argentina, and lives in Amsterdam since 2005, where he graduated from the School for New Dance Development. With a focus on creative processes and new artistic methodologies his work explores ethical questions through bodies and minds in movement.

Henry A. Giroux currently holds the Global TV Network Chair Professorship at McMaster University in the English and Cultural Studies Department. His primary research areas are cultural studies, youth studies, critical pedagogy, popular culture, media studies, social theory, and the politics of higher and public education. In 2002, he was named as one of the top 50 educational thinkers of the modern period in Fifty Modern Thinkers on Education: From Piaget to the Present as part of Routledge's Key Guides Publication Series. In 2005, he received an honorary doctorate from the Memorial University in Canada. He is on the editorial and advisory boards of numerous national and international scholarly journals, and he serves as the editor or coeditor of four scholarly book series. He has published numerous books and articles and his most recent books include *Youth in a Suspect Society: Democracy or Disposability?* (Palgrave Macmillan, 2009), *Hearts of Darkness: Torturing Children in the War on Terror* (Paradigm, 2010), *Zombie Politics and Culture in the Age of Casino Capitalism* (Peter Lang, 2011), *On Critical Pedagogy* (Continuum, 2011), *Education and the Crisis of Public Values* (Peter Lang, 2011), *Twilight of the Social: Resurgent Publics in the Age of Disposability* (Paradigm, 2012), and *Disposable Youth: Racialized Memories and the Culture of Cruelty* (Routledge, 2012). His forthcoming books are *Youth in Revolt: Reclaiming a Democratic Future* (Paradigm, in press) and *The Education Deficit and the War on Youth* (Monthly Review Press, 2012). His website can be found at www.henryagiroux.com.

Sandy Grande is an Associate professor and Chair of the Education Department at Connecticut College. She is currently working on developing an indigenous think tank, *The Tecumseh Institute,* based in New York City. Her research and teaching are profoundly inter- and cross-disciplinary and interfaces critical and Indigenous theories of education with the concerns of Indigenous education. Her book, *Red Pedagogy: Native American Social and Political Thought* (Rowman and Littlefield, 2004) has been met with critical acclaim. She is also working as principle evaluator of The

American Indian College Fund's project *Wakanyeja* "Sacred Little Ones" Project, a Tribal College Readiness and Success by Third Grade Initiative funded by the W. K. Kellogg Foundation. She has also published several book chapters and articles including: "Confessions of a Fulltime Indian," *The Journal of Curriculum and Pedagogy*; "Red Land, White Power: A Pedagogy for the Dispossessed." In *The Havoc of Capitalism: Education for Social and Environmental Justice*. J. Suoranta, D. Houston, G. Martin, and P. McLaren (eds); and "American Indian Geographies of Identity and Power: At the Crossroads of Indigena and Mestizaje," *Harvard Educational Review*.

Tricia M. Kress is an assistant professor of Leadership in Education at the University of Massachusetts, Boston. She received her PhD from the City University of New York Graduate Center. Her research interests include using critical pedagogy and critical research methods with teachers and students to rethink learning environments to be generative and liberating for students and teachers. She is the single author of *Critical Praxis Research: Breathing New Life into Research Methods for Teachers* (Kress, 2011) and coeditor of *Imagination and Praxis*, a new book series with Sense Publishers.

Robert Lake is an associate professor at Georgia Southern University. He teaches both undergraduate and graduate courses in multicultural education from both a local and global perspective. Robert is the author of *Vygotsky on Education* (2012) for the Peter Lang Primer Series. His other books include *Dear Maxine: Letters from the Unfinished Conversation with Maxine Greene* (2010) and *Dear Nel: Opening the Circles of Care (Letters to Nel Noddings 2012)* published by Teachers College Press. He is also coeditor along with Tricia Kress of *Imagination and Praxis*, a new book series with Sense Publishers.

Peter Mayo is professor in the department of Educational Studies, University of Malta, where he teaches/researches in sociology of education, adult education, comparative and international education, and sociology in general. He is also a member of the Collegio Docenti for the Doctoral program in educational sciences and continuing education at the University of Verona. He is the author or editor of many books including his most recent *Learning with Adults* (with Leona English, Sense, 2012), *Echoes from Freire for* *a Critically Engaged Pedagogy* (Continuum, 2012), and *Politics of Indignation* (Zer Books, 2012).

Peter McLaren is a professor at UCLA **and** the author, coauthor, editor, and coeditor of approximately 40 books and monographs. Several hundred of his articles, chapters, interviews, reviews, commentaries, and columns have appeared in dozens of scholarly journals and professional magazines since the publication of his first book, *Cries from the Corridor* (Methuen, 1980).

Some of the journals in which Professor McLaren's work has appeared include *The Journal of Advanced Composition, Ethnicities, The Harvard Education Review, Cultural Studies & Critical Methodologies, Philosophy and Social Criticism, Cultural Studies, Educational Theory, Social Text, Strategies, Polygraph, Australian Journal of Education, The International Journal of Qualitative Studies in Education, American Journal of Semiotics, Semiotic Inquiry, Discourse: Theoretical Studies of Media and Culture, Interchange, International Journal of Leadership in Education, Educational Philosophy and Theory, Theoria, Journal of Thought, Educational Policy, Cultural Critique, Monthy Review and Socialist Review.*

Professor McLaren's most recent books include *Academic Repression: Reflections from the Academic Industrial Complex* coedited with Stephen Best and Anthony Nocella (AK Press, 2010), *The Havoc of Capitalism,* coedited with Donna Houston, Greg Martin, and Juha Suoranta (Sense Pubications, 2010), and *A Critical Pedagogy of Consumption,* coedited with Jennifer Sandlin (Routledge, 2009), *Critical Pedagogy and Marxism* (Continuum, 2013), *Capitalists and Conquerors* (Rowman and Littlefield, 2005), *Teaching Against Global Capitalism and the New Imperialism,* with Ramin Farahmandpur (Rowman and Littlefield, 2005), *Red Seminars: Radical Excursions into Educational Theory, Cultural Politics, and Pedagogy* (Hampton Press, 2005), *Marxism Against Postmodernism in Educational Theory,* with Dave Hill, Mike Cole, and Glenn Rikowski (Lexington Books, 2002), and *Che Guevara, Paulo Freire, and the Pedagogy of Revolution* (Rowman and Littlefield, 2000).

Raymond Morrow is a recent Emeritus Professor of Sociology at the University of Alberta (Edmonton, Canada). Besides having published numerous articles and chapters, he is the author of *Critical Theory and Methodology* (Sage Publications, 1994) and *Reading Freire and Habermas* (Teachers College Press, 2002), and the coauthor, with Carlos Alberto Torres, of *Social Theory and Education* (SUNY Press, 1995).

Nel Noddings is Professor of Philosophy and Education at Teachers College, Columbia University, and Lee L. Jacks Professor of Child Education Emerita at Stanford University. She has 10 children and has been married for 63 years. She credits her early educational experiences and her close relationships as key in her development of her philosophical position. She is the author of numerous books and articles and is still in great demand around the globe as a presenter on care theory, moral philosophy, and democratic education.

William Reynolds teaches in the Department of Curriculum, Foundations and Reading at Georgia Southern University. His two most recent books *are Expanding Curriculum Theory: Dis/positions and Lines of Flight* (Routledge, 2004) *and The Civic Gospel: A Political Cartography of Christianity* (Sense, 2009).

Melissa Winchell is an instructor of English at Massasoit Community College in Brockton, MA. A doctoral candidate in the Leadership in Urban Schools program at Boston's University of Massachusetts, Melissa's research interests include critical pedagogy, critical race theory, co-teaching, and participatory action research.

INDEX